D0085431

THE
STATUS AND APPRAISAL OF
CLASSIC TEXTS

THE
STATUS AND APPRAISAL OF
CLASSIC TEXTS

An Essay on Political Theory,
Its Inheritance,
and the History of Ideas

CONAL CONDREN

WITHDRAWN

Princeton University Press
Princeton, New Jersey

Burg,
JA
71
copy1   .C568
         1985

Copyright © 1985 by Princeton University Press
Published by Princeton University Press, 41 William Street,
Princeton, New Jersey 08540
In the United Kingdom:
Princeton University Press, Guildford, Surrey

All Rights Reserved
Library of Congress Cataloging in Publication Data will be
found on the last printed page of this book

ISBN 0-691-07670-7

Publication of this book has been aided by a grant from
the Paul Mellon Fund of Princeton University Press

This book has been composed in Linotron Electra.
Clothbound editions of Princeton University Press books
are printed on acid-free paper, and binding materials are
chosen for strength and durability. Paperbacks, although satisfactory
for personal collections, are not usually suitable for library rebinding

Printed in the United States of America by
Princeton University Press, Princeton, New Jersey

WITHDRAWN

TO A. C.
AND IN MEMORY OF W. J. AND B. E. M. C. AND P. C.,
WHO SHOULD HAVE OVERSEEN THE FINAL STAGES.

CONTENTS

SOCRATES:
Now then you agree in rejecting with me
the Gods you believed in when young,
And *my* creed you'll embrace *"I believe in wide space,
in the Clouds, in the eloquent Tongue."*

STREPSIADES:
If I happened to meet other Gods in the street,
I'd show the cold shoulder, I vow.
No libation I'd pour: not one victim more
on their altars I'll sacrifice now.

Aristophanes
The Clouds,
trans. Benjamin Rogers,
which ran last in 423 B.C.

"And it occurs to me that running a programme like this is bound to create an enormous amount of popular publicity for the whole area of philosophy in general. Everyone's going to have their own theories about what answer I'm eventually going to come up with, and who better capitalize on that media market than you yourselves? So long as you keep disagreeing with each other violently enough and slagging each other off in the popular press, and so long as you have clever agents, you can keep yourselves on the gravy train for life. How does that sound?"

The two philosophers gaped at him.

"Bloody hell," said Majikthise, "now that is what I call thinking. Here Vroomfondel, why don't we think of things like that?"

"Dunno," said Vroomfondel in an awed whisper, "think our brains must be too highly trained Majikthise."

So saying, they turned on their heels and walked out of the door and into a lifestyle beyond their wildest dreams.

Douglas Adams,
The Hitch-Hiker's Guide to the Galaxy,
which did rather better in A.D. 1979

PREFACE

This book is largely a study of academic mythologies—in part, a professional act of deconstruction. Put more simply, it is a book about reading books and the reasons we give for requiring others to read them also. Such a book is in danger of a mandarin seriousness and self-indulgence; furthermore, it is one that has taken nearly as long as it took Mr. Gibbon to scribble off his *Decline and Fall*, and so teeters on the edge of a double jeopardy. Thus in order to avoid a tedious pomposity, I have tried to keep in mind the tag Nietzsche used in *The Case of Wagner, ridendo dicere severum* (through the laughable say what is serious). I hope this compensates for any lapses of intellectual taste.

The essay began one dull London Sunday as a very serious, if short, paper (it would have been longer had I then heard of deconstruction) which I showed a few days later to my tutor. He encouraged me to develop its themes further, and so it grew into an enthusiastic and hasty Ph.D. thesis. Since then it has become a somewhat more skeptical journey through my professional self and (broadly) my academic environment. And, whatever its limitations, the questions it raises must be important to anyone sufficiently interested in books to have read this far. What makes them good, and why are some forgotten? Why is a nodding acquaintance with a few educationally *de rigueur*—"you mean you haven't read von Aardvark?" To reply "Why should I?" often hovers on the edge of impertinence, while the reasons for reading seem so often to have the whiff of rhetorical defense mechanism about them. The impertinent question is asked, or feared, the machine switched on, and out come well-stamped words like "original," "revelant," or "classic." But the questions are too important for this species of familiar response really to be good enough, especially for those enmeshed in an academic world which flows past largely in print. These are questions about how we spend our time and how we persuade others to do likewise. Put in these somewhat political terms, it is clear to me that what follows could be explored much further in the zealous interests of intellectual *thorough*; and had I world enough and time, it could be further refined in those of arboreal responsibility. But as things stand, operating at the intersection of a number of academic industries, the argument remains schematic, its illustration incomplete, and above all preoccupied with the praises heaped upon political theory texts, as well as the criticism of the professional theorists who heap the praise, then wield the texts at each other: in short, with the institutionalized study of a handful of classic texts and the rhetoric of their promotion. Considered then as a study of classicism per se in the idiom of Sainte-Beuve, this work retains a certain *raku* roughness, and the term *essay* in the title (like Burckhardt's famed subtitle *ein versuch*) is intended to remind the reader of this.

At any rate, the work has stopped and, like that mythical Norwegian Blue parrot, now confronts its maker. After so long I have good reasons for letting it rest in peace. I doubt that I could improve much upon it, and it is in any case only the second of four related studies. In the first, I suggested a vocabulary for historical comparison on which, metaphorically, I have drawn. The third will be a detailed study of a text and its history—a test case for the principles sketched here; and in the fourth, I hope to explicate the theory of language which underpins what I have to say and the way in which I have consistently tried to say it. There is a lot to do. It is this interconnectedness of my work which also explains what may seem the undue number of references to my previously published papers. They have in truth all been footnotes in search of a text; this text, therefore, is the context which will make more, if belated, sense of them all.

The longer one takes to write, the more debts one incurs. My last and most enjoyable task is to rehearse the most important of them, as a sort of testament of intellectual rakishness—though, as even Strepsiades knew, to rehearse one's debts no matter how pleasurably and publicly is not to repay them. I owe much to Michael Oakeshott, who late in my formal education showed me the excitement of intellectual life and the enjoyment of hard work. It was fitting that he should comment on the penultimate draft of the essay. My thanks are due also to Dorothea Sharp and to Robert Orr, a tolerant and constructive tutor who guided this patiently through its early stages; and to David Cameron and Harro Höpfl, not least because they suffered the early days of my hallelujah zeal with friendship and civility. Doug McCallum's high tolerance of intellectual eccentricity has provided an atmosphere in which my research could overlap with some of my teaching. As a result I owe thanks for stimulation to numerous students, most notably Dr. Raia Browning and especially Dr. Damian Grace, encourager, reader, discussant, and friend. The library staff at the University of New South Wales have set a peerless example of kindness and expertise. Over the final stages of revision, my friends in the Sydney History of Ideas Group have been splendid hosts, literally and metaphorically. Professor John Gunnell did me the great service of suggesting I send my manuscript to Princeton and provided constructive comments. John Pocock's generosity in criticism and encouragement have been extraordinary. Sandy Thatcher's help and kindness have made the final stages much easier than I had any right to expect; and Renetta DeBlase's fastidious copyediting has been much appreciated.

Naturally, like most academics I owe much to those I think wrong: but for our communal "priviledge of Absurdity," as Hobbes had it, few of us could survive. And certainly, if political theory did not exist, I would have to invent it. It is precisely because of this that I can easily seem less grateful than I am to a number whose works have been invaluable in helping me define aspects of my own position. Even at the risk of sounding like Frederick Crews' dreadful Myron Masterson, I should single out the following whose works have provided a stimulation inadequately reflected in my argument: Alan Gewirth, Frank Kermode, Michael Oakeshott, Chaim Perelman, Gregorio Piaia, John Pocock, W. V. Quine, Nicholas Rescher, Richard Rorty, Quentin Skinner, Stephen Toulmin, Stephen Ullmann, and David Wiggins. I regret that P. D. Juhl's recent study *Interpretation: An Essay in the Philosophy of Literary Criticism* and the recent works of Stanley Fish have come too late to my attention for me to make use of and to discuss. To the classic texts of political theory, like a good parasite, I have owed my living; in particular, Plato's exquisite aesthetic sense and Hobbes' metaphorical decorum have proved irresistible suns at which to fly. I apologize for any abuse of them and (especially in the case of Ovid) dubious translation.

I should like to thank Pan Books for permission to quote from Douglas Adams' *The Hitch-Hiker's Guide to the Galaxy*; Frederick Crews and E. P. Dutton, Inc., for permission to quote from *The Pooh Perplex*, copyright Frederick C. Crews, 1963; A. D. Peters & Co., for permission to quote from Frank Kermode, *The Classic*, Faber & Faber, London, 1975; and Benteli Verlag, Bern, and Faber and Faber to quote from Paul Findlay's English translation of Paul Klee's *Über die moderne Kunst*, fifth impression, 1962. Dr. Max Lake kindly gave permission to quote from his essay *Cabernet: Notes of an Australian Wineman*, Rigby, Adelaide, 1977; the lines from the lyrics of *Sergeant Pepper* are reprinted by kind permission of ATV Northern Songs, Pty. Ltd.

Personal thanks are due to Col. George Raby and Tom Faithful, who never begrudged my giving up cricket for writing; to Brig. Leslie Rush and Nora Rush in whose idyllic Tuscan home so much of this book was finally written—their hospitality was a constant test of my seriousness; to Gail Pryor, who unscrambled my manuscript with a skill worthy of a cryptographer.

For services of various sizes both Aoise and Allegra Condren deserve to have their names in print. The essay is dedicated partly to my parents who, ironically, I can never thank: my father for a life of friendship and a daunting standard of excellence; my mother, for love and courage; both for unquestioning support. Partly the essay is dedicated to Averil, who will not begrudge this sharing despite having done more than anyone to keep my prose upon its feet. Greater love hath no woman than to lay down her own work for someone else's book. To have done so with such constructive grace has made much of it hers. Naturally, I refer only to the good parts—the good men write is oft attributed to their friends, the bad not reckoned among their loans. Sometimes this makes for a pretty rough justice; but with so many friends and so much help, I can hardly complain.

ABBREVIATIONS

The following abbreviations are for those journals which are most commonly cited in the text, or which have the longest titles.

AHR	*The American Historical Review*
AJPS	*American Journal of Political Science*
APSR	*The American Political Science Review*
CQ	*The Classical Quarterly*
CSSH	*Comparative Studies in Society and History*
EHR	*The English Historical Review*
Hist. & Th.	*History and Theory*
HJ	*The Historical Journal*
IPP	*Il Pensiero Politico*
JCH	*The Journal of Contemporary History*
JHI	*The Journal of the History of Ideas*
JMH	*The Journal of Modern History*
JP	*The Journal of Politics*
NLH	*New Literary History*
P & R	*Philosophy and Rhetoric*
PSQ	*The Political Science Quarterly*
Pol. Stud.	*Political Studies*
Pol. Th.	*Political Theory*
Proc. Arist. Soc.	*Proceedings of the Aristotelian Society*
Proc. Brit. Academy	*Proceedings of the British Academy*
RP	*The Review of Politics*
SR	*Social Research*

PART ONE

One told me, Heraclitus, you were dead; and left me
weeping,
As once more I remembered how often down the west
We talked the sun to setting.
        Callimachus of Cyrene, on Heraclitus
        of Hallicarnassus, trans. F. L. Lucas

L——d! said my mother, what is all this story about?—
A Cock and a Bull, said Yorick—And one of the best of its
kind, I ever heard.
        Laurence Sterne, *Tristram Shandy*

Introduction

————————— I —————————

Great books are less written than they are read. That is, designations of qualitative status (good, bad, indifferent, classic, or a waste of trees) are less simple descriptions of the facts of authorial achievement than they are evocations of the expectations and criteria of judgment the reader brings to bear upon a text. These constitute what I shall call *appraisive fields*. On occasion we may find such fields specific to a discipline or activity in which we place a book—hence we do not read a viticultural treatise as we would a pastoral idyll. Commonly, however, our expectations are abridged into a more general appraisive field in terms of which we organize a wide range of reading, through which we can begin to make comparisons between apparently different sorts of work while justifying our conclusions, and under which we even subsume more specific criteria of judgment.

The very general appraisive field with which I shall be concerned consists largely of a familiar net of terms and their cognates and associated notions: *originality, coherence, contribution, influence, ambiguity*. Indeed, so familiar is this field and so widespread its use that its principal members form an international currency in and beyond the academic world; furthermore, so much are its items taken for granted that they are sometimes reified into characteristics seen as quite independent of our interpretive expectations and priorities. As a field, they help structure our judgments on an extraordinarily wide range of intellectual enterprises, past, present, and future. We expect theses to be *original*, essays to make *contributions*, arguments to be *coherent*, concepts to be *unambiguous*. And what we deem 'the great books' of the past are commonly held, ideally, to be paradigmatic confirmations of these expectations. Our own field of appraisal is thus easily assumed to explain the qualitative, even classic,

3

status of a given work. It is also used habitually to reaffirm or dispute that a book is worthy of a certain standing, as well as to set down the terms of debate through which we most naturally justify studying the textual remnants of the past.

This essay is largely a critical overview of the main items in this appraisive field of textual analysis: it is an attempt to reform it, to refine the vocabulary through which we tackle the problems of textual status and appraisal. As I will eventually argue, what I take to be the principal items in the field do little to help answer the questions surrounding such status, and the air of paradox consequent upon this conclusion means that what I have to say must be seen as a rule for reading, and not as some sleazy handbook to insure the scribbler's immortality.

In whatever language we seek to justify and explicate it, the predication 'classic' has a special, even paramount, place in the vocabulary of textual appraisal—not least because it always invites a consideration of relationships between past and present.[1] Any work called a classic is close to being placed, as Kermode has stressed, in "a privileged order of time," as a perpetual contemporary, immune from qualitative decay.[2] This is true of what he refers to as the Horatian notion of the classic, that is, a work called a 'classic' by virtue of the fact that it is continuously read; it is even more true of what he calls the imperialist theory of the classic, that is, the notion that the classic is a timeless reservoir of cultural identity and understanding—a paradigm of experience. The Horatian, or, as it were, *de facto* notion of classicism invites empirical inquiry into the means, ends, and mechanisms of industrious rereading. The imperialist theory, so closely associated with Matthew Arnold and T. S. Eliot, is an attempt to explain what the *de facto* understanding of classicism recognizes.[3] It carries a good deal of metaphysical baggage uncongenial to any historical explanation of *de facto* classicism, and the

[1] Frank Kermode, *The Classic* (London, 1975), pp. 15ff.

[2] Ibid., p. 19.

[3] Matthew Arnold, "The Modern Element in Modern Literature"; T. S. Eliot, "What is a Classic?," discussed in Kermode, *The Classic*, chap. 1; see also Eliot's related papers, "Virgil and the Christian World," in *On Poetry and Poets* (London, 1957), and *The Classics and the Man of Letters* (Oxford, 1942).

final chapter of this work is antithetical to it, although in its own classic form the imperialist theory of Eliot will not be dealt with directly since it is devoted to works largely to one side of those in whose qualitative status I am most interested.

Obviously enough, the more a canon of acceptedly major works is important to an intellectual activity, the more the question of their qualitative status becomes a means of exploring the activity itself. The argument here is pursued largely through an exploration of the established academic activity of political theory, a loosely structured enterprise geared to the reading of a set of 'classic' texts to a degree surpassed perhaps only by disciplines devoted to the study of national literatures.

At a time when a potent lineage is a fitting credential for little more than a racehorse and a royal family, it is curious that academic political theory has created and disseminated a serious image of itself through a lineage of ancestral 'classic' texts. This lineage stretching from Plato to Marx and beyond is, as I shall suggest, no mere subject matter; rather, it forms a *religio*, providing a community rhetoric, an educational strategy, and distinctive notions of politics and political theory: to the political theorist, expressions such as 'the great books,' 'the masters,' and 'the classics' are almost clichés reflecting the pedigree's potent and binding force. The outsider might think that the use of these expressions to refer to a heap of papers, parchments, and papyrus rolls, in blissful ignorance of which most of the world has managed to hobble along, signifies the relationship between an arcane order and its sacred books. Such a view would be, of course, nearly unfair. Nevertheless, the religious analogue can help frame the questions about political theory which stimulated my argument as a whole and led to an analysis of the appraisive field on which it relies. In the light of what criteria, then, do we distinguish major from minor prophets? By what process do books become a Bible, the corpse an ancestor, the dead immortal and divine? Could any of the authors of our 'classic' texts, like the dying Roman emperor, feel themselves becoming gods? Why should we spread their words to our students? As important as I think they obviously are, these questions have not been commonly asked or pursued with any tenacity. This may well be because the answers might seem straightforward.

An initial Identikit response might suggest that the great works of political theory are deemed so because, for all their blemishes, they are models of the search for political understanding. If we seek political truth, we can but follow in the footsteps of the masters and achieve some enlightenment, even by seeing how and where they stumbled. We work in their vineyards that we may all tramp the vintage of political wisdom.[4]

Superficially at least, such an idiom of response seems to inculcate an imperialist understanding of classicism. But few political theorists would be prepared to adopt Eliot's view in any precise sense. The criteria of classic status he had in mind (maturity, metropolitanism, even latinity) are not clearly appropriate to works of political theory; not all theorists would argue that their 'classics' are models to be followed; and few if any would assert, as did Eliot, a discrepancy between classicism and supreme quality. The most that can be said here is that political theorists recognize themselves as dealing with a deservedly *de facto* or Horatian body of classics which are sometimes explicated with a top dressing of imperialist rhetoric, such as when they are referred to as 'timeless,' or 'paradigmatic'—expressions appropriate to their often being treated almost as contemporaries.

More clearly, such a form of response intimates that political theorists enjoy a common activity, with its own *telos* as well as specific standards of excellence and criteria of qualitative appraisal. It certainly suggests a curriculum which we are prepatterned to study in certain ways. Questions concerning the classic status of political theory texts in a Horatian or a diluted Eliot-

---

[4] Numerous works in and around political theory reflect this general view, from the articulate and defensive—e.g. S. S. Wolin, "Political Theory as a Vocation," *APSR* 63 (1969); Andrew Hacker, "Capital and Carbuncles: The Great Books Re-Appraised," *APSR* 48 (1954)—to the more simple and introductory, important precisely because they may be thought to be trading in agreed postulates: e.g. J. Harmon, *Political Thought From Plato to the Present* (New York, 1964); Leslie Lipson, *The Great Issues of Politics* (New Jersey, 4th ed., 1970); and from the old to the new—e.g. Robert Blakey, A *History of Political Literature* (London, 1854); R. Fitzgerald, ed., reflecting some of the contributions in *Comparing Political Thinkers* (Oxford and Sydney, 1980).

esque sense are, then, intimately bound to the character, real or supposed, of the political theory community itself. As I shall suggest in Part One, beyond the level of evocative rhetoric, common standards of textual appraisal specific to political theory are chimerical; and so, as it were, through a consideration of the community, we are forced to confront the more general appraisive field on which it relies.

Within the context of political theory's established conventions of discourse, I am concerned, then, with the appraisive field of textual analysis which, with slight modifications, is shared by political theory and its neighboring academic communities. Since I am concerned with the character, recognition, and origin of Holy Writ, what follows may be seen as an exercise in hermeneutics, both in a modern and in the ancient sense of rendering the sermons of the Church intelligible.

A more precise identification of the nature and limits of my argument, however, is not easy. To some extent, as it is concerned, for example, with the refinement of a conceptual vocabulary, it is readily recognizable as philosophical; but it also engages in the interpretation of some nonphilosophical texts and their fortunes in the hands of others. And so, spasmodically, the essay is historical. But, to use an unlovely word, methodology is the activity with which overall it may most closely be associated. At its center, the methodological is in some respects a dubious region to which my own attitude is a trifle ambivalent. The risk of self-conscious operation in and around this area may be to suggest irony, insouciance, and, above all, a degree of *asebeia* which I hope will not be seen as too arrogant, or as totally corrupting.

First warnings aside, the remainder of the Introduction is intended to outline in more detail the plan of the essay, and then finally to explain my spasmodic use of symbols, indicating the most general level on which the essay operates.

The argument as a whole is continuous. Part One, however, should be seen largely as a contextual and ground-clearing exercise. The apparently tangential Chapter 1 is concerned with the pervasively important phenomenon of methodological argument per se[5] which, because it is too easily oversimplified and depressingly often mistaken for a panacea rather than a purgative, requires preliminary delineation. In outlining its intellectual character, significance, and dangers, I am providing, as it were, a theoretical center from which my own arguments move toward theory and practice; at the same time, I am providing a theoretical context for the previous methodological animadversions about political theory and the history of ideas which overlap with my own. From a context for the character of my argument, I move to one for the main subject of dispute: thus the remainder of Part One surveys political theory in the light of the methodological attention it has already attracted, but in such a way as to focus upon the complex of questions concerning qualitative appraisal and classic status. Chapter 2 begins by outlining largely *in abstracto* the discursive character of political theory which, among other failings, mitigates against the political theory community's achieving any clear, uniform criteria of textual appraisal of its own. I then turn in more detail to consider two major articles of faith which, despite the difficulties inherent in the discursive character of political theory, might be of value in explaining classic status.

A discussion of the faith in what I shall call the issue-orthodoxy (the belief that politics consists of a finite set of basic, universal issues) takes up the remainder of Chapter 2; the belief that the 'classic' texts of the theorist constitute a genuine tradition of speculation takes up Chapter 3. On the surface, these two complementary articles of faith seem to provide a sound basis from which we might explore problems of status and appraisal within political theory. For the issue-orthodoxy might appear to suggest

[5] Richard Bernstein, *The Restructuring of Social and Political Theory* (London, 1979 ed.), p. 9.

8

the elemental subject matter for the political theorist and to circumscribe the terms of debate through which appraisive categories could be articulated; the tradition might be thought of as
displaying a full list of those who, by degrees, have succeeded in
living up to any requisite standards in their discussions of the
political verities.

On closer inspection, however, both look like Arbuthnot's "proof
articles," which, if swallowed, facilitate the digestion of almost
anything else.[6] Deservedly, both articles have attracted the ire of
methodologists of little faith since the 1960s, but it is not my
purpose to rehearse what others have already argued at length.
Rather, it is to emphasize the explanatory poverty of these two
articles of faith if used to approach questions of status and appraisal, in which process it has been necessary to extend and add
to the arguments of others.

The conclusion to Chapter 3 provides a natural transition to
the problems canvassed in Part Two, insofar as the question of
whether the contemporary political theorist is the inheritor of a
genuine and long-standing tradition of master works is itself predicated on the acceptance of the individual works as classics themselves. To abandon the notion that Marx, say, dealt with the
basic issues of politics and did so well that his works became a
part of a tradition of similarly successful classics is not to abandon an interest in Marx. Rather, it is to highlight the difficulties
involved in appraising him and explaining his status; it is to strip
away the moribund creed of a community and force us to consider the more general categories on which that community also
relies.

I introduce Part Two by sketching in the appraisive field of
textual analysis as a whole. The sorts of terms forming allegedly
basic issues in politics, and around which the improving slogans
of a political society coagulate, are used explicitly as an area of
metaphorical and analogical expansion for understanding the *clef*

---

[6] "Of such a nature [the author] takes transubstantiation to be in the Church
of Rome, a proof article, which if anyone swallows, they are sure he will digest
everything else . . . ." (John Arbuthnot, *The Art of Political Lying*, 1712, in *Political Pamphlets*, comp. A. F. Pollard [London, 1897], p. 120).

mots of textual appraisal. In this way, the rhetorical and structural similarities between political and academic language are
drawn together from a pattern of allusion which informs the whole
argument. The chapters immediately following take each of the
major items from the appraisive field in turn, just as a political
theory textbook might have an introductory chapter about politics and then go on to discuss individually such topics as democracy, obligation, and freedom. The progression is roughly from
those terms of most rhetorical and least classificatory and explanatory power to those of most explanatory power.[7] In this way,
the argument in Part Two sustains the largely negative and ground-
clearing tone of Part One, although Chapter 7 is in this respect
transitional. After a very short introduction, Part Three offers a
more positive unity insomuch as it suggests the basis of a reformed appraisive field which I take also, in the final chapter, to
provide a more viable framework for understanding the actual
interpretive history of given texts in political theory than any
reliance upon the established field can provide. As a corollary,
in the final stages, I return again to the matter of political theory's tradition; to the conventional structure of the activity; to the
relationships between past and present in which notions of 'classicism' are implicit; and to the generation of the particular historicist idiom which has such an important, but potentially de-
structive, role within the 'classic'-minded political theory
community, and around which so much methodological dispute
has already pivoted. Thus in the end is the beginning, as we

---

[7] Two related senses of the term *rhetoric* should be kept in mind here: as the
repertoire of persuasive devices used in a particular discursive form and separable
from cogency of argument; and as the persuasive dimension of any argument,
predicated upon the existence of a discriminate and potentially disputatious audience. These meanings may most easily be seen as constituting two poles of a
discursive vector. Both are used in this essay, depending upon the context of
argument, and they are explicated further in Part Two, the Introduction, and in
Chapter 6. For more discussions of rhetoric in the specific sense, see e.g. Henry
W. Johnstone, Jr., *Validity and Rhetoric in Philosophical Discourse: An Outlook
in Transition* (University Park, 1978): and for the more general meaning, Ch.
Perelman, *The New Rhetoric and the Humanities* (Dordrecht, 1979); and Paolo
Valesio, *Novantiqua: Rhetorics as a Contemporary Theory* (Bloomington, 1980).

return to method and to the question already posed: What is it that makes a 'classic' text and how should we organize our reading of it, or of any text for which some notion of qualitative appraisal is a relevant consideration?

III

Having stood upon the order of my writing long enough, I shall now begin by explaining the rationale for its symbolic punctuations, by explicating its most general level of operation, and by elucidating its philosophical presuppositions. My argument presupposes that the intellectual world is in principle divisible into different discursive unities (Foucault's expression) which, if not coextensive with, are apparent in established areas of communal activity such as political theory. These unities provide an abstract, yet effective, means of imposing conceptual order upon the world, of identifying its parts and discerning the connections between them, as well as providing distinguishable but inseparable principles of connection and classification. Such principles combine to delineate a manageable area of experience, to individuate the interesting and problematic within it, and to reform the whole in a more intelligible manner. Their use enables us to tell tree from tree in Carroll's nameless wood; to impose an improved order upon a Heraclitan world of partially understood flux which never independently makes total sense.[8]

The term *time*, for example, provides synoptic clues to the diverse principles of interconnection and classification which produce our always modal understandings. Temporal change may be seen as progressive, repetitious, causal, or random; first this, then that, just one thing after another. Thus under the rubric of time we may find quite different species of change, a persistent

[8] Michael Oakeshott, *On Human Conduct* (Oxford, 1975), pp. 1ff.: the intellectual world is thus an analogue of his *Societas*. See also Stephen Toulmin, *Human Understanding* (Oxford, 1972), 1:35.

and single-minded concern with any of which may be taken as suggesting different discursive unities. These, in turn, may become sufficiently established and habitual to be reflected in continuous self-conscious communities of intellectual activity which leave middens of accumulated textual output.

In these schematic terms, then, we can see that the question of how reference to time should be modified is the central issue of modern historical methodology and the philosophy of history. The different answers to that question expand or contract the *de facto* historical community and circumscribe its ways of imposing order upon that area of experience called the past. Or, again with respect to the philosophical community, to answer the question of what are philosophical connections between different items is to classify or reclassify argument as philosophical or otherwise. If the connections are restricted to those of certain sorts of entailment between only the most stable of items, then the domain of philosophy, as Wittgenstein suggested in the *Tractatus*, will be small, albeit potentially certain.[9] The vaster reaches of human experience, being beyond its dispensation, are proffered to the singing poet.[10]

Now, what I refer to as discursive unities might seem to be little more than the heuristic and hypothetical extensions from existing conventional matrices of intellectual activity; but they can also be defined roughly as discourse rid of the uncertainties and ramified untidiness of its communal and temporal dimensions. If, for example, we were to follow Vico, Cassirer, or Müller on myth, Hegel or Klee on art, Cicero on rhetoric, or Oakeshott on history, we might well claim for these phenomena the status of discursive unities. In this essay putative discursive unities will be indicated hypothetically by the symbolic series *A, B, C, D*. Their postulation attests to the belief that we may properly seek *in abstracto* diverse, or diverging, principles of classification and interconnection as cohering threads running through the complex fabric of established conventional intellectual activity. The

[9] *Tractatus Logico-Philosophicus* (London, 1961 ed.), author's Preface.
[10] Richard Kuhns, *Literature and Philosophy: Structures of Experience* (London, 1971), p. 272.

symbolic series A, B, Γ, Δ will be used to indicate hypothetically such established conventional matrices themselves, where I wish to state a position at a level independent of the contingent and sometimes contentious identifications suggested by such labels as 'history,' 'philosophy,' 'ideology,' and 'poetry.' By conventions I refer in the most general way to identifying regularities of language."[11] Under their aegis I subsume such diverse phenomena as distinctive vocabularies and conceptual fields, techniques and procedures of argument, specific rhetorical *tropes* and *topoi*, characteristic assumptions, and, of course, distinctive standards of appraisal (brilliance in chess, elegance in mathematics, decorum in rhetoric), as well as the principles of classification and interconnection marking members of the series A . . . Z. What, in short, differentiates A . . . Z from A . . . Ω is any inherited, semi-institutionalized pattern of linguistic convention to be found in members of the latter.[12] Thus where A might stand for quin-

[11] D. K. Lewis's preliminary definition of a convention is useful here: "A regularity in the behaviour of members of a population P when they are agents in a recurrent situation S is a *convention* if and only if in any one instance S among the members of P 1. everyone conforms to R; 2. everyone expects everyone else to conform to R; 3. everyone prefers to conform to R on condition that the others do" (*Convention: A Philosophical Study* [Cambridge, Mass., 1974 ed.], p. 42). Despite strong criticisms (Alasdair MacIntyre, *Against the Self Images of the Age* [London, 1971], pp. 211ff.; Richard Bernstein, *The Restructuring*, p. 63), Peter Winch's *The Idea of a Social Science* (London, 1958) remains one of the most stimulating and suggestive formal accounts of conventionality relevant to the themes of this work. Similarly so are Ch. Perelman and L. Olbrechts-Tyteca, *The New Rhetoric: A Treatise on Argumentation*, trans. J. Wilkinson and P. Weaver (Notre Dame, 1968); and Toulmin, *Human Understanding*. There are, of course, numerous historical studies of value which have explored the character and transformation of activities as matrices of conventional behavior and expectation. See e.g. the recent comments of J. G. A. Pocock, "The *Machiavellian Moment* Revisited: A Study in History and Ideology," *JMH* 53 (1981), esp. pp. 50–51 on his own historical work.

[12] As a corollary it is not my purpose to reduce established activities ABΓΔ each to no more than one totally exclusive set of classificatory and connecting principles, or to say that if we did we would have necessarily an adequate understanding. After all, it will always be possible to show that from the perspective of a given member (A) of the series A . . . Ω, certain principles of classification must be presupposed *a priori* to be common to all in the series, lest from the standpoint of A (the crucial but trivializing qualification) the world becomes

tessence of Clio, History as some ideal type; A may become the Göttingen or Annales school of Historians; B might become the schools of the Second Sophistic; for Γ we might read the established university study of English literature or political theory. In terms of these two series of symbols, perhaps a few very general rules of analysis could be elicited for an equally unspecific series of texts cum authors (for which the series $a \ldots z$ will be used); and for a range of different discursive items such as ideas, statements, arguments, images, for which the series $\alpha \ldots \omega$ will be employed. If we add a means of representing terms used per se as covering terms (the series $\bar{A}, \bar{B}, \bar{C}, \bar{D}$ will be used),[13] and if we were to provide a means of signifying items in an appraisive field when functioning as predicate variables (which proves unnecessary), we would have the basic notational capital for developing an argument in blithe disregard of all political theory and its texts. Pursued at such a level of abstraction, the argument would either be reached quickly and inconsequentially by stipulative fiat or, by first passing through the difficult straits of set theory, it would end where all philosophy is apt to end and begin again, that is, in the tensions of paradox.

The nature of methodological argument as I understand it, however (see Chapter 1), forecloses alike upon the purely symbolic presentation of a case, the imposition of a stipulative order upon all relevant language, and upon an indifference to the untidiness of the world to which appeal must be made for reform to be urged. Just as equally it shuns unreflective participation in any activity subject to its eye of rationality. The consequent difficulties of this interstitial status we must come to later, but it is important for the whole essay to stress here that whatever might

---

unintelligible. Thus it happens that the philosopher can argue (who else would try?) that the Yoruba who claims to carry his head tucked underneath his arm in a cowrie-shell covered box, must be assumed to share the same logic (same principles of classification and connection) as philosophers. For a defense of the cowrie-shelled philosopher, see Martin Hollis, "Reason and Ritual," in A. Ryan, ed., *The Philosophy of Social Explanation* (Oxford, 1976 ed.), pp. 33–49.

[13] These symbols will be adhered to throughout except where I resort to diagrams, and where I cite Russellian notation (Chap. 1, n. 22) and where I discuss Wiggins' reformulation of Leibniz' law of identity (Chap. 2.II).

be said with safe and tautologous nicety at the level of symbolic relationship is compromised when translated into established categories of discourse, where edges are blurred, pictures imprecise, with their figures sometimes fading into a mottled sepia mass. The closer we wish to come to a coincidence of social and intellectual complexity, the more we are perforce required to trade in loose concepts, or to cash in strict ones with a certain tolerance of exchange. Hence when I trade in terms such as 'history,' 'philosophy,' and 'ideology'—especially when I am outlining the general conventional character of political theory—I shall do little to refine or stipulate away from familiar usage. Therefore, the temptation to delineate our sepia world with thin gray lines will be resisted. The consequent incompleteness is both a matter of competence and priority. A joke does not have to become a pantomime, a sketch a Sistine ceiling. In this respect at least, there is some grim compensation in the fact that the hallowed rhetoric of calling upon philosophers to fetch everything "from the first items in every reckoning," or to explore ideas *"dans toutes leurs conséquences théoriques,"* constitutes a strictly impossible injunction—especially for those who spend time perpetuating different forms of it.[14] It may, of course, remain a valuable ideal to fail by, for, as Martin Hollis has recently remarked with an element of truth, "There is no methodological snag about outrageous de-

---

[14] Hobbes, *Leviathan*, pt. 1, chap. 5; Alexis de Tocqueville, *De la Démocratie en Amérique* (Paris, 1948 ed.), 1:25; cf. Quine's sound remark so pertinent to political theory: "The less a science has advanced, the more its terminology tends to rest on an uncritical assumption of mutual understanding" (*The Ways of Paradox* [Cambridge, Mass., 1975], p. 77).

Not being able to take back every word to first reckonings, it has seemed advisable to distance myself, if only temporarily, from unwanted complications, which I would ask the reader to hold in abeyance, that the main argument might proceed. To this end I have used single quotation marks. This is not part of any covert strategy of "neutralising success words," as David Stove might put it, *Popper and After: Four Modern Irrationalists* (Sydney and Oxford, 1982), p. 7f. Rather, this is simply to suggest, as it were, communal quotation and to signal awareness of terminological contentiousness. I have italicized words used as words, as abstract concepts, or as members of an appraisive field. The use of both devices, however, can be distracting, so where possible I have relied upon the context of argument to clarify usage of, or reliance upon, a particular word.

mands."[15] But fail by it we must. If the philosopher is haunted by Heraclitus through the need to make stable sense of a shifting world, he is concomitantly mocked by Humpty Dumpty's definitional megalomania and is dissipated by what may be called Shandy's Disease, death by terminal digression. How such difficulties endanger the "cock-and-bull" stories of the methodologist we will shortly see.

The point, then, of the occasional employment of my five symbolic series is to help delineate general argument from the untidiness and digressive infections of concrete illustration. Furthermore, the series will help avoid the confusions that may arise from a total reliance on terms such as 'history,' 'concept,' and 'argument,' many of which, still inhabiting a fluxionary world, are themselves unstable and haloed by often unwanted connotations.

The deployment of these series, then, signals on the one hand the difference between the refinement of a vocabulary for textual appraisal and the difficult and detailed business of its application, while on the other the rudimentary nature of its elaboration displays my reluctance to leave the world of the interpretive practitioner for the rarified airs of the logician. The argument is intended to apply, ultimately, to a specific range of texts, not to a purely hypothetical host of Norman Anonymi. It contains rules, regulations, and righteous calls for reform addressed largely to members of the political theory community, not just a set of hypothetical imperatives for members of community Ξ. But before idly doling my laws and distributing caps to whomsoever they might fit, I must, like Aeschylus's sea-lifted suppliants, plead my exile from the political theorist's and the formal philosopher's more certain realms. The symptoms of Shandy's Disease notwithstanding, the gentle reader may find it useful to be given a more detailed account of the character of methodological argument in order to contextualize and help draw the boundaries on the whole enterprise.

[15] Martin Hollis, *Models of Man* (Cambridge, 1977), p. 131. See Chap. 1, p. 26, for the significant qualification.

CHAPTER 1

Methodology:
Its Character and Significance

Behold, how good and how pleasant it is for brethren
to dwell together in unity!
                    Psalm 133, verse 1.

All the King's men got on their horses and got ready
to ride back to the palace. The captain took off his
bright red helmet and bowed to Mrs. Dumpty. "I'm
very sorry, Madam," he said, "we did all we could to
mend your son. The King will be sorry too, for
Humpty was the only really egg shaped boy in the
kingdom; but as you see, we cannot do a thing for
him. May I suggest that you sweep up the pieces into
a brown paper bag and throw them into the dustbin."
                    William Joseph Condren,
                    The Humpty Dumpty Story, Part Two

I

Arguably, we live in an age of methodology, and if Shelley was
right in stating that each deifies its greatest sins, are we, when
confronted with such terms as *methodology*, *metatheory*,
methodeutic, in the presence of a trinity—aspects of the god of
rationalistic excess?[1] Possibly, but we are given to worse failings,
for this has also been called the age of wastepaper and rubbish.

[1] "Ours has been the methodological century in the Social Sciences," Arnold
Brecht, *Political Theory* (Princeton, 1959), p. 5; see also Bernstein, *The Restructuring of Social and Political Theory* (London, 1979 ed.), p. 9

For good or ill, few modern, major intellectual figures have not been concerned with problems of method. Moreover, we are prone to delineate intellectual activities, above all else, by their methods;[2] and the condition of an activity neither sharing an established method nor claiming one of its own looks much like a body in search of a soul.[3] Right method, it may seem, gives the keys to the kingdom of man.[4]

As the *OED* indicates, the term 'method', from *methodus*, a following after, covers a multitude of sins.[5] From the eighteenth century, however, *méthodologie* appears as the science of method; like hermeneutics in its general sense, it is a concern with the art of inquiry. More precisely, methodology may be seen as the reduction of an activity to its guiding principles. It is certainly a faith in rule books, as well as distillations of principle, that underpins our preoccupation with method.

[2] For example, A. J. Ayer, *The Problem of Knowledge* (Harmondsworth, 1962 ed.), with respect to philosophy; or E. R. A. Seligman and A. Johnson, eds., *The Encyclopaedia of the Social Sciences* (New York, 1963 ed.), 9–10:389: "The progressive character of science shows that its essence is to be sought not in the content of its conclusions but rather in the method whereby its findings are made and constantly corrected."

[3] See e.g. Northrop Frye, *The Anatomy of Criticism*, Polemical Introduction (Princeton, 1971 ed.), passim; or A. R. Radcliffe-Brown, *Method in Social Anthropology* (London, 1966 ed.), esp. chap. 3, for anthropology's search for a method of its own.

[4] *Novum Organum*, Bk. 1, aphorism 68; Wolin, e.g., traces the beginnings of the preoccupation with "methodism" to Bacon, in "Political Theory as a Vocation," *APSR* 63 (1969): 1062.

[5] The *OED* indicates that method can cover the whole pursuit of knowledge, referring also to systematic procedures in logic and rhetoric, and to a concern with how things are done. Hence the plausibility of Mill's notion that most disputes were in the end about methodology, cited in R. Cumming, *Human Nature in History* (Chicago, 1969), 1:11.

The wide field of reference for the term can be organized initially into a continuum stretching away from the residue of everyday activity. Along it, there is first tactical methodology, which, assuming the goals of an activity, concentrates upon the means of their achievement. Second, and further from the activity, is strategic methodology, the process of legislating goals and of specifying the questions that the activity's practitioners may legitimately ask. Third, there is structural methodology, the attempted distillation of the overall principles to be found in the activity. Though distant from diurnal practice and equipped with no *apparatus belli*,[6] it remains (to echo the dictionary) concerned with the way things are done and is still a following after. This extended use of the term *methodology* suggests the elaboration of a full cartography of the intellectual world for which a perspective of Zarathustran distance is necessary: to recall a related balloon image of understanding, methodology hovers around the clouds of a systematic inquiry well removed from the streets in the city below.[7]

This continuum makes clear a firmer bifold distinction which I take to indicate the quintessence of methodological discourse from which much common usage diffuses. Tactical and strategic methodologies are forms of intrinsic regulatory inquiry, differing principally with respect to the details of their recommendations; they assume or articulate prescriptive principles derived from the subject activity or held to be appropriate to it. For both, appeal is to the conventions of the activity under scrutiny. Conversely, structural methodology is extrinsic and nonregulatory inquiry in that the characteristic conventions of discourse to which it appeals are not those of the scrutinized activity. Its end is not to prescribe but rather to render intelligible from beyond the confines of the activity.

My suggestion is that the central characteristic of methodolog-

[6] Bernard Bosenquet, A *History of Aesthetics* (London, 1892), p. xi.

[7] Nietzsche, Preface to *The Case of Wagner*, and *Thus Spake Zarathustra*, for the eagle eye; Bertrand de Jouvenel, *The Pure Theory of Politics* (Cambridge, 1963), pp. 11–12, expresses the balloon variant beautifully.

ical discourse is its propensity to hover (Socratically in a basket?) at the nexus of extrinsic and intrinsic inquiry, the area around the nexus being tarred with the same terminological brush.[8] This identification of the methodological nexus, however, presupposes the recognition of conventional distance between activities. This, briefly, is the degree to which patterns of convention form into discernibly different (in Rorty's expression, "incommensurable") activities. Be it slight or great, the difference between extrinsic and intrinsic inquiry is a function of this conventional distance. Generally, the greater it is, the more clear the delineation between activities, and the greater the task of translating between them. More specifically, it should be borne in mind that the greater the distance, the more activities will exhibit their own discriminate standards of appraisal for works created under their aegis, and the more a common appraisive field of terms is needed as a means of traversing conventional distance in the consideration of works from different genres.

As a corollary, much hinges upon the nature of translation itself. Four forms of translation should be mentioned. In the intensive sense we have linguistic and by slight extension idiomatic translation (from thieves' cant to Fowler). In a more extended sense we have also dialectic translation, where the categories of one putative discursive unity are cashed into the terms of another.[9] Finally, there is discursive translation where material intimately bound with the conventional structure of one discernible activity is carried over into that of another. Thus as exercises in discursive translation one could chase words such as *paradigm*, *relativity*, *evolution*, and *archetype* around the hu-

---

[8] Thus we find that in *The Encyclopaedia of the Social Sciences*, 9–10:389, the meaning of method "varies from that of abstract, or formal logic applicable to all statements to that of the technique which may be peculiar to a particular science or even some special field of it." For similar identifications see e.g. Maria Falco, *Truth and Meaning in Political Science* (New York, 1973), p. 45; Martin Landau, *Political Theory and Political Science* (Atlantic Highlands, 1979 ed.), p. 70; and Vernon van Dyke, *Political Science: A Philosophical Analysis* (Stanford, 1967 ed.), pp. vii and 94–95, where despite his use of the term *philosophy*, he locates his own work as operating at the methodological nexus.

[9] See e.g. E. Kedourie, *Nationalism* (London, 1961 ed.), pp. 34ff. for an account of Fichte's adaptation of Kant's metaphysics.

manities and social sciences. Frequently, such processes of translation are compound. Marshall's translation of the *Defensor Pacis* was linguistic ("out of Latyn into Englysshe") and indubitably discursive (from the ideological conventions of fourteenth-century Italy to those of sixteenth-century England).[10] These forms share a common creative and approximate mode of operation. Even in its simplest referential forms, as Quine has shown, translation never trades in synonyms or standards of absolute sameness.[11] The translator's art is that of the pessimist practiced by the optimist; what signifies is knowing what to sacrifice.

All this is well enough known with respect to idiomatic and linguistic translation,[12] but it is the case with dialectic and discursive also. Principles of classification and connection expanded into different networks of activity with their own preoccupations, priorities, procedures, and even specific rhetorics of persuasion prohibit translation from being simply a matter of substitution, the function of which is to reveal an essential sameness in the world. To think in substitutional terms is to undermine the very processes of delineation on which any precise understanding of the world is based; it is to confuse translation with description; and the world is not best seen as some potential cosmic monoglot (if they can't speak English we can always shout). In other words, assertions of the sameness always depend upon selection; salt is not in all respects the same as NaCl, as Bloomfield had it;[13] ξ is not the same as π except (the crucial qualification) that it is seen

[10] For a full discussion see Gregorio Piaia, *Marsilio da Padova nella Riforma e Nella Controriforma* (Padua, 1977), pp. 143–165. See also Chap. 9 of this study.

[11] W. V. Quine, "Meaning and Translation," in J. Fodor and J. Katz, eds., *The Structure of Language: Readings in the Philosophy of Language* (Englewood Cliffs, 1964); and "On Synonymity," in *From A Logical Point of View* (New York, 1961 ed.).

[12] For a delightful example compare Lear's *The Owl and the Pussy Cat* with the French translation cited and discussed in G. Steiner, *After Babel* (Oxford, 1975), pp. 405–406; or consider Marlowe's translations of Ovid. The general point, which Steiner makes at length, seems at least to have been attested since Herder, on whom, in this context, see Isaiah Berlin, *Vico and Herder* (London, 1976), p. 189.

[13] L. Bloomfield, *Language* (New York, 1933), p. 139.

from a different perspective.[14] Perspectives are all we can see from; and too often we mistakenly use the translations we are able to make from a given perspective as evidence for that perspective's universality.[15] Ultimately, to emphasize this species of error is to prepare the ground for criticism of a good deal of fallacious orthodoxy which characterizes political theory and the history of ideas (see Chapters 2 and 4). Immediately, however, it is to underline both the significance of conventional distance and the ambivalence of the methodologist if he is to be located at the junction of intrinsic and extrinsic inquiry.

If that is the correct location, then a notion of conventional distance becomes crucial for assessing the specific character of any particular methodological argument. The greater the distance, the more we are likely to be presented, as Julienne Ford put it, with "methodological jelly-pie"—a challenge alike to taste and digestion.[16]

In effect, the tolerance of methodological plausibility depends upon the conventional distance between what is accepted as philosophy and the scrutinized activity. For philosophy has become established and is often held to be an ultimate court of intellectual appeal.[17] Its great rhetorical achievement has been to persuade us of the universality of its principles and standards of appraisal without accepting (any more) the obligation to make everyone a philosopher as a participant in a distinct discipline. The general position we have reached might be expressed in Figure 1.

[14] *Contra* Friedrich Waisman, "Language Strata," in A. Flew, ed., *Logic and Language* (New York, 1965), p. 247.

[15] The ghost of the headless Yoruba raises his cowrie shell box again (see Introduction and n. 12). Toulmin's remarks on Carnap's essay, "The Logical Foundations of Probability," and his comments on notions of implicit logic are also pertinent. See *Human Understanding* (Oxford, 1972), pp. 65 and 157–158.

[16] Julienne Ford, *Paradigms and Fairy Tales* (London, 1975).

[17] For an acute and critical discussion see Richard Rorty, *Philosophy and the Mirror of Nature* (Princeton, 1979), esp. chap. 8. Although it may properly be said that philosophy has no authority beyond philosophical discourse, it is difficult to see how discussion of the character of an activity does not in practice dissolve into or attract what we normally recognize philosophy to be. Therefore, it is this which lends so much plausibility to anyone operating at the methodological nexus. See also n. 31 of this chapter.

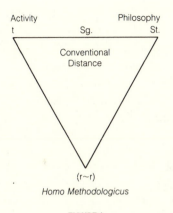

Homo Methodologicus

FIGURE 1

It might appear from this that my identification of the characteristic methodological nexus is simply a sentence of purgatory upon *homo methodologicus* for the congenital breach of Hume's Law. But this is too simple, and we can get a more precise understanding of the character of methodological statements by paying further attention to the understanding of statements in discourse per se. Although the matters raised here will be returned to in the Appendix, enough can be said now in a provisional fashion to help prepare the ground for the understanding of discursive items such as ideas, arguments, and concepts in political theory. At its simplest level, in identifying a statement ξ in public discourse, we are identifying something as being an example of, or the evidence for, discriminate human action. More specifically, ξ as statement presupposes a stater with some intention in addressing ξ to an audience.[18] That is, the identification of ξ entails the implicit acceptance of a framing explicatory vocabulary of intention and audience.[19] The intended force of, or in,

[18] P. F. Strawson, *Logico-Linguistic Papers* (London, 1974), chap. 9; and "Meaning, Truth and Communication," in N. Minnis, ed., *Linguistics at Large* (St. Albans, Herts., 1973 ed.), pp. 91ff.; and more generally, Ch. Perelman and L. Olbrechts-Tyteca, *The New Rhetoric* (Notre Dame, 1968), secs. 1–9. How we specify the ξ, however, can affect the issue. See the Appendix.

[19] This question is again taken up in the Appendix. For the moment, however, it is to be stressed that the vocabulary is easily misused. The necessity for the

the ξ only becomes intelligible in terms of how a discriminate audience is expected to act, or react. What may be called the potential force (which may well be discrepant from the intended force) becomes intelligible through the ways in which receptive groups take on the role of audience. In other words, statements understood as having meanings evoke, point to, or may be relocated in networks of discursive convention which pattern and limit audience understanding. Only then may they be said to be understood as 'saying' something and not 'saying' something else. Therefore, one of the things involved in concluding that a statement is meaningless is precisely that it evokes and can be tied to no discernible conventional network. No reactions are intimated, none ruled out;[20] clearly, the qualitative assessment of ξ is the function of the fit between force and conventional expectation.

Whatever permutations we may play with the explicatory vocabulary entailed by the family of terms specifiable under ξ (often the absence of an intending author gives much room for maneuver),[21] what the vocabulary makes clear is that ξ always carries some normative force designed to restrict potential force and to persuade us of its adherence to some discriminate convention or minimal communicative standards.[22]

---

vocabulary does not mean we have made any discovery by deploying it. Intentions may be withheld, confused, or mixed. Similarly, the postulation of an audience does not enable us necessarily to read into it any specific character. We may hypothesize that *Beowulf* was written with some audience in mind, but it is quite another matter to glean from the poem a homogeneous audience at a specific stage of religious and artistic sensitivity, as in D. Whitlock, *The Audience of Beowulf* (Oxford, 1951). However, see J. Opland, *Anglo-Saxon Oral Poetry: A Study of the Traditions* (New Haven, 1980), chaps. 1 and 8, for a more careful treatment.

[20] Even Gadamer, *Truth and Method* (New York, 1975), and *Philosophical Hermeneutics* (Berkeley, 1977), whose arguments are concerned to assert the autonomy of the text from the mind of the intending author, does not regard texts as giving *carte blanche* for any capricious reading.

[21] The point has been made strongly by Paul Ricoeur, "The Model of the Text," *SR* 38 (1971); and by Charles Tarlton, "Historicity, Meaning and Revisionism in the Study of Political Thought," *Hist. & Th.* 12 (1973).

[22] In the context of the *Principia Mathematica* and the audience to which it

In this light, then, objectivity is best seen as an appropriate normative mode.[23] It is precisely because *homo methodologicus* stands between two discernible activities (Ξ and Π) that the normative force of his statements, being grounded in different values and priorities, can be rendered objective by no single set of standards. With one exception (on which see Chap. 1, p. 29), it is, then, this compound normative appeal that characterizes what I have called the methodological nexus. Methodological discourse is marked by what will later be defined as coalescent ambiguity (see Chap. 7, p. 187). It is ironic that the methodologist who, in the social sciences, has been so preoccupied with the problem of objectivity is thus denied an objective voice of his own—he is unable to speak in any single normative mode. It is equally ironic that methodological argument, which

---

was addressed, the notation $p \supset q$. $\sim p \supset \sim q$ carries the force that we should accept it as an adequate symbolic picture of a proper philosophical procedure. Either or both of these recommendations might be resisted not as disputable positive statements, however, but as matters of discrepancy between the notation and its force, on the one hand, and the perceived conventions of philosophical discourse, on the other. This seems to be Hamblin's attitude. See *Fallacies* (London, 1970), pp. 279–280.

It is against such a background that Johnstone draws his distinction between a *reductio* in philosophy and in pure mathematics, in *Validity and Rhetoric in Philosophical Discourse* (University Park, 1978), pp. 26–27. Or, to give a rather different instance, when F. R. Leavis, "Criticism and Philosophy," in *The Common Pursuit* (Harmondsworth, 1963 ed.), p. 217, states that Blake is not a philosopher, he is telling critics they ought not to confuse conventions of philosophy with literary criticism in reading Blake.

[23] See Gadamer, *Philosophical Hermeneutics*, pp. 9 and 15; Charles Taylor, "Objectivity in Political Science," in Ryan, *The Philosophy of Social Explanation* (Oxford, 1976), pp. 139ff. Gadamer insists strongly that our values are the necessary conditions of our understandings, but as both are of different types, the ubiquity of the former is, strictly speaking, entailed by the modality of the latter. For a sympathetic and lucid discussion see Gunnell, *Political Theory: Tradition and Interpretation* (Cambridge, Mass., 1979), chap. 4, and the refreshingly civilized discussion by Gunnell and Pocock, *Annals of Scholarship* 1 (1980):2–62. For a more general treatment of Gadamer's theories see Rorty, *Philosophy*, pp. 357ff.

It is, of course, this general picture of the functioning of statements within the structures of linguistic convention which also enables the connection to be made between rhetoric in its specific and general senses. See Introduction, n. 7; Part Two, Introduction; Chap. 6; and Appendix.

is so intimately concerned with the qualitative assessment of what goes on in a subject activity, has only an approximate fit with any activity's appraisive expectations: hence only the partial truth of Hollis's statement that "there is no snag about outrageous methodological demands." From the perspective of practice, there is always a snag. However, that is not the only perspective involved. *Homo methodologicus* must persuade and appraise according to scrutinized convention, but by degrees, and janus-like.

This simple picture of the elusive intellectual location of *homo methodologicus* is rendered more complex and his position more difficult if the scrutinized activity itself is conventionally composite and marginally unstable, exhibiting differing appraisive expectations. Although remaining under the auspices of activity Ξ, an author x may in fact shift between patterns of value that Ξ has come to embrace. Various established academic activities could be used to illustrate this general point, for example, anthropology or the study of national literatures such as English—and the more interdisciplinary they claim to be, the more apposite they become; but as I shall suggest, political theory provides an apt enough instance of the incentives and difficulties which face the methodologist who would reform a conventionally composite activity.

----------- III -----------

This general survey of the intellectual location of methodological discourse reveals clearly enough the limitations to which an essay such as this will be subject and provides a statement as well as a warning as to the nature of the terrain I am covering. Similarly, we are in a position to appreciate the sorts of criticisms which are commonly leveled at methodological argument, and despite them we can appreciate the intermittent significance of methodological discourse in the very process of reformulating intellectual activity and its standards of judgment.

The first ill to which *homo methodologicus* is heir is what must seem to be a terrible weakness of self-reference. Hence what Steiner has called the mandarin idiom is dominant in methodological discourse. It is the tendency of writers "to deal more with each other's previous papers and animadversions than with the intrinsic question."[24] Steiner's impatience is understandable, but this is surely what we should expect. For, once placed in an equivocal context of discourse, any "intrinsic question" itself becomes questionable. The certainty of knowing exactly what is at issue does depend upon the very stability of a context of convention at the edges of which *homo methodologicus* operates. He is obliged to take less for granted than those living in the security of their daily research round. The second major ill also arises directly from his interstitial status; he is only equivocally a member of any established community. He is arguably first cousin to Oakeshott's theoretician, neither practitioner nor fully a theorist, an impostor in the Cave.[25]

Consider the crossfire in which Sir Karl Popper's scientific theories have been caught. Feyerabend sees Popper as prescribing a set of strategies within, and detrimental to, scientific activity, as a perpetrator of "law and order science." For Margaret Masterman, on the other hand, he is setting up a philosophical model of explanation so far removed from scientific activity that it is largely a curious irrelevance.[26] Or more directly, consider some of the judgments made of Skinner's seminal essay "Meaning and Understanding in the History of Ideas." For Steiner it

[24] Steiner, *After Babel*, p. 162.

[25] *On Human Conduct* (Oxford 1975), p. 30, and p. 26 on theoreticians. Or consider the remarks of S. Humphries, "The Historian, His Documents and the Elementary Moves in Historical Thought," *Hist. & Th.* 19 (1980):1. Barry Hindess, *Philosophy and Methodology in the Social Sciences* (Sussex, 1977), pp. 3–4.

[26] Cf. Margaret Masterman's contribution to I. Lakatos and A. Musgrave, eds., *Criticism and The Growth of Knowledge* (Cambridge, 1970); Toulmin, *Human Understanding*, pp. 62–63, who groups Carnap, Frege, and Hempel with Popper; and more generally, Eugene Meehan, *Explanation in Social Science: A System Paradigm* (Homewood, 1968), chap. 1, and the Foreword by Norton Long: with Paul Feyerabend, *Against Method* (London, 1975), index for "Law and Order Science"; and Toulmin (again) on philosophy as intellectual authoritarianism, *Human Understanding*, p. 46.

covers well the real difficulties of the historian of ideas, but it is philosophically naïve; for Mulligan, Richards, and Graham, it is historically unworkable (the snag about outrageous demands); for Gunnell it is a philosophy of history which has been mistaken as a harbinger of method.[27] All these criticisms testify to the methodological position of an author without realizing the full significance of the designation, each like an independent fix on an unknown transmitter needing another to locate its whereabouts.

In short, a writer operating at the methodological nexus is as vulnerable to half-true accusations of irrelevance, superficiality, and half-baked interference as he is to misunderstanding. Certainly, the qualitative assessment of his own argument is less straightforward than we are apt to think. I am not, of course, making a plea for indiscriminate tolerance: any methodologist who finds it necessary to tell historians (twice) that they will not find questionnaires of too much help, since their subjects are usually dead, deserves just about all he gets, and perhaps a little more.[28]

The intermittent significance of the methodological idiom has been considerable; it has, perhaps, been the principal mechanism of disciplinary mitosis that has marked Western thought for over two thousand years; and throughout this period, philosophy has been a relatively stable point of reference in methodological dispute. The qualification is important because we cannot assume philosophy to have a static and trouble-free identity, like some moth, transfixed in the unmoving context of its own genus.[29] And, although it has never been so capricious as to avoid

---

[27] Steiner, *After Babel*, p. 136; L. Mulligan, J. Richards, and J. Graham, "Intentions and Conventions: A Critique of Quentin Skinner's Method for the Study of the History of Ideas," *Pol. Stud.* 27 (1979):84ff.; Gunnell, *Political Theory*, pp. 102 and 116ff. See also the Pocock-Gunnell exchange, *Annals of Scholarship*, esp. pp. 42–44 and 60–61, which reveals that care is needed not to oversimplify work located at the methodological nexus.

[28] Nils Kvasted, "Semantics in the Methodology of the History of Ideas," *JHI* 38 (1977):162, and for the reminder, 167–168.

[29] For a discussion around this theme see Rorty, *Philosophy*, and Toulmin, *Human Understanding*, passim.

all nets and labels, the covering term *philosophy* can disguise and be applied to genuine discursive differences; as Iris Murdoch has elegantly remarked, McTaggart states that time is unreal, Moore that he has just finished breakfast. So the eye of philosophy turned inward provides the basis of all we understand to be philosophy in any discriminate sense. Narcissus, not Socrates, is the guide and moth catcher who holds the lantern in the dark. The reflexive core of philosophy is important to stress here for two reasons. First, it provides an exception to my rule of method; in reflexive philosophy, the methodological tension between regulatory and nonregulatory inquiry seems overcome through the eradication of conventional distance. Perhaps only in philosophy do we have a point at which the methodologist has a respectable occupation, a home in which the mandarin idiom is the supremely authentic voice and where *praxis* is inescapable.[30] Second, insofar as philosophers have been fundamentally concerned with the nature and limits of their own activity as discipline, they have tended to erode the established domain of philosophical discourse, leaving an increasingly extensive area of discourse which they see as extrinsic to their own inquiry, yet over which a residue of indirect philosophical authority in a more general sense of the term *philosophy* remains. The net result is to reveal an increasingly large territory over which *homo methodologicus* can wander in his accustomed fashion with justifiable plausibility.[31]

[30] Michael Murray, *Modern Philosophy of History: Its Origin and Destination* (The Hague, 1970), p. 1.

[31] To some extent one result of this residuum of indirect philosophical authority is to modify the conventional distance between philosophy (as discipline) and other activities, and perhaps it may even help maintain contradictory expectations that conventional distance can be overcome without the erosion of a subject activity. The general belief that somehow the philosopher has an authority beyond his own domain certainly helps maintain a naïve faith in the positive results to be expected from anyone working at the methodological nexus. Thus Vernon van Dyke, *Political Science*, accepts the conventional distance between philosophy and political science but nevertheless sees the philosopher's role as legislative (Feyerabend's law and order [political] science). More negatively, and from the perspective of a subject activity, that Geoffrey Elton could be gleeful, or disappointed (I'm not sure which), that philosophers have failed to

At this point, the image of the philosopher's stone might be appealing: in the beginning, philosophy as undifferentiated love of wisdom seems like some giant, unworked, neolithic flint, heavy, blunt, but capable of being cut for many specialized purposes. Gradually it is transformed, its many shards being cast away, some to be shaped for supplementary purposes (pure physics), others ultimately to be abandoned as worthless (alchemy). So one can hear *homo methodologicus* working the stone in the echoes of Socrates' teachings; one can also hear the claims that it has achieved its almost polished shape in the acclamations of philosophical revolution and achievement which have echoed down the centuries.

Even if the stone has to be polished with a little salt (not least because it places a stable core of philosophy necessarily at the center of a changing world), it is nevertheless unnecessary to suggest a very different history of philosophy in order to illustrate both the periodic importance of sustained methodological discourse and the concomitant significance of reflexive philosophy which provides both the exception to, and the grounds for, methodological dispute. Whereas Plato spent his life asserting the overarching authority of philosophy in whose demeaning shadow all other intellectual activities lay, Aristotle emphasized the potential integrity of some degree of intellectual diversity. By defining and accepting the conventional distance between philosophy, its aims and methods and standards of appraisal, and those of rhetoric, he provided the initial conditions necessary for the firm, methodological separation of rhetoric and philosophy affected by figures such as Cicero, Quintilian, and, much later, Valla.[32] In the fourteenth century, again with an emphasis on method, philosophy was separated from religious faith through

---

advance historical study, attests to his recognition of the conventional distance between the relevant activities and also to the belief that somehow it should have been the philosopher's task to overcome it by becoming a strategic methodologist. See *The Practice of History* (London, 1969).

[32] Thus for Aristotle when in the context of rhetorical discourse, the *enthymeme* is not a malformed syllogism, but the structural analogue of syllogistic argument. So it can be said that the fit between ξ as *enthymeme* and the context of argument in which it is found determines whether ξ is a fault or a virtue.

the work of Ockham and Autrecourt; in the sixteenth and seventeenth centuries philosophy, scholastic and natural, were separated. The nineteenth and twentieth centuries have seen a veritable cornucopia of discursive and disciplinary developments, with conceptions of philosophy and its methods impinging on most of them, and methodological dispute central to them all.[33] History, for example, divided first from rhetoric, has been given some formal and methodological independence from both political ideology and scientific explanation (see Chap. 9. v). The social sciences have claimed a methodological identity distinct from both social philosophy and history. Sociology now grapples with the conflicting claims of post-Weberian and post-Marxian methodologies, both of which are rooted in differing conceptions of philosophical reasoning. Political science, divorced from moral philosophy and history by a nineteenth-century image of scientific methodology, itself promises to exhibit increasing divisions in the heat of philosophical controversy over the nature of scientific method, and in the light of its failures to fulfill the expectations raised by its own almost Baconian methodological manifestoes. In the context of these general remarks alone, it would be surprising if political theory, which during the 1950s and 1960s was considered as either dead or on balance worthy of extinction, should not itself be the subject of marked methodological attention.

So, as a prelude to an outline of methodological dispute in political theory, one can evoke a catalog of names of self-proclaimed methodological revolutions which have been such a feature of the twentieth century—the phenomenological, the Leavisite, the structural, the Wittgensteinian, the Namierite, the Saussurian—all have involved emphatically, some perhaps almost exclusively, proclamations of the method needed to lead us from the dark into the light, proclamations of new aims, new techniques, words, rules, and gospels. Moreover, given the hardly

---

[33] See e.g. Toulmin, *Human Understanding*, pp. 232ff., for an account of the methodological dispute between Planck and Mach, the work of the "plage" group in forming the activity of molecular biology, and for an account of the methodological difficulties of particle theory and their ramifications for the character of physics.

relieved darkness of the past and confusion in the present to which they have all pointed, they exhibit a faith in the future which, if I have located *homo methodologicus* rightly, must seem touching.

> No analysis of a literary work, *Winnie-The-Pooh* not excepted, can, in this age of conflicting critical schools, afford not to rest itself upon a thorough consideration of methodological principles.[34]

In short, where there is dissatisfaction with the existing boundaries and conventions of established intellectual activities, we can anticipate that what we recognize most generally as philosophy will be a touchstone for the clustering altercations of *homo methodologicus*, a figure attracted by the merest whiff of disorder, messenger of hope, peace, progress, and rationality, a harbinger of principles on tablets in whose wake is turmoil. And, insofar as *homo methodologicus* is involved in the formation and reformation of discrete intellectual activities, he is instrumental in the formation and reinforcement of the differing standards of textual appraisal appropriate to them. Where some hope of discriminate qualitative analysis is fulfilled, however, the more any existing general appraisive field will have to carry the burden of the translator's art; just as, to repeat and prefigure, where an activity lacks a particular and singularly authoritative set of standards of its own, the methodologist's attention must sooner or later be drawn to the common appraisive field on which it relies.

The existence of *homo methodologicus* is, as it were, a condition of the diversity of intellectual life. The price he pays for his *de facto* and occasional significance is in the coinage of exile. He is an itinerant, bardic or sophistic, wandering among the *poleis* of the intellectual world, seeking out (for each one's own good) weaknesses of *nomos*, *logos*, and *techne*. Although less kindly perhaps, given his interstitial status, the analogue of the witch may be more fitting; and the methodologist's being frequently misunderstood (if not persecuted) by the various groups between

---

[34] Duns C. Penwiper, "The Complete Analysis of *Winnie-The-Pooh*," in F. Crews, ed., *The Pooh Perplex* (London, 1972), p. 87.

which he peddles his spells may be a sort of Salem effect. From the perspective of those securely behind the walls of self-confident and unified activities (possibly still basking in revolutionary glow of previous turmoil), *homo methodologicus* haranguing from the walls of a neighboring acropolis may seem to be but the stirring in a teacup or a belated effort to sift something of value from the lees. But a teacup deftly stirred, as Jane Austen knew well enough, can be a foreboding and an intimation of greater things to come. As it has been justly written, if there are those who consider Jane Austen merely tea–tablish, there are those who think that Mozart tinkles.

CHAPTER 2

Political Theory,
Its Conventional Structure,
the Issue-Orthodoxy, and
the Assessment of Texts

Do not be troubled by the fact that languages . . .
consist only of orders. If you want to say that this
shews them to be incomplete, ask yourself whether
our language is complete;—whether it was so before
the symbolism of chemistry and the notation of the
infinitesimal calculus were incorporated in it; for these
are, so to speak, suburbs of our language. (And how
many houses or streets does it take before a town
begins to be a town?) Our language can be seen as an
ancient city: a maze of little streets and squares, of old
and new houses, and of houses with additions from
various periods; and this surrounded by a multitude of
new boroughs with straight, regular streets and
uniform houses.

Wittgenstein, *Philosophical Investigations*

My advice is this: take two mistresses at once—
He is stronger who can manage more;
When the attention, thus distracted,
Runs from this to that,
One passion saps the other's force.
Great rivers weaken when divided into brooks.
Fierce flames gutter when fed on scattered fuel.

Ovid, *Remedia Amoris*

Were he more than the creation of metaphor, *homo methodologicus* would migrate in droves to the *polis* of political theory, where certainly the methodological idiom is now heard with a frequency which is difficult to ignore.[1] So pervasive is it that an overview of methodological dispute about political theory can almost serve as a means of describing the community itself.

An identification of the political theory community, however, is by no means straightforward; the covering term itself overlaps with expressions such as 'political philosophy' and 'thought' and is sufficiently porous to include with degrees of certainty scholars who are involved in rather different intellectual activities which themselves are marginally unstable. Thus we may be told that political theory and science are different, that political theory is a logico-normative field within political science; that it is a branch of moral philosophy, or largely an aspect of the history of ideas; that it always involves a blend of logical, empirical, and normative reflection. Such identifications as these (in all of which there is some truth) attest to a methodologically irritating endemic state of terminological *laissez faire* and to a complex and fluid conventional structure, which I shall identify impressionistically in quite familiar terms.

Most notably, the habitual methods of the political theorist usually reflect some of the conceptual rigor of the philosopher:[2] the theorist is expected to observe logical procedures and to impose firm and unequivocal conceptual order upon his material, to avoid arbitrary termini and conclusions which are not logically compelling. At the same time, he is expected to be at home in

[1] "It is perhaps an unwonted parody of Hegel's aphorism about the Owl of Minerva . . . that the decline of political theory should be accompanied by a heightened interest in how political theory should be studied. . . . Methodological issues dominate the current literature of political science." Richard Ashcraft, "On the Problem of Methodology and the Nature of Political Theory," *Pol. Th.* 3 (1975): 5.

[2] Hence Field's notion of theory being "quasi-philosophical," *Political Theory* (London, 1963 ed.), p. xiii; see also P. H. Partridge, "Politics, Philosophy and Ideology," in A. Quinton, ed., *Political Philosophy* (Oxford, 1977 ed.), pp. 33ff.

35

tracing the contingent, nonlogical connections between and within past sequences of events and ideas, without imposing upon them conceptually stereotyped and anachronistic patterns of unity.[3] In addition, his arguments are expected to be (and are frequently promoted as being) of practical guiding relevance to the political world in which the theorist lives. To this last extent, the theorist is commonly supposed to be concerned not with what has been, is, or logically must be, but with what ought to be.[4]

To put the matter more abstractly, and irrespective of the familiar but approximate labels, at least three different principles of classification and connection jostle for ascendancy: those of logical inference, preferential possibility, and contingent chronological sequence. These may be seen as the main currents in the conventional rivers from whose junction the marsh of the political theory community spreads.[5]

As a whole, each major conventional stream is rather like

[3] So, what might be seen as a philosophically legitimate inference may also be seen as historiographical sleight of hand. See e.g. J. H. Hexter's comments on J. G. A. Pocock, *The Machiavellian Moment* (Princeton, 1975), in *Hist. & Th.* 16 (1977): 308. Numerous studies in or about political theory attest to the important (but limited) role of historical, or more broadly, empirical discourse in political theory: see e.g. Field, *Political Theory*; Elizabeth James, *Political Theory: Introduction to Interpretation* (Chicago, 1976), chap. 4; Andrew Hacker, "Capital and Carbuncles: The Great Books Re-Appraised," *APSR* 48 (1954); L. J. Macfarlane, *Modern Political Theory* (London, 1970), pp. xv–xviii. See also Chap. 3 of this study.

[4] Hence not only the vulgar textbook designations of political theory as simply the 'normative branch' of political science, but the more carefully argued backing of Gewirth, *Political Philosophy* (New York, 1975), pp. 1ff., that political philosophy is but a branch of moral philosophy; and the common image of political theory among its academic neighbors. See e.g. Max Gluckman, *Order and Rebellion in Tribal Africa* (London, 1963), p. 5, citing Fortés, Evans-Pritchard, and Radcliffe-Brown.

[5] J. R. Lucas's ironic apology in *The Principles of Politics* (Oxford, 1966) is indicative of the conventional structure which also has a clear institutional dimension. As an activity in universities, political theory grew from, and between, departments of history and philosophy with its early practitioners being often involved in political programming and ideological promotion. For further comment on the institutional background of political theory, see Editorial, *Pol. Stud.* 1 (1953): 1; C. Condren, "Political Theory," in D. Aitkin, ed., *Surveys of Australian Political Science* (Canberra, forthcoming).

Machiavelli's depiction of the papacy in Italy—too strong for another to dominate the peninsula, too weak to do so itself. But the very existence of the community is a sign that the situation is not as intolerable as methodological Machiavellis might imagine. Indeed, despite earlier rumors of death, political theory is a modish activity, heavily populated at its center by a relatively unreflexive corpus, a rump which is apparently happy to wriggle from one set of priorities to another, despite the incitement this becomes to *homo methodologicus.*[6]

The forms and degrees of methodological reaction have been various. Discussion of extrinsic political phenomena is sometimes used as a means of urging an alteration of the community's intrinsic conventional balance.[7] More directly, since the Second World War, there have been expostulations of dismay at the incantatory gestures in the direction of such magic words as 'logic' or 'analysis,' which have passed for philosophical reasoning within the community.[8] At the same time, but with often greater ur-

[6] Consider Ruth Bevan, *Burke and Marx: A Revisionist View* (La Salle, 1973), p. 15, where in almost as many words we are told that the essential point of political theory is to be found in logic, in historical biography, and in its political value for us. Gunnell, *Political Theory: Tradition and Interpretation* (Cambridge, Mass., 1979), p. xvii, has commented dryly on the traditionally unreflective nature of the community; and N. A. McDonald and J. N. Rosenau have remarked that the inner contradictions of the activity are so fully accepted that they are hardly matters of concern for political theorists, in "Political Theory as Academic Field and Intellectual Activity," *J.P.* 30 (1968): 319. See M. Cowling, *The Nature and Limits of Political Science* (Cambridge, 1963), p. 69, for a critical account of some of the confusions attendant upon political theory's structural diathesis. Understandably, then, Bernstein, *The Restructuring of Social and Political Theory* (London, 1979 ed.), pp. 235–236, looks toward the sort of dialectical change that can be predicated only on an awareness of contradiction.

[7] For illustration see Condren, "The Quest for a Concept of 'Needs,' " in R. Fitzgerald, ed., *Human Needs and Politics* (Oxford and Sydney, 1977), pp. 244ff.

[8] Margaret McDonald, "Natural Rights," *Proc. Arist. Soc.* 47 (1947): 225ff.; T. D. Weldon, *The Vocabulary of Politics* (Harmondsworth, 1953). The tone of irritation infuses such works as Brian Barry, *Political Argument* (London, 1965); Lucas, *The Principles*; Cowling, *The Nature and Limits*. A good deal of this seems understandable, and certainly for all the frequent references to 'logic' and 'analysis,' just what is meant by these terms is often unclear to me.

gency, there have been common cries that political theory is insufficiently informed by the correct ideological priorities.[9]

Perhaps the most sustained and interesting calls for methodological reform, however, have come from the historians in and around the community. Ten years ago, John Pocock was confident that at least the historians of political theory were already living through a methodological transformation of their discipline. Confrontation and self-awareness were finally giving hope of systematically good work. For,

> good work done in a context of methodological confusion is in a sense done by chance, or by some co-incidence of *virtù* and *fortuna*: it is done despite the available methods, and lacks the critical autonomy which comes only when the method is operating positively to produce the work. The transformation we can claim to be living through is nothing more or less than the emergence of a truly autonomous method.[10]

Here speaks the authentic voice of *homo methodologicus*, in a manifesto reminiscent of the *Novum Organum*, *Scrutiny*, and *The Complete Analysis* of Duns C. Penwiper.[11]

But largely because of the community's conventional struc-

---

[9] Examples are legion, but see Neil Wood, "The Social History of Political Theory," *Pol. Th.* 6 (1978): 345ff.; William Leiss, "Critical Theory and Its Future," *Pol. Th.* 2 (1974): 330ff.; Ashcraft, "On the Problem," is a particularly intelligent example; F. von Hayek, *The Constitution of Liberty* (London, 1960), is a monumental one. The cries for a strategic reorientation are closely associated with getting political theory somehow closer to something called the 'real world.' A clear example is to be found in Carole Pateman's remarks in S. Benn, ed., *Political Participation: A Discussion of Political Rationality* (Canberra, 1978); another is to be found in Brian Barry's remarks that political theorists are uninteresting because they write only about other political theorists. See "Do Neighbors Make Good Fences?" *Pol. Th.* 9 (1981): 296–297. A parallel body of literature has grown of the behavioralist movement. The work of Christian Bay and Leo Strauss and his followers link the two activist manifestations. See e.g. G. J. Graham and G. W. Carey, eds., *The Post Behavioural Era* (New York, 1972), esp. chaps. 5 and 9.

[10] J. G. A. Pocock, *Politics, Language and Time* (London, 1973), p. 11.

[11] "In this light almost all the methodologies we might otherwise be tempted to sample appear inadequate and dangerous; whatever good results they may have produced 'have been achieved,' as R. S. Crane puts it, 'to a considerable extent

ture, this optimism may seem misplaced. As we will see (pp. 50–52, 76–77, 283ff.), unalloyed historical discourse can even be seen as threatening to the community's *raison d'être*.[12] It is not surprising that there has been considerable resistance to what has been seen as a simple historicist imperialism,[13] associated most strongly with Pocock and Skinner.[14] However, resistance on these grounds is itself an oversimplification given the conventional complexity of the activity to which, in part, they are appealing. The advocacy of historical rigor and authority has come by turns wrapped in a coating of political benefit[15] and philosophical subordination,[16] resulting in a blend of conclusions that might not

in spite of the critics' addiction to principles of enquiry and knowledge ' " Duns C. Penwiper, "The Complete Analysis of *Winnie-The-Pooh*," in F. Crews, ed., *The Pooh Perplex* (London, 1972), p. 88.

[12] See David Easton, "The Decline of Modern Political Theory," *JP* 13 (1951), concerning theory's *decline* into history; see also Hacker, "Capital."

[13] See esp. C. D. Tarlton, "Historicity, Meaning and Revisionism in the Study of Political Thought," *Hist. & Th.* 12 (1973): 307ff.; Margaret Leslie, "In Defence of Anachronism," *Pol. Stud.* 18 (1970): 433ff.; B. Parekh and R. N. Berki, "The History of Political Ideas: A Critique of Skinner's Methodology," *JHI* 34 (1973): 163ff.

[14] Of Skinner's essays, "Meaning and Understanding in the History of Ideas," *Hist. & Th.* (1969), has attracted most attention, but for further references and discussion, see "Political Thought and Political Action: A Symposium on Quentin Skinner," *Pol. Th.* 2 (1974): 251ff.; for Pocock, see *Politics, Language and Time*, esp. the first and last essays; the discussion with Gunnell in *Annals of Scholarship* 1 (1980); and the essay that perhaps began the whole historical attack, "The History of Political Thought: A Methodological Enquiry," in P. Laslett and W. G. Runciman, eds., *Politics, Philosophy and Society*, 2nd ser. (Oxford, 1962), pp. 183ff. See also some of the writings of John Dunn, notably, "The Identity of the History of Ideas," *Philosophy* 43 (1968): 85ff.; B. A. Haddock, "The History of Ideas and the Study of Politics," *Pol. Th.* 2 (1974): 420ff.; Gunnell, *Political Theory*, chaps. 1–3.

[15] Skinner, "Meaning and Understanding," ends echoing Keith Thomas on the uplifting note that good history is the key of self-awareness; Pocock ends *Politics, Language and Time* suggesting that historical understanding is a useful guard against unpalatable ideological mythologizing (p. 291).

[16] Skinner, ibid., a view which is reflected in his readings of Hobbes and his criticisms of Warrender. Since Skinner in particular draws on philosophers such as Collingwood, Wittgenstein, and Austin, all of whom stressed the philosophical importance of concrete detail and substantive illustration, it is not difficult to see how this rapprochement between philosophy and history comes about in Skinner's writings.

be so far removed from those of mainstream theorists such as Hacker and Berlin.[17] So, it is difficult to say how far the new methodological critics have been attempting to readjust the conventional distance between philosophy and history, have compromised a strict historicity by appealing to the mixed standards of the established political theory community, or have simply attempted to alter by new arguments a traditional balance of dispositions. In sum, even this most cursory glance at the literature indicates how the inherent tendencies of methodological discourse, when directed to the conventional structure of an activity like political theory, result in a certain dissipation of normative force. Atempted reform has brought with it heat, frustration, and confusion in which Minerva's armies have failed to clash by dusk.[18] Such a glance, moreover, serves precisely to underline the political theory community's lack of common standards of qualitative assessment.[19] This is a lack, however, which may be indicated further by noting a countervailing trend in the community to an even greater conventional eclecticism. Leaving aside the main conventional rivers, minor tributaries such as social psychology or behavioralism should be borne in mind as perhaps increasingly important to the community. Although one could not accuse the political theorist of being a Wildian worshiper of whim, or a conceptual kleptomaniac,[20] Brian Barry has noticed the con-

---

[17] Hacker, "Capital"; Berlin, *Four Essays on Liberty* (New York, 1970), p. 4; Field, *Political Theory*, "Some Historical Preliminaries"; and others too numerous to mention.

[18] See the comments of McDonald and Rosenau, "Political Theory"; J. G. A. Pocock, *Politics, Language and Time*, p. 5. For a sustained wave of heat see John Keene, "On the 'New' History: Quentin Skinner's Proposal for a New History of Political Ideology," *Telos* 47 (1981).

[19] Hence Judith Skhlar's impatience with Pocock for his failure to share her priorities as to who is worth studying, *Pol. Th.* 6 (1978): 551ff. Pocock's ironic remarks in his discussion with Gunnell, in *Annals of Scholarship*, precisely underline this lack of shared sense of priorities. See also the very different appraisive conclusions reached from similar beginnings by Mark Francis and Richard Dagger concerning Carole Pateman, *Political Obligation, Australasian Journal of Politics and History* 27 (1980), and *Pol. Th.* 8 (1980), respectively.

[20] Political theorists have traditionally shown little awareness of stylistic problems, for example, which is surprising, given the lip service paid to the literary

siderable variety of newly embraced disciplines which political theorists have previously shunned.[21] Such enrichments to the conventional infrastructure of political theory may result, as Barry hopes, in that desirous consummation, an autonomous sphere of discourse; more likely, however, is an increase in the theorist's superficiality. To converse in his *agora* he will need yet another phrase book; and the most sanguine of methodologists will be driven totally to distraction.

The methodological demands, then, for a more severe discursive identity, or the hopes for a constructive interdisciplinary libertarianism, may constitute a balance of disadvantages for many calling themselves political theorists. As things stand, although the theorist's domain may be vulnerable to methodological attack, the force and direction of the attack are difficult to sustain; the theorist may shift ground without abandoning territory or conceding any palpable hit.[22]

Whether this is, in fact, a consequence of the *status quo* which commends itself to the political theorist, the composite conventional structure of the activity, much as I have depicted it, has had no shortage of defenders. And it is in the latitudinarian defense of "old-fashioned political theory"[23] against all comers that

---

excellence of so much of their subject matter. James T. Boulton's *The Language of Politics in the Age of Wilkes and Burke* (London, 1963) is an exception (written by a literary critic) and an indication of just how much could have been done.

[21] Brian Barry, "The Strange Death of Political Philosophy" *Government and Opposition* 15 (1980): 287–288; de Jouvenel, *The Pure Theory of Politics* (Cambridge, 1962), p. x. Precedent was clearly set by Anthony Downs, *An Economic Theory of Democracy* (New York, 1951); Christian Bay, *The Structure of Freedom* (Stanford, 1958).

[22] See John Plamenatz' (anticipatory?) disclaimer with respect to *Man and Society* (London, 1963) that he is not a historian, but a theorist. This proved insufficient to stop Skinner gazetting him as a historical blunderer, in "Meaning and Understanding," pp. 15 and 22; Hacker, too, is given honorable mention, pp. 4 and 5. He also would argue that he is a theorist, not a historian, and so historical critique misses the mark. The attempt to condemn such writers in a purely historical court of appeal raises an interesting discrepancy in Skinner's own writings, on which Gunnell has commented, *Political Theory*, pp. 24–25, 96–97.

[23] Hans Kohn, "Political Theory and the History of Ideas," *JHI* 25 (1965): 303.

one can see perhaps most easily the lack of a uniform or distinctive standard for appraising the community's inherited and potentially important work.

William Blackstone, for example, explicitly defending political theory against any form of "reductionism," argues that political theory should aspire to adequacy, the criteria for which constitute a syndrome of moral seriousness, logical coherence, empirical accuracy, and scientific testability.[24] "Adequacy," in fact, looks just like a defensive reflex for the conventional structure of political theory as we know it, and it reminds me forcibly of Lorenzo Valla's view of the strengths of the rhetorician over the weaknesses of the philosopher.[25] It is precisely because the philosopher adheres to a single set of conventions that a single error can wreck his whole argument; but the rhetorician, eclectic, flexible, freed from the authority of any overriding procedural standard and cohesive criteria of appraisal, remains immune from the collapse of any part of his argument.

> Do I contradict myself,
> Very well, I contradict myself,
> For I am large,
> I contain multitudes.

Now is not the time to labor my belief that, if 'gentlemen of the wide swallow' like Professor Blackstone are right, what we need is less adequacy (not least because as logical consistency is one of his criteria, his position is inherently self-contradictory); neither should it be stressed unduly that his criteria for adequacy, capacious as they are, cannot cover all we consider important in political theory. Even if *Utopia* is morally serious, and we add an appreciation of dialectic to a criterion of logic, it is difficult to see how notions of empirical accuracy, let alone scientific testability, are much help in understanding the work.

[24] W. T. Blackstone, *Political Philosophy: An Introduction* (New York, 1973), p. vii, pt. 1, and pp. 183ff.

[25] Lorenzo Valla, *Dialecticarum Disputationem*, Libri 3, Praefatio 1, cited in Linda Janik, "Lorenzo Valla and the Demoralisation of History," *Hist. & Th.* 12 (1973): 390; Sidney, *Defence of Poesie*, puts a similar case with respect to the strengths of poetry over philosophy.

What does emerge starkly from the political theorist's questing after "adequacy" and "completeness," as well as from the shunning of "reductionism" and the "single-minded approach" in the appraisal of political theory, is the difficulty of finding any authoritative standards and defining criteria of judgment, especially if, as Professor James innocently puts it, "all approaches" can constitute "the best route to understanding great theory."[26] This sounds a little like the Dodo after the Caucus Race—but as the Dodo realized sensibly enough, if everybody gets a prize it matters not what the shape and length of the course are. The formal point to emerge from this is simply that however we specify the conventional structure of political theory, once its composite nature is accepted, then the methodological questions revolving around the qualitative status of its inheritance become as difficult as they are central—for, manifestly, not every approach does get a coconut at the fair, nor every text a victor's crown. Moreover, as differing intellectual activities produce diverging qualitative expectations, then the more intellectually composite an established activity is, the less it can give rise to its own commonly approved and specific criteria of qualitative appraisal. Whatever else it is, the desire to contain multitudes is a bulwark against appraisive rigor; to offer coconuts for all approaches is not much help. "There hath," wrote Francis Bacon wagging his methodological finger,

> been also laboured and put in practice a method, which is not a lawful method, but a method of imposture . . . being nothing but a mass of words of all arts . . . like a fripper's or a broker's shop, that hath ends of everything, but nothing of worth.[27]

It seems there hath, indeed, and the result is to place a heavy burden upon the general categories of an appraisive field under which any qualitative conceptions pertaining to the activity of

---

[26] The expressions are taken from Blackstone, *Political Philosophy*; George Kateb, *Political Theory: Its Nature and Uses* (New York, 1968), p. 174; and James, *Political Theory*, p. 16, for "all approaches"; see also Leslie Lipson, *The Great Issues of Politics* (Englewood Cliffs, 1970 ed.), pp. 24–25.

[27] Bacon, *The Advancement of Learning*, Bk. 2.

political theory can be subsumed. And it may be added, reliance on the members of this field provides a common, if variously negotiable, currency which has its place in creating the illusion of a single disciplinary form to which Professor James, for example, still refers despite her urging a warm and woolly embrace of all approaches. Thus we are led to a direct assessment of the appraisive field the theorist employs when dealing with the more or less adequate texts which are supposed to exemplify the 'discipline's' major modes of discourse. However, before we can begin to approach this problem directly, there are two barriers to be overcome in the shape of the orthodox theorist's belief in a fundamental or basic set of political issues and in his faith in an ongoing tradition of classic political theorists. Adherence to what I shall call the issue-orthodoxy involves a range of methodological injunctions for the political theorist among which, it might be thought, can be found considerable hope of approaching questions of qualitative status despite the difficulties posed by conventional structure, while the great tradition would seem *prima facie* to reveal all the qualities necessary for any text's achieving classic status.

II

To begin with, the issue-orthodoxy may be identified as the general belief that politics can be defined in terms of a finite range of distinct universal or 'basic' issues, encapsulated by such terms as *power, justice, sovereignty, obligation, state,* or by such expressions as *the public good* or *the limits of government,* upon which political theory should focus.[28] The number and formu-

[28] Affirmations of the issue-orthodoxy are so widespread that Elizabeth James suggests that belief in the "perennial questions of politics" is shared by all traditional political theorists (as opposed to activist critics on the one hand and behavioralists on the other). The generalization is a reasonable one, although many behavioralists and some activists (such as Bay) would embrace the issue-orthodoxy, and some otherwise traditional theorists would seem to reject it. See Pate-

lation of the allegedly basic issues varies from theorist to theorist,[29] but specification notwithstanding, the faith in a range of basic issues denotes a distinct understanding of politics, language, and political theorizing.[30] In this way, it provides a strategic method for political theory, regardless of the conventional balance of the activity, for perception of the issues would seem to have priority over the mode of their explication. Moreover, it may appear that the inheritance of political theory texts can be assessed qualitatively with reference to the issues, in whose light they may be appraised, and their achievement, or not, of classic status be explained.[31]

Dealing in some way with the 'basics' is the least we should expect from a great political theorist. An examination of this expectation could take us back immediately to the conventional structure of political theory, since an interpreter's view of the quality of a past theorist's treatment of an issue will depend largely upon his own discursive priorities. Returning to this sort of terrain will be unfruitful, not least because the coventional distance between philosophy, history, and ideology is in part a function of the different qualitative criteria of judgment inherent in each matrix of discourse. A philosophically poor discussion of an issue like consent or property (such as Bumbling Mr. Locke is often

---

man, *Political Obligation*, holding that obligation is a distinctly modern political problem.

[29] For d'Entrèves, "Obligation," *Philosophy* 43 (1968): 104ff., there is only one basic issue; for Lipson, *The Great Issues*, pp. 13ff., there are certainly only five; for C. J. Friedrich, *An Introduction to Political Theory* (New York, 1962), there are half a dozen or so; for von Hayek, *The Constitution*, p. 5, there is an unspecific plurality. The seventy-eight section headings in Lucas, *The Principles*, provide an almost full range of the candidates for such perennial status.

[30] Lipson, *The Great Issues*, p. 17; J. B. Miller, *The Nature of Politics* (London, 1962), p. 282, instructing the instructors as to their duty, writes that the student "must also be convinced that there are certain central problems of politics which occur in any system."

[31] Hence Friedrich's treatment of Machiavelli and Hobbes as both theorists of power, *An Introduction*; Lipson, *The Great Issues*, p. 17; Margaret Judson, *The Political Thought of Sir Henry Vane The Younger* (Ann Arbor, 1982 ed.), provides a clear example of the belief that dealing with the basic issues is a firm index of greatness, and because Sir Harry Vane did, he should not be ignored now. See pp. 5, 15, 36, and 51.

accused of providing)[32] might even be a condition of an author's ideological success. The historical perception of a writer like Guicciardini could well mitigate against his achieving philosophical standing.

We can, however, deal with the issue-orthodoxy more directly—although, as befits and illustrates the conventional structure of political theory, quite differently grounded objections will be needed before the orthodoxy can even be encircled properly and its poverty as a basis for the appraisal of political theory's inheritance be revealed. The orthodoxy takes both an empirical and a metaphysical form. As a preliminary, however, it is worth canvassing some logical problems common to both forms, partially in order to emphasize that, in either manifestation, the issue-orthodoxy has not been elaborated or defended with the rigor appropriate to its communal significance.

Whether understood empirically or metaphysically, the issue-orthodoxy looks, if only in a weak sense, like a child of what Leatherdale has called "alphabetism."[33] This is the notion that the understanding of complex phenomena is essentially a matter of isolating an inherent and finite range of stable elements and charting the range of their permutations. It is a notion of understanding, he argues, that gains strength from the alphabet as a model, from musical notation, the Arabic number system, and precious little else. Acceptance of the model presupposes that, even if we cannot find all or even any of them, the elements exist, although we have no other reason to assume a range of such elements and often search vainly for them and the evidence for their kaleidoscopic potential. The model, in short, provides an exception rather than a rule, a paradigm of misunderstanding, offering at best an initial way of perceiving provisional identities.

[32] See John Dunn, *The Political Thought of John Locke* (Cambridge, 1969), p. 77, for the ironic appellation. For a good example of the sort of thing he has in mind, see W. D. Mabbott, *The State and the Citizen* (London, 1948).

[33] W. Leatherdale, "The Alphabet as a Model in the History of Science" (paper read to the *Sydney History of Ideas Group*, December 1981); this is especially clear in de Jouvenel, *The Pure Theory*, for whom science is an analogical ideal for political study and who is intent on defining the basic elements (Preface, p. 11, and Conclusion).

Precisely because the issues are viewed as unchanging in essence, and constitutive of political activity, their ancestry looks Cadmian, and in terms of this ancestry, the issue-orthodoxy would seem to require a considerable act of faith, for few would be bold enough to claim for the issues (however specified) the simple noncontentious identity of the letters of the alphabet. Indeed, it is only by gliding over a sea of identification problems that the issue-orthodoxy can sustain its common appeal.

When terms such as *justice, obligation,* and *power* are designated 'fundamental,' 'basic,' or 'enduring' issues, they are functioning, in part, as general covering terms under the auspices of which specific statements, theories, and ideas are classified as having a certain significant sameness about them. Thus Plato's *Republic* and Lilburne's *The Just Man's Justification* may be seen as comparable discussions of the same issue, *justice.* Valid assertions of sameness, however, are contingent upon the stability of the relevant covering terms. The point is stressed strongly by David Wiggins in his reformulation and defense of Leibniz' law of identity.[34] As he states most simply, assertions of sameness always invite the question "The same as a what?"[35] It is a question which will echo throughout my discussion. Precisely because Wiggins is discussing phenomena a good deal more stable or easily distinguishable from each other than those we call political, his discussion of the logical preconditions for valid assertions of identity is worth citing. Formally, he expresses Leibniz' law of identity as:

$$(a = b) = (\Phi \text{ (a) as an } f \equiv \Phi \text{ (b) as an } f)$$
$$f$$

where f represents the covering terms for items a and b and Φ an unspecified range of predicate variables. The formulation only holds if f is unequivocal. The crucial contrast with the issue-orthodoxy is that the instability of the allegedly basic issues is widely accepted, their controversial nature is even stressed, or they

[34] David Wiggins, *Identity and Spatio-Temporal Continuity* (Oxford, 1967).
[35] Ibid., pp. 1–2.

might be thought, echoing Gallie, to be essentially contestable. [36]
In this light, the failure of the political theory community to
agree on the range of the issues constituting the political become by stipulative definition which will afford considerable
terms such as *obligation, democracy,* and *equality* can be overcome by stipulative definition which will afford considerable
precision and classificatory power, but the very stipulative process, by its managing to exclude so many inherited and traditional
uses, must undermine the scope of claims that can be made
under the auspices of the stipulated concept. Furthermore, it
must render the concept increasingly irrelevant to any question
of the qualitative assessment of the wealth of excluded material.
On the one hand, to fulfill the logical preconditions necessary
for valid assertions of sameness, on which the issue-orthodoxy
relies, the very universality of the claims made in terms of the
'basic' issues has to be sacrificed. On the other hand, for the
theorist to remain satisfied with the instability of the 'basic' issues
as classifiers weakens not only the significance of assertions of
sameness made under their aegis but also the ground for qualitative comparison between texts. If, say, justice is an unstable
classifier f, for us to subsume specific theories a, b under its
auspices may well tell us little and may be distracting or misleading. Yet if f is given the requisite precision to be informative, we may no longer be able to subsume either a or b, or both,
beneath it.

A sort of conceptual inflation will thus be encouraged, resulting in an ever-expanding syndrome of 'basic' or 'fundamental' or
'enduring' issues, which by its existence robs such predicates of
their meaning. Or the political domain will be narrowed tau-
tologously to the scope of the intensively refined issues, sufficient
to exclude from political purview a large proportion of that literature we have inherited as political and 'classical.'

Depending on circumstances and what we wish to achieve,
there is nothing wrong with either loose concepts or extremes of
precision. What logically seems wrong with the issue-orthodoxy
is that it sails between the Scylla of hard-edged classifiers, which

[36] W. B. Gallie, *Philosophy and the Historical Understanding* (London, 1962),
chap. 8.

it would seem to presuppose, and the Charybdis of porous ones, on which it must rely in order to perpetuate the leaky unreliability of its claims. Beewax against the siren song of the logician would seem an invaluable protection, perhaps taking the form of Aristotle's advice that there should not be too much rigor in the discussion of politics. To stop at this point, however, would be to beg the question as to precisely what are the claims made in terms of the issue-orthodoxy.

III

At first sight the claims would seem to be of an empirical nature, to be tested in a historico-linguistic court of appeal, for the issue-orthodoxy appears to tell us what the political theorists of the past have commonly regarded as the central problems of political life. In this form the orthodoxy has been subject to a forceful attack by Quentin Skinner, arguing that political theorists (among others) have confused the categories of their own mental "sets" with the priorities of past thinkers.[37] To recall the vocabulary of Collingwood's nightmare, the issue-orthodoxy predisposes us to mistake triremes for third-rate steamships;[38] this easily results in confusion and puzzlement when it is used as a basis for assessing the quality of a work: if politics is basically about an issue such as obligation, and Hooker fails to deal with it in any adequate fashion, one can begin to wonder why he is considered to be a classic political thinker.[39]

Skinner's conclusion is that we have no *a priori* reason for expecting previous political thinkers to reveal any interest or awareness of our 'basic' issues. This is a conclusion which is

[37] Skinner, "Meaning and Understanding," p. 4; Hanna Pitkin, *Wittgenstein and Justice* (Los Angeles, 1972), pp. 181–182, for related remarks; Pocock, *"The Machiavellian Moment* Revisited," *JMH* 53 (1981), for comment on how his own work has focused on issues as functions of the languages in which they occur. All these works point to the more formal linguistic problems of the issue-orthodoxy discussed in this chapter.

[38] R. G. Collingwood, *An Autobiography* (Oxford, 1939), pp. 63–64.

[39] Skinner, "Meaning and Understanding," pp. 14–15.

strengthened if one sees the issue-orthodoxy in the context of Leatherdale's alphabetism. It is, moreover, a conclusion which two dominant and related principles of modern synchronic linguistics, sketched in by Saussure and variously elaborated for example by writers such as Quine, Ullmann, Trier, and Steiner, would lead us to expect.[40] The first is that the abstract vocabulary of a society is to be understood in terms of reciprocally related fields of terms, and that a change in any one item in a given field has direct or indirect ramifications for the whole. The second is that such fields cannot act as substitutes for each other since they are themselves the means by, and through which, a facet of experience is perceived and organized.[41] Translation, then, in any of its four primary modes, by being creative, fractures continuities and undermines any apparent sameness and stability between apparently common ideas.

In addition to other problems, then, it seems plausible to hold that there is one set of basic issues with which political theorists have been concerned only if we believe naïvely that translation is a simple matter of conversion, the imposition of superficial changes between languages, and conventions of discourse which are images of each other. If we shout loudly enough, Plato will have to reply in English. The faith in the empirical form of the issue-orthodoxy recalls Andrew Lang's remark (*Moly and Mandragola*) on something similar:

> This reminds me of the preacher who demonstrated the existence of the Trinity thus: "For are there not, my brethren, one sun, and one moon and one multitude of stars?"

If, in any empirical sense, there is no clear evidence for a fixed cosmic agenda, then there seems little to stop political theory's collapse into a sort of historical linguistics. It is this danger,

---

[40] Ferdinand de Saussure, *Cours de linguistique générale* (Paris, 1916), the founding text; Jost Trier, *Der deutsche Worschatz im Sinnbezirk des Verstandes. Die geschichte eines sprachlichen Felds*, vol. 1 (Heidelberg, 1931); on which see esp. Stephen Ullmann, *Semantics: An Introduction to the Science of Meaning* (Oxford, 1972), pp. 244ff.; Quine, "Meaning and Translation" and "On Synonymity"; Steiner, *After Babel* (Oxford, 1975).

[41] See Ullmann, *Semantics*, for an especially lucid account of Trier's semantic field (*sprachlichen feld*).

I think, which has alarmed theorists about Skinner's polemic; however, as one might expect, in the context of the conventional structure of political theory, a historically mounted attack on something as central and elusive as the issue-orthodoxy is bound to be inconclusive. Fortunately, if for the political theorist history is only on tap, then it can be turned off.[42] The theorist may both retreat from historical convention (or for that matter even more easily from logical or linguistic convention) without abandoning claims to being a political theorist and may use a faith in the issue-orthodoxy as a barrier against the possibility of historical "reductionism"; for it may be construed not in historical but metaphysical terms.

In its metaphysical form, the issue-orthodoxy is a belief that beneath the diversity of language and institutional forms lies a substratum of ideas which is only inadequately expressed in the language of any people, and toward the common understanding of which the great political theorists (together with their modern legatees) have struggled.[43] Thus the very confusions attendant upon a past theorist's not using, say, a vocabulary of sovereignty may index his laboring to unearth, despite his language, the underlying idea of such an issue.[44] In this way, we cannot reasonably expect any theorist to deal adequately with the issues—although the striving to do so is clearly an indication of intellectual status; neither can we expect the historian, tied to the surface of language and events, to be able to appraise this sort of theoretical significance. Although the historian may expostulate that such a line of argument is little short of a rationalization for the systematic circumnavigation of evidence, the theorist could reply that,

[42] Hacker, "Capital," p. 775, alluding to Laski.

[43] Presumably, the import of Glen Tinder's remark that eight or ten ideas have acted as "lanterns" for Western civilization, *Political Thinking: The Perennial Questions* (Boston, 1970), p. 6; Macfarlane, *Modern Political Theory*, p. xiii.

[44] C. W. Previté-Orton, "Marsilius of Padua," *Proc. Brit. Academy* 21 (1935): 143, on Marsilius' struggle toward the concept for which Austin later had the words; W. K. Hancock, "Machiavelli in Modern Dress," *History* 22 (1933): 98, to which Previté-Orton approvingly refers; Ernst Cassirer, "Giovanni Pico della Mirandola: A Study in the History of Renaissance Ideas," *JHI* 3 (1942): 137 and 345, for the "buried treasure" of Pico's thought which Pico himself was unable to unearth. For devastating comment see W. Craven, *Giovanni Pico della Mirandola: Symbol of His Age* (Geneva, 1981), p. 13.

regrettably though understandably, the historian has too limited a notion of evidence; consequently it is the very task of the theorist to get beyond this in order to uncover its universal sense.[45]

It is worth dwelling on the shortcomings of this alternative form of the issue-orthodoxy, partly because they adversely affect its apparent capacity to provide criteria for assessing classic status; partly because we will have to return to very similar problems when discussing the more general notion of originality as an appraisive category; and partly because beliefs in a structuring range of independent ideas underlying the diversity of the written word are too extraordinarily widespread to be ignored.

They are to be found, for example, most succinctly and plausibly in Quintilian's potent imagery of the body of ideas subsumed under *res* as opposed to the decorous clothing of *verba*.[46] They underwrite the faith in the existence of literary archetypes and the distinction between form and content.[47] They provide the *raison d'être* for progressive histories of mankind,[48] and most pleasingly provide motifs for poets such as Marlowe and Sheley.[49] There is a sufficiently strong family resemblance between all such beliefs and Plato's theory of forms (when read as opposing a stable world of *eide* to the transient world of *to horomenon*) for us to suggest that all are similarly vulnerable to the same species of metaphysical critique which has, since Aristotle, been leveled at the Platonic *eide*—namely, that they are redundant and so inaccessible as to be mere items of faith. Even if we are convinced of the formal possibility of the existence of ideas in-

[45] Hacker, "Capital," p. 784, where history is clearly one of the hurdles in the way of the search for timelessness; Lipson, *The Great Issues*, pp. xvii and 17–18, where only the issues make sense of history; de Jouvenel, *The Pure Theory*, p. 11, for reaching down to the elements which might not be found in any previous theories.

[46] *Institutio Oratia*, Pref. 21.

[47] Vladimir Propp, *The Morphology of the Folk-Tale*, trans. L. Scott (Austin, 1975 ed.); W. A. Hendricks, *Grammars of Style and Styles of Grammar* (New York, 1976), pp. 4ff. and 19ff.; J. J. Bachhofen, *Myth, Religion, and Mother Right*, trans. R. Manheim (London, 1967), pp. xxvi and 199–200, for a classic nineteenth-century statement.

[48] The Introduction to Hegel's *History of Philosophy* is perhaps the finest statement of the underlying ideas that enable us to see the progress of history.

[49] *Tamberlaine*, pt. I.5.1; cf. Shelley's image of the cooling fires of inspiration.

dependent of language, what signifies with respect to appraising the written word is whether it is necessary to hyposthesize such independence, and what are the interpretive consequences of so doing. In practical terms, there may be as many candidates for an underlying ideational reality as interpreters have imaginations, and it is difficult to see how their proliferation can be governed. Thus we might explain why political theorists having faith in a single set of basic issues cannot really agree on the range and content of the set; and until they can, the issues themselves must seem to constitute a somewhat capricious set of standards through which the works of the past are appraised.

More formally, it can be stated that the postulation of an underlying ideational reality independent of language is a confused extension of a tenable position. It can be granted that people use language in ways which leave their ideas and beliefs by degrees less than completely explicit, and for the purposes of explication the interpreter may well find strata metaphors (referring to planes, levels, substructures, superstructures, surfaces, and so forth) to be of considerable use. However, this does not warrant or seem to require the postulation of an underlying independent set of general ideas, the *idées fixes* of nature. Strata metaphors, familiar as they are, are used almost, as it were, subconsciously, in a way which facilitates our tripping over our own world projected as *sub specie aeternitatis*.[50] There are three related propositions which should be kept distinct here:[51]

[50] In Leatherdale's neologism, we trip over our own "mentefacts." It is easily done, for there is a thin line between reification and the abridgment of argument. See Stephen Toulmin's remarks on "deep structure" and the notion of generative grammar where he notes that Chomsky's Locke Lectures switched equivocally between using "generative" as a procedural predicate and as a reified "inner psychic agency," itself guaranteeing grammatical structure, in *Human Understanding* (Oxford, 1972), 1:472, n. 1.; or cf. T. H. Huxley's comments on reification (of mathematical symbols and materialist terminology) with his own propensities to reification in "On the Physical Basis of Life," in *Method and Results* (London, 1901), esp. p. 165.

[51] For further discussion, and on which I am drawing generally here, see Nicholas Rescher's fine study, *Conceptual Idealism* (Oxford, 1973), pp. 14ff.; for a similar view with respect to sociology see Julienne Ford, *Paradigms and Fairy Tales* (London, 1975), chap. 5; Richard Rorty, *Philosophy and the Mirror of Nature* (Princeton, 1979), pp. 275ff.

(1) that the world is ordered and understood through mental constructs ('ideas');
(2) that the world has no existence independent of and prior to our ideas of it;
(3) that our₁ ideas have an independent and prior existence to our₂ perception and elaboration on them.

Proposition (1) is true, but it gives no sanction for (2), which requires a *deus ex machina* such as Berkeley's mind of God to stabilize the absurdity of a solipsistic universe,[52] or for (3). With respect to (3), 'our' needs some unpacking. If our₁ refers to a stable existent community, and our₂ to an individual as part of that community, then (3) may be contingently true and is not necessarily at odds with (1). But if 'our' on either occurrence is taken to refer to anything but a person's or a community's specific mental operations, then it exemplifies what may be called the Pythagorean fallacy.

By thinking that because everything in the world could be counted (that is, numbers could be classifiers and enumeration a principle of classification), Pythagoras may have come to the conclusion that the idea of number was the underlying reality of the world. The Pythagorean fallacy, then, is a special form of reification. Rooted in the otherwise conceptually invaluable propensity to objectification characteristic of many tongues, it consists in the illicit shift from recognizing the explanatory or classificatory power of a concept to granting a prior objective existence to any awareness of it. The fallacy confuses the imposition of order upon the world with the discovery of new-found lands which have been waiting patiently for us. So, while we may properly speak of a Columbus discovering new lands, the physical provides a dangerous analogue for a world of mental operations; thus Wittgenstein's care to say that Newton imposed a uniform description upon the world rather than telling us anything about it.[53]

Similarly, we may choose if we wish to impose a set of solar

---

[52] Rescher, *Conceptual Idealism*.
[53] *Tractatus Logico-Philosophicus* (London, 1961 ed.), 6: 34–36; on which see Toulmin, *Human Understanding*, pp. 169–170.

and meteorological categories upon the complex world of *märchen*, but this does not mean that a nursery rhyme is an obscure but decipherable remembrance of a weather report.[54] Although decoding requires rewriting, rewriting is not necessarily decoding, as Straussians (the tribes of Lévi and Leo) often give the impression of believing.

In political theory, the so-called basic issues oscillate between historical, logical, and metaphysical critique. If they can avoid the methodological critique of the historically orientated, they are still, however, used as classifiers; as such they activate the logical problems involved in assertions of identity. If they transmogrify into underlying ideas, they activate charges of redundancy, arbitrariness, and explanatory spuriosity.

The issue-orthodoxy probably operates best as a sort of introductory noble lie, which is not to say much, for propaedeutic protection is often the last refuge of a superannuated belief; however, the orthodoxy also enables the theorist to engage in several activities at once and yet be judged systematically by the standards of none of them. A truncated and conceptually translated past and some general or quasi-philosophic reasoning can both be brought to bear on an ideologically perceived present in which, if nowhere else, the main candidates for basic issue status are likely to be found alive and well.[55] So the issues can foster the belief that the political theorist is engaged in an activity which is academically respectable, cosmically significant, and socially responsible. Set against this, the cost of a little historical, linguistic, logical, and metaphysical dubiety may be thought a tolerable one to pay.

Nevertheless, the fact remains that, in the context of the main themes of this essay, the promise that the issue-orthodoxy holds out for providing a framework specific to political theory in terms

[54] "To opinions like those which Sir George Cox has advanced with so much earnestness, and in such a captivating style of eloquence, it has always been objected that there is an improbable monotony in the theory which resolves most old romance into a series of remarks about the weather" (Andrew Lang, Introduction to *Grimm's Household Tales* [London, 1910], in R. Dorson, ed., *Peasant Customs and Savage Myths* [London, 1968], 1:290–291).

[55] As Lipson, *The Great Issues*, recognizes.

of which texts may be qualitatively appraised and, where we find it, classic status explained, is one that is written on the water. We must turn, then, to a related article of faith which has both done so much to hold the political theory community together and which must have a strong claim to provide the most immediate context in which qualitative assessment can operate: we must turn to the belief in the existence of a tradition of classic texts.

CHAPTER 3

Political Theory
and the Faith in a Tradition
of Classic Texts

Thou, O King, sawest, and, behold, a great image.
This great image, whose brightness was excellent,
stood before thee and the form thereof was terrible.
This image's head was of fine gold, his breast and his
arms of silver, his belly and his thighs of brass, His
legs of iron, his feet part of iron and part of clay.
                    Daniel 2:31–33

What do you see when you turn out the light,
I can't tell you but I know its mine.
Oh I get by with a little help from my friends.
            J. Lennon and P. McCartney,
            Lyric from *Sergeant Pepper*

I

In turning to consider the established tradition of political theory, we move from the rivers of discord into the oceans of controversy. The tradition has attracted more direct attack and defense than the problems of the issue-orthodoxy or the conventional
structure of political theory on their own; it is, after all, a more
stable phenomenon than either, providing a means through which
they may easily be discussed.[1]

[1] The most important discussions are: J. G. A. Pocock, "The History of Political Thought: A Methodological Enquiry," in P. Laslett and W. G. Runciman,
eds., *Politics, Philosophy and Society*, 2nd ser. (Oxford, 1962), pp. 183ff.; and

57

In its simplest received form, the tradition resembles a slain list or a biblical begattery. Of the undisputed first rank are the names of Plato, Aristotle, Augustine, Aquinas, Machiavelli, Hobbes, Locke, Rousseau, Hegel, Marx, and Mill, whose major works are the sibylline books of the political theorist. Behind these stand such impressive figures as Cicero, Dante, Marsilius, More, Bodin, Hume, Bentham, Burke, Paine, and de Tocqueville. Behind these are the lesser prophets and distant cousins, Rabbit's friends and relations, who cluster around the great; so, in Sabine's pages, Halifax and Harrington nestle in the shadow of Locke, Bakunin in the beard of Marx.

This "Expotition" of the great and not so great constitutes more than a rich but passive subject matter for the theorist, and, indeed, no single member is an obligatory focus of attention. It has been rather, as I indicated at the outset, a binding force, like the *religione*, which, Machiavelli tells us, held the virtuous republican Romans together despite internecine tension and external threat. So, references to 'the tradition,' or 'classical political theory,' the 'great books,' 'the master works,' or to clusters of its most prestigious names can seem like beads shared in an academic game, the deft manipulation of which identifies one political theorist to another.

Concomitantly, a *religio* requires an educational policy to insure the continuity of the community; thus the process of becoming acquainted with the tradition and its members is still seen in many universities as an educational obligation for the theorist, and can be coextensive with an induction into the community itself. Assurance in the manipulation of the lineage is a marker of mystery competence, and the theorist, once a full-fledged member of the community, may then locate his own work, as von Hayek and Rawls have done, in the context of this portentous pedigree. So large has loomed the tradition in the

---

"Time, Institutions and Action: An Essay on Traditions and Their Understanding," in P. King and B. Parekh, eds., *Politics and Experience* (Cambridge, 1968), reprinted in *Politics, Language and Time* (London, 1973), chap. 7; Quentin Skinner, "Meaning and Understanding in the History of Ideas," *Hist. & Th.* 8 (1969); John Gunnell, *Political Theory: Tradition and Interpretation* (Cambridge, Mass., 1979); and "The Myth of the Tradition," *APSR* 72 (1978): 122ff.

minds of some theorists that they have drawn little distinction between it and political civilization itself: thus Leo Strauss, distressed at the decadence of the modern world, stood togaed for a generation in the image of a latter-day Cato and bemoaned the abandonment of classical political theory.[2]

Moreover, failing a universally accepted formal understanding of what political theory is or should be, and differences of opinion as to the number and range of its basic issues, the tradition, molded sufficiently in the likeness of a flexible present, provides an anthropomorphic picture of the established activity as a whole recognizable to all. It becomes a sort of conceptual surrogate enabling past and present to be used reciprocally as a means of legitimizing and holding a tensile community together around what might seem to be a common enterprise of understanding.[3] Nevertheless, as we shall see, faith in the tradition is detrimental to understanding its members and is an unfortunate source of expectation for confronting the problems of explaining classic status.

II

Now despite the antiquity of some of its most august members, the notion of the tradition of political theory per se has a strikingly short history, and hardly predates the existence of an identifiable professional community of political theorists. Until recently, its character and credentials as a genuine historical phenomenon have gone unchallenged, its generation unexplored; it was assumed to exist, so its inventor was ignored. However, the effects of the opiate are perhaps wearing off. *Nostra religione* may be passing from a stage of Romanesque religious innocence to something analogous to an impious Florentine frailty. If this is so, there are sufficiently good methodological reasons for it, and the consequences for the community as a whole are

---

[2] Gunnell, ibid.
[3] See e.g. W. Bluhm, *Theories of the Political System* (Englewood Cliffs, 1965).

not to be underestimated.[4] Yet before testifying to my own lack of faith in the existence of the tradition, it is necessary to give due credit to its putative Numa, but for whose work perhaps a felicitous order in the community might not have been maintained for as long as it has.

In 1855, Robert Blakey, better known in the annals of angling as Hackle Palmer and sometime editor of the radical papers *Black Dwarf* and *Politician*, published *A History of Political Literature from the Earliest Times*.[5] In so doing, he first suggested much of the elementary structure of what was to become the tradition of political theory. His justification was significantly twofold: he was filling a historical lacuna and his subject was of the greatest importance to the welfare of man.[6] He proposed to point out,

> as distinctly as possible, those various progressive step[s] or landmarks, in the great framework of European thought, on legislation and general government.[7]

Despite the difficulties stemming from bias, doubt, complexity, and confusion, the task, he urged, was feasible because Western political speculation was bound together by the two permeating ideas of liberty and tyranny.[8] The political writers who had grappled with these concepts were at the present time

> thrown into a promiscuous heap . . . [where] individual distinction [could] be made.[9]

The task, then, was to sort these wheat from chaff so that the individual contributions to the progress of political science could be made clear and the dross be cast away.[10]

With the now largely unread Blakey, we have most of the characteristics (five unmistakable marks) that typify histories of political theory, and which are associated with common concep-

---

[4] Machiavelli, *Discorsi* 1, 12, 13.
[5] I have used the reprint edition, New York, circa 1960.
[6] Ibid., Preface, pp. vi–vii.
[7] Ibid., p. vi.
[8] Ibid., Introduction, p. xvi.
[9] Ibid., pp. xxiv–xxv.
[10] Ibid., and Preface, p. vii.

tions of the tradition disseminated to the undergraduate. There is the claim that exploration of the tradition is both historically and practically (politically) important, a claim which later grows to reflect two of the main discursive propensities in the established community of political theory. We have the claim that there is an ongoing, unified, indeed progressive tradition of thought, together with the belief that such progress can be plotted in terms of individual contributions. We have a belief in a set of universal, abstract, political issues which generate all political thought worthy of the name, and which the tradition encapsulates. Finally, we have, in Blakey's two volumes, nearly all the names and texts that are later to be distilled into the 'classics' of political theory.

Nearly fifty years later, Dunning (while rejecting Blakey's effort) follows a recognizably similar pattern.[11] After Dunning, a host of authors, perhaps culminating in Sabine's monumental tome,[12] have done their best to maintain the aura of significance and historical reality[13] by refinements and by ritual acts of reaffirmation and reiteration.

> 'Just the place for a Snark! I have said it twice:
> That alone should encourage the crew.
> Just the place for a Snark! I have said it thrice:
> What I tell you three times is true.'

The 'histories' show little sign of abating, though some are prefaced with a whiff of embarrassment about producing yet another history of political theory.[14] Moreover, they are supplemented by anthologies of the tradition's major texts suitably cut to size,

---

[11] W. Dunning, A *History of Political Theories* (New York, 1902); see also Sir Frederick Pollock's slightly earlier study, An *Introduction to the History of the Science of Politics* (London, 1890).

[12] G. S. Sabine, A *History of Political Theory* (New York, 1937).

[13] See Gunnell, *Political Theory*, pp. 12ff., for further elaboration. One need not count the pages Sabine devoted to fascism and communism to see how seriously the different discursive claims are taken; or see R. H. Tawney's Introduction to J. P. Mayer et al., *Political Thought: The European Tradition* (London, 1939), even citing the tradition itself as precedent, pp. vi–vii.

[14] J. Harmon, *Political Thought from Plato to the Present* (New York, 1964), p. v.

glossed, and introduced, thus saving the busy student the necessity of reading the originals. Studies of general abstract issues, such as Blakey's liberty and tyranny, habitually assume the tradition as a context of discussion, as do the analyses of any individually important political theorist—one thinker acting as a bookend for another.[15] The rejection of political theory by 'objective' political science,[16] or, more tolerantly, its designation as the 'normative branch' of political science,[17] has been a rejection or tolerance of the tradition, while the alleged death of political theory was, above all, an obituary for the extinction of a once fertile family line.[18] In fine, the history of political theory from Plato to Marx and Mill constitutes Kohn's "old-fashioned" political theory in its most readily digestible and sometimes only form.[19] As a corollary, the tradition and its fate are intimately tied to the community as a whole, its sense of identity and purpose.[20]

For some time now, however, in a piecemeal way, the received tradition has been increasingly revealed as complex and

[15] Hence Gunnell, *Political Theory*, citing Wolin from a wider field: "The core of Wolin's claim . . . is the assumption that whatever the immediate problem the theorist concerned himself with, and no matter what the concrete circumstances of his thought, his participation in the tradition of political theory is the primary factor in interpretation, and his participation is also a source of the tradition" (pp. 84–85).

[16] The rejection was frequent during the "behavioral revolution," and continued in the revolution's idiom thereafter; see Eugene Meehan, *The Theory and Method of Political Science* (Homewood, 1965). See Kateb, *Political Theory: Its Nature and Uses* (New York, 1968), esp. chap. 4, for an attempt to relegitimize the tradition in the eyes of the political science student.

[17] See R. A. Kahn et al., *An Introduction to Political Science* (Ontario, 1972), p. 7; McDonald and Rosenau, "Political Theory as Academic Field and Intellectual Activity," *JP* 30 (1968): 314–315; Gewirth, *Political Philosophy* (New York, 1965), pp. 1ff. for a brief but careful statement.

[18] See Gunnell, *Political Theory*, chaps. 1 and 2; see also C. Condren, "The Death of Political Theory: The Importance of Historiographical Myth," *Politics* 9 (1974): 146ff.

[19] Hans Kohn, "Political Theory and the History of Ideas," *JHI* 26 (1965): 303; the point is made by McDonald and Rosenau, "Political Theory," p. 320.

[20] Gunnell, *Political Theory*, persuasively argues the point especially with respect to Leo Strauss (see also "The Myth of the Tradition"), for whom, notably among Hannah Arendt, Eric Voegelin, and Wolin, the tradition is "a regulative paradigm" and an "*a priori* article of faith," p. 66.

diverse. The cumulative effects of the continual exploration and reassessment of its members have been to undermine its viability as a tradition. The peculiar dialectic to which Pocock drew attention, between the disintegration of political mythology and the processes of exploring, refining, and defending it, is at work in the community of political theory.[21] In the fourteenth century, the search for a clear authoritative model of the Early Christian Church, and the concomitant discovery of an alien world, possibly led some Christians, such as Lapo da Castiglionchio in the fifteenth century, to a belief in the irrelevance of the Early Church to Christian life.[22] So it may be that the attempts to delineate the tradition after Blakey, and to understand political theorizing in terms of it, are giving rise to suspicions about its historical credentials, its relevance, and adequacy for understanding and appraising the classical political thinkers who constitute its basic structure. Do we have a historical tradition or a myth?

The term 'tradition' is capable of both equivocal and extensive usage, and as the word is used to embrace both variety and degree of historical continuity, we must perforce deal with a sliding scale punctuated by a series of loose concepts—classifications flexible enough not to caricature unduly, but nevertheless capable of affording some approximate identifications. At its most general, the term 'tradition' refers to a chronological series, a sequence by virtue of certain continuities shared by its members, transmitted from one to the other. Barely subsumed even by this most general characterization and terminating one end of the continuum, 'tradition' refers to any chronologically arranged series of names whose fate it is to be assembled into the same book,

[21] J. G. A. Pocock, *The Ancient Constitution and the Feudal Law* (Cambridge, 1957), passim; "The Origins of the Study of the Past: A Comparative Approach," *CSSH* 5 (1962–1963), on which see also Chap. 9. v; Kermode, *The Classic* (London, 1975), p. 16, remarks of the Renaissance, "It is also the best illustration of the truth that efforts to see models clearly make them seem further off in time."

[22] On Lapo, *De Curiae Romanae Commodis*, see Hans Baron, "Franciscan Poverty and Civic Wealth as Factors in the Rise of Humanistic Thought," *Speculum* 13 (1938): 30–31.

and who might have little but their commentator's narrative style in common. In this trivial and uninformative sense, in which the continuities are either nonexistent or historically spurious, we have at least a minimal standard of misuse for the term 'tradition'; one so extended that it suggests a mythological characterization of the past.[23]

To specify the residue excluded from this extreme, however, it is necessary to consider both what is transmitted in sequence and the literality of the transmission process. First, either topics, the subject matters (material objects) of discourse, or the conventions (formal objects) of discourse may be the principal items of transmission. A sequence cohered by the transmission of any widely available topic is likely to show altogether more disparity than one cohered by transmitted conventions. Subject matter on its own is a weak cement, for it tells us little about how people have written or what their problems might have been; the more naked a singularity it is, the more it provides only a contingent starting place for the processes of speculation. In relative contrast, traditions exhibiting transmission of convention are considerably more discriminating and, we may expect, will provide tighter and more informative connections between members of the sequence. Of course, in practice traditions may exhibit both items of transmission (astrology); and traditions of mainly conventional continuity may be more porous than they seem (science fiction);[24] but in principle the items of transmission provide a workable criterion for distinguishing types of tradition. But it is still necessary to consider literality of transmission.

We may speak of a relatively literal process of transmission insofar as it is possible to detect tradition awareness among the members of the sequence. In a highly developed form, tradition awareness gives rise to much reflexive activity—where members of the sequence develop themes and variations on the work of their predecessors. Conversely, insofar as there is a high degree

[23] E.g. see B. Mazlish and J. Bronowski, *The Western Intellectual Tradition* (Harmondsworth, 1963 ed.); B. Russell, *A History of Western Philosophy* (London, 1950).

[24] Brian Aldiss, *Billion Year Spree* (London, 1973), p. 10, on the search for "illustrious ancestors."

of tradition nescience, the very notion of transmission as a process of handing on (whether topics or conventions) becomes hopefully euphemistic. The postulated tradition may be revealed as a pattern of affinities and mnemonics that act as surrogates for any specific or direct historical connections between members of the sequence. The distinction between tradition awareness and nescience thus affords a second criterion for the classification of traditions; together the two criteria suggest a number of permutations, the most likely and relevant resulting in conventional-aware traditions and topical-nescient ones. These major possibilities suggest, in turn, a distinction between what I shall call autochthonous and synthetic traditions,[25] which may be placed as points along a continuum of extended usage; autochthonous traditions mark one extreme, mythical the other, with synthetic ambivalently in the center.

Briefly, we may say that autochthonous traditions come to the historian as self-made continuities of activity. Secondly, that any such tradition as a whole provides an invaluable context for the analysis of any one of its members (especially where, as in the tradition of Western music between, say, Monteverdi and Berg, there is a high degree of reflexivity). Thirdly, we may say that although all traditions of speculation may be misleadingly abridged into a simple series of classical names, and arbitrary exclusions, autochthonous traditions can suffer a high degree of compression and filtration because the combination of shared conventions and tradition awareness gives rise to fairly specific and common criteria of significance as well as clear credentials of membership from within the tradition itself. Terms of appraisal may be specified to fit a continuing genre or form of activity: in this way, autochthonous traditions furnish standards of excellence for those involved in the activities they display and are paradigmatic of the initiatory processes necessary to sustain complex forms of intellectual conduct.

With respect to all three points, synthetic traditions provide a contrast. With these it is the historian's task to impose a line of

---

[25] Gunnell, *Political Theory*, p. 86, draws a similar distinction between "analytic" and "historical" traditions.

continuity between various figures by virtue of some synthetic principle of which, per se, the members of the proposed tradition may be unaware.[26] The historian thus has an enhanced opportunity for the imaginative reconstruction of the past, but he runs the risk of being accused of propagating spurious connections and providing arbitrary delineations. Similarly, as such principles may cut across tradition awareness, synthetic traditions provide a less *certainly* valuable context of undertanding for the figures deemed to constitute them.[27] Finally, synthetic traditions are, with less plausibility than autochthonous ones, compressed into a series of great names for which there are clear, common, and relevant criteria of qualitative assessment. Synthetic traditions, then, stand at the borderline of an extended usage of the term 'tradition' at the edges of a slide into mythology. The location of the tradition of political theory has a crucial relevance to the whole question of qualitative appraisal.

However, to make the forms of tradition clearer, consider first the notion of chess *qua* tradition. The autochthonous tradition of chess-play analysis is an identity that in large measure the historian may take for granted. It is a self-conscious tradition of esoteric and clearly circumscribed rules, notations, criteria of judgment, which suggest uniform standards of appraisal, abridgment, and inclusion appropriate to members of the chess-playing sequence. Indeed, members of this tradition, like many artists, composers, and mathematicians, have proved able to both formulate and justify figurative abridgments of their highly reflexive activity from, say, Ruy Lopez to Tal. To identify a figure as a member, especially as a significant member, of the chess tradition tells us a good deal precisely by providing a clear context of understanding through the conventions of the activity and the articulated modes of their transmission.

[26] Consider e.g. Michael Oakeshott's principles of Rationality, Will, and Rational Will, in his Introduction to *Leviathan* (Oxford, n.d.); W. H. Greenleaf's principles of Order and Empiricism in *Order, Empiricism and Politics* (Oxford, 1964), and applied by R. Eccleshall, *Order and Reason in Politics* (Hull and Oxford, 1978).

[27] See V. S. Pritchett's criticisms of F. R. Leavis's tradition of the English novel, constructed by "putting the roof of Henry James on First," cited in F. R. Leavis, *Letters in Criticism* (London, 1974), p. 43.

At the same time, chess may also provide a principle for the construction of a synthetic tradition. As a topic common to a number of activities, the autochthonous chess tradition is subsumed as a part of a larger whole. Thus, in addition to the reflections and recorded games of chess players, we would have to include chess as metaphor for language, chess as model for political analysis, chess as a branch of mathematics, chess as a medium for artists, chess as therapeutic, and chess as propaedeutic. Once we have a synthetic principle of organization telescoped into a traditional sequence, which clearly includes much more both qualitatively and quantitatively than the autochthonous tradition, much else is lost. There are no common standards of comparison and appraisal; the tradition provides little context for historical analysis—for to designate someone part of the chess tradition is uninformative, and the abridgment of its major figures begins to look peculiar: Saussure, Wittgenstein, Josiah Wedgewood, Lewis Carroll, and Ingmar Bergman standing in sequence with Morphy and Alekhine.

Given that the established activity of political theory is structured principally by differing and mutating conventional patterns of discourse, we may expect that what functions in part as its 'tradition' reflects these differences. Most simply, philosophers, ideologues, and historians may all be found under its aegis; and there are other and potentially more fragmenting ways of detailing conventional diversity of political theory which might be pursued by calling on discursive distinctions I am subsuming under the schematic headings of philosophy, history, and ideology. Even a superficial glance at the members of the tradition would reveal that it is marked more by topical than by any singular conventional continuity. And, in relative contrast to a topic such as chess, there is less topical continuity than one might think—to the extent that the nature and limits of political activity are themselves theoretical problems. Much the same can be said about theory (see Chap. 2.1), the usage of which in conjunction with its surrounding net of expressions has remained unsettled.[28]

---

[28] Arnold Brecht, *Political Theory* (Princeton, 1959), p. 14; McDonald and Rosenau, "Political Theory," pp. 312–316; James, *Political Theory: Introduction to Interpretation* (Chicago, 1976), pp. 3n. and 76n.—all attest to the fact.

In this light we should expect, perhaps, the established subject matter of the tradition to provide an uncertain minimum in the way of topical continuity; we should even expect to see a series of radically opposed conceptions of the tradition (no one tradition at all) or a tradition so general and eclectic as to cover all possibilities suggested by the compoundedly flexible expression 'political theory.' Of course, in fact we have nothing of the sort; the received tradition is highly refined, at its heart a handful of 'great names' and in its specification extremely repetitive.[29] It begins to look as if the tradition is a mythical projection of the academic *status quo.*[30]

Such suspicions are heightened if we turn to consider the lack of tradition awareness its members reveal. This is especially evident with the subseries of giants who span the early modern period, Machiavelli, Hobbes, and Locke. There is no firm evidence to suggest that Machiavelli either saw himself as continuing or departing from the 'medieval' tradition of political theory.[31] He claims to be original, it is true, but does not specify any tradition of political reflection from which he is departing, and the very idea of medieval society, let alone a typically medieval mode of political theorizing, was undeveloped at the time Machiavelli was writing. Hobbes, who, in terms of the abridged

[29] C. Northcote Parkinson, *The Evolution of Political Thought* (London, 1952), notes the parochialism (arbitrariness) of the tradition, but the tradition's historical credibility *qua* tradition is hardly enhanced by his willingness to toss in a miscellany of non-European figures. Much the same could be said of the tradition outlined by Kahn et al., *An Introduction.*

[30] The political philosopher, writes Robert Cumming, "cannot adequately canvass the problems of his discipline, while insisting on the centrality of any one problem or adhering to any fixed subject matter; the problems of political philosophy were philosophical only so long as they were enmeshed in shifting relations between subject matters." "Is Man Still Man?," *SR* 40 (1973): 508. Cf. Northrop Frye's remarks with respect to English literary criticism: "There is no question of accepting the whole of literature as the basis of study, but a tradition (or, of course, 'the' tradition) is abstracted from it and attached to contemporary social values, being then used to document those values" (*Anatomy of Criticism*, [Princeton, 1973 ed.], p. 23).

[31] The passages usually cited in this context are from *Il Principe*, chap. 15, and from the Introduction to *Discorsi*, Bk. 1; but see the pertinent remarks of Sydney Anglo, *Machiavelli, A Dissection* (London, 1969), pp. 172–174.

tradition, follows Machiavelli, may well have been familiar with the Florentine, but nowhere discusses or mentions his work; indeed, his own conception of his originality assumes a tradition of speculation that has a somewhat different structure from the accepted tradition of political theory, a difference which is clearly confirmed in Lawson's critique of him.[32] Moreover, as has been shown some time ago, figures quite extrinsic to the accepted tradition of political theory (such as Harvey and Galileo) are of at least as much contextual relevance to understanding his thought as are his 'predecessors' within it.[33] Locke, who closely follows Hobbes, nowhere in the *Two Treatises* discusses Hobbes.[34] Spinoza, like Machiavelli, is unspecific in his rejection of political speculation, and we certainly have no reason to assume that his readers would have been so familiar with the tradition for him not to have needed to name names. Although James Mill's *Essay on Government* is a little more specific, much of Bentham's work must be read in the context of Blackstone's legal commentaries which are yet to establish a certain place in the tradition; and de Tocqueville leads most directly to Pascal and Descartes—writers even more beyond the pale of political theory.

Although not a major political thinker himself, T. H. Huxley is also instructive in this context, partly because writing circa 1890 he stands between Blakey and Dunning, and precisely because he was such a consummate popularizer. In his collected essays, *Method and Results*, although we do find a sense of tradition in political thinking—which certainly has a family resemblance with what later is established as *the* tradition—the differ-

[32] George Lawson, *An Examination of the Political Part of Mr. Hobbs, His Leviathan* (London, 1657), pp. 43 and 67.

[33] J.W.N. Watkins, *Hobbes's System of Ideas* (London, 1965); and "Philosophy and Politics in Hobbes," in K. Brown, ed., *Hobbes Studies* (Oxford, 1965), pp. 237ff.

[34] On the irrelevance of Hobbes to an understanding of Locke, see Laslett's Introduction to *The Two Treatises of Government* (Cambridge, 1963), pp. 67ff.; John Dunn, *The Political Thought of John Locke* (Cambridge, 1969), pp. 77–83—with the pointed remark that a more adequate context would be most inconvenient for all those who give their lectures on Locke after delivering on Hobbes.

ences are striking. Abstracting from his most explicit abridgment, his tradition reads roughly as follows:[35] Aristotle, the Roman jurists, the Dark Ages, Hobbes, and Locke, at which point it divides into two schools, the "regimental" (consisting of Morelly, Mably, and Rousseau) and the "anarchistic" (consisting of von Humboldt, Dunoyer, Stirner, and Bakunin). Between these is a free-floating Fichte. Although Huxley, like so many modern political theorists, drew up his tradition as part of the good fight against contemporary evil (in his case the sin of *a priori* method), in this context we must still ask where in his abridgment are such potent names as Plato, Augustine, Aquinas, Machiavelli, Spinoza, Hegel, and Bentham; and where art thou now in the textbooks O Mably, Morelly, Dunoyer, and free-floating Fichte? In other words, some authors now deemed great may well have been aware of networks of received convention entangled with patinated topics of inherited concern, and in such autochthonous traditions they may certainly be placed; others, like Huxley and even Blakey, may have been employing a more synthetic sense of tradition; but of *the* tradition in which the major names of political theory are now habitually placed, there has been until recently only a shadowy or nonexistent awareness.

If the received tradition, *qua* tradition, begins to look untenable as an autochthonous phenomenon, there are at least hallowed verbal maneuvers which sustain an illusion of autochthony. One is to cast the tradition in the form of a debate, in which the roster of great names can even be drawn up as competing teams, such as totalitarians versus constitutionalists, engaged in something like a *Battle Fought Last Friday*; or there is the looser ventriloquistic rhetoric of an ongoing dialogue.[36] Again,

---

[35] T. H. Huxley, "Government: Anarchy or Regimentation," in *Method and Results: Essays* (London, 1901 ed.), 1:383ff.

[36] See W. Y. Elliott and N. A. McDonald, *Western Political Heritage* (New York, 1949), for two Cold-War debating teams. See also S. S. Wolin, *Politics and Vision* (Boston, 1960), pp. 22 and 25; Dante Germino, "The Contemporary Relevance of the Classics of Political Philosophy," cited among others by Gunnell in *Political Theory*, p. 90; even Margaret Leslie, "In Defence of Anachronism," *Pol. Stud.* 18 (1970): 447, whose argument seems intended to show otherwise, writes of the "dialogue" between Machiavelli (loud voice) and Gram-

one can see a family resemblance between the common rhetorics surrounding terms like 'anticipation,' 'insight,' and 'perception' which can be used alike to create an aura of traditional continuity. Marsilius 'anticipates' Hobbes and Marx; or he had an 'insight' into what they later developed. Machiavelli 'anticipated' or had 'insight' into theories of the modern state; and 'insightful,' 'perceptive' Aristotle 'anticipated' nearly everyone. Individually, such claims operate to press a thinker upon our attention, but *en masse*, they help close the gaps in the tradition. Furthermore, by translating the thought of one thinker into the terms of another or into the terms of our own priorities, they become, in Kermode's expression, "strategies of accommodation," rendering the tradition more uniform than close inspection reveals.[37]

More significantly, in the absence of any sustained overall autochthony, there is a plethora of synthetic principles, a whole family of attempts to encompass the tradition as a whole. To varying extents, such principles have proved illuminating or obscuring with respect to the individual members of the tradition. It is certainly not my purpose to discuss any individual principle in detail but, as a final stage in a ground-clearing exercise, to outline their familiar types and to indicate what I take to be the shared dangers of reliance upon them.

First, the tradition may be gathered with the net of a single general principle such as 'political science,' 'the political life,' or 'the art of politics.'[38] Here an apparently synthetic principle is

---

sci (good hearing), or vice versa; and James, *Political Theory*, for varied use of the dialogue *trope*.

[37] Kermode, *The Classic*, pp. 16 and 39ff.; Skinner, "Meaning and Underanding," p. 11, has a few general comments on anticipation; Hermann Segall, *Der Defensor Pacis des Marsilius von Padua: Grundfragen der Interpretation* (Wiesbaden, 1959), has particularly acid remarks on the rhetoric of anticipation in the interpretation of Marsilius; for a good example of 'insight' at work, see Hanna Pitkin, *Wittgenstein and Justice* (Los Angeles, 1972), the closing peroration. The general point concerning the translation of one thinker into the terms of another as a means of sustaining the tradition is essentially Pocock's in "The History of Political Thought."

[38] See e.g. J. Roucek, *Classics in Political Science* (London, 1962); A. Hacker, *Political Theory: Philosophy, Ideology, Science* (New York, 1961); Gaston Bou-

able to cover the received tradition only by virtue of being un-informative and indiscriminate. At best, a single overarching principle is a way of indicating, at worst, a marginally misleading way of restating that the tradition is a topical classification. The rudimentary subject matter of the tradition is 'politics.' To be told this is to be told very little, and is to be provided with no clear means of accounting for the discrepancies between those who are *de facto* members of the tradition and those who are not; let alone can it help explain degrees of significance within the tradition. On a similarly general level, we may be told that the tradition consists of the combined attempts to deal with a single question, such as "What makes the state legitimate?"[39] Such questions (ignoring translation) can no doubt be formu-lated in a way general enough to cover all members of the tra-dition, but concomitantly they are thus made too unspecific to elicit any range of exclusively appropriate answers, and moreover cease to be sufficiently discriminating to suggest criteria for ex-cluding many who are beyond the received tradition.

More satisfactory are dualistic principles such as Wolin's pol-itics and vision; Voegelin's gnosticism and transcendentalism; or Weldon's distinction between mechanistic and organic theories of society.[40] All these sets of paired oppositions have potentially the advantage of being specific and, to some extent, discriminat-ing. They do not attempt to catch the tradition under a single heading which to be successful has to be vacuous. Nevertheless, their scope potentially stretches well beyond the tradition to which they are applied (arbitrarily), while those figures within the tra-

thoul, *L'Art de la Politique* (Paris, 1962), p. 22, e.g.—but given that Roucek and Bouthoul provide the most extraordinary miscellaneous anthological gleanings, it is difficult to see how they could use any more informative covering term.

[39] Jeffrey H. Reiman, *In Defense of Political Philosophy* (New York, 1962), pp. xx–xxi.

[40] Sheldon Wolin, *Politics and Vision*; Eric Voegelin, *The New Science of Politics* (Chicago, 1952); T. D. Weldon, *States and Morals* (London, 1946). Gunnell's general discussion, *Political Theory*, chap. 2, is instructive; so, too, are some specific remarks by Susan Tenenbaum, "Women Through the Prism of Political Thought," *Polity* 15 (1982): 90–92, on the failure of the dualistic prin-ciples of household and polity even to encompass reflections on women within the received tradition.

dition (and because of its diversity there are always some) who do not conform to the principles have to be cut to fit, or ignored. More specific still, and perhaps achieving the worst of all possible worlds, is the "shopping list" approach[41] of writers such as Friedrich and Tinder,[42] who designate a syndrome of general 'issues," by virtue of a concern with which it appears a figure is deemed a 'classic' political theorist, his traditional credentials established.

Conversely, the tradition of speculation about these issues (Blakey's permeating ideas augmented) is seen as the tradition of political theory. All that needs to be noted in this context is that in resorting to a whole range of general issues, or in the looser expression 'problem areas,' in order to encompass the tradition, we are paying tribute to its lack of unity.[43] Such a widely cast net anticipates a teeming ocean of fish. If it is necessary to impose so many synthetic principles upon the material in order to weld it into a single tradition, in what sense can one speak of *a* tradition? And as the potential scope of such 'issues' or 'problem areas' as *justice* or *freedom* remains far greater than their habitual application, it becomes difficult to see how such a notion of the tradition can provide any reliable qualitative guide to political theory.

III

The various synthesizing principles and rhetorical devices employed by political theorists do not convince of the tradition's autochthony; as a corollary, they sustain something close only to a protective mythology of autochthonous standards of appraisal. They are successful, however, in adding some diachronic depth to the allegedly basic issues and to the major patterns of discourse

---

[41] I have taken the expression from Robert Orr, "Reflections of Totalitarianism Leading to Reflections on Two Ways of Theorising," *Pol. Stud.* 21 (1973): 481ff.

[42] Tinder, *Political Thinking: The Perennial Questions* (Boston, 1970); Friedrich, *An Introduction to Political Theory* (New York, 1962).

[43] Friedrich, ibid., Preface.

which vie for dominance within the contemporary political theory community. Hence when we are told that the tradition is really about, or is cohered by, this issue,[44] or aspires to be philosophy,[45] or has only been vital when really ideologically committed,[46] we can suspect, as with the manipulation of all living myths, that what is primarily at stake is a modification or reinforcement of the infrastructure of the contemporary community that has projected the myth and uses it as an internal idiom of persuasion. Reference to the tradition is thus frequently a sort of pidgin history. Werner Stark has shown how even the most obscure religious communities have been able to project on a universal scale their myths and sense of self-awareness, thus making their societies and their local problems the center of a whirling cosmos of strife.[47] Political theorists, largely professional academics writing for other professional academics, sometimes achieve a similar effect. When Professor Bay writes about human needs in Plato, we can be reasonably sure that his arguments are not unconnected with his belief that responsible political theorists should ride bicycles. In this sense, too, Strauss' crisis of the great tradition has been splendidly decoded by Gunnell as only an idiom of contemporary concern, the tradition's study being a "ritual therapeutic."[48]

The parallels with the legitimizing role of lineage-polishing in premodern society, which seems so quaintly primitive to the

[44] E.g. Christian Bay, in R. Fitzgerald, ed., *Human Needs and Politics* (Oxford and Sydney, 1977), who insists that classical political theory was about human needs as a prelude to stressing the centrality of this issue now.

[45] George Kateb, *Political Theory*, esp. pp. 1–8, in company with Wolin and Sabine, who also hold the tradition to be essentially philosophical, although it is not always clear in the literature whether philosophy is distinguished from the morally improving.

[46] Easton, "The Decline of Modern Political Theory," *JP* 13 (1951), and, more recently, Neil Wood (also following a strand in Sabine), "The Social History of Political Theory," *Pol. Th.* 6 (1978):345ff.; W. J. Stankiewicz, *Aspects of Political Theory* (London, 1976), Introduction, links the revival of political theory (after its outbreak of death) with its political vitality.

[47] Werner Stark, *The Sociology of Religion* (London, 1967–1972), 4 vols.

[48] Gunnell, *Political Theory*, pp. 36–40, on Strauss and, more generally, p. 68.

modern rational mind, are also rather strong: we know the political theorist who evokes the right names and manipulates passages from their arguments to focus upon contemporary concerns is in a way universalizing those concerns, achieving a dramatizing perspective which affirms his involvement in an important activity. Just so, we knew the stranger who came in the night and recited his lineage in verse to be no ordinary mortal.

> Then to the hall-door Wulfgar went, and brought the message from within: "My conquering lord, chief of the Eastern Danes, bade me inform you that he knows your noble blood (*æpelu*), and that ye men of brave intent are welcome to him hither over the sea-billows."
>
> *Beowulf*, trans.
> J. R. Clark Hall

It makes little difference here if the theorist extols the success or bemoans the failure of the tradition to deliver what we require of it. Although satisfaction or discontent might seem to distinguish the conservative from the radical political theorist, their therapeutic expectations spring from the same source of eternal hope. So, too, it made little difference if the stranger was at one with or estranged from the *cneoris* or the *oikos*, which ideally infused him and his listeners with a sense of the divine cosmos. Believing that, as your grandmother, Frig or Hera should come to your aid precedes the conclusion that she has failed or properly succored you.

By way of conclusion, and in the light of the previous chapter, we may say that the received range of classic names has been manipulated into a tradition which is a projection of the discursive structure of political theory, which is made to illustrate and reflect competing versions of the issue-orthodoxy, and which insofar as it is presented as a pre-existing empirical phenomenon is an example of the Pythagorean fallacy writ large. So, a highly selective past becomes a more or less mobile army of metaphors for ourselves, carrying our parochialism under the colors of continuity, universality, and timelessness. In this way, too, we may list the main thrusts of the tradition's major critics: Pocock first focused upon the tradition as a projection of what the modern professional theorist regards as the proper level of rational discourse for politics;[49] Skinner then attacked the tradition as a reservoir of what we think are the mandatory issues of politics;[50] and Gunnell has underlined and explored the tradition's reified character.[51] Understandably, many historians in and around the community seem increasingly skeptical of its credentials and of discourse operating within its terms—although some might perhaps be prepared to defend or accept it as a philosophical crutch, or, like the issue-orthodoxy, as an educational one. This takes us back to the balance of discursive forms within political theory. The tradition can in a way be seen as a microcosm of the community because, as an article of faith, its continued propagation in the face of its historical shabbiness stands for the restricted authority of historical convention within community discourse.

If we can now place the tradition of political theory from Plato to Marx along the abstract spectrum of traditions, then we must do so somewhere toward the mythological extreme. The dangers to some extent inherent in the creation of all synthetic traditions, of inventing spurious continuities and of making arbitrary delineations, are found in an acute way in histories of the classic tradition. It is in particular this second species of danger which raises the problems of the qualitative assessment of the tradition's members; it is this that reveals the full sense of Blakey's "promiscuous heap." If the tradition does not have intrinsic to it (that is, formulated and sustained by its own self-conscious members) a clear and stable set of criteria of inclusive and qualitative assessment, then on what grounds do we go to its members for guidance; on what grounds are some thinkers great, others greater, and some considered not at all? Reference to the tradition to answer such questions could be of much help only if that tradition were autochthonous; in fact, when it is realized not to be, it becomes no more helpful than appeal to the issue-orthodoxy

---

[49] Pocock, "The History of Political Thought."

[50] Skinner, "Meaning and Understanding."

[51] Gunnell, *Political Theory*, p. 86: "The idea of the tradition as a scholarly convention came to be conceived as a pre-existing historical phenomenon."

which, too, has played its part in obscuring questions of status and appraisal.

The inquiry into what makes a classic text is central to any inquiry into political theory and precedes, logically, the question concerning whether or not such texts merit the collective noun 'tradition.' But it is a question that now needs some unpacking. First, in the conventionally eclectic field of political theory it is a question which is apt to put emphasis on historical criteria of judgment, especially as it can be to ask for a detailed account of how a given series of texts became the traditionally studied ones. Secondly, it may be to ask for the general categories of analysis that structure the qualitative appraisal of historically significant texts, and in terms of which the analysis of a potentially important text, claiming admission to the tradition, should be organized. In short, the initial question that doubting the self-evident truth of the tradition raises itself breaks down into the related fields of the history and historiography of political ideas, and of the methodology of textual analysis.

How we have come to study a given series of works as 'classics' in the Horatian sense is apt to shade into questions concerning the qualities we take, and should take (the methodological nexus), to identify a 'classic.' Blakey had his answer; the study of the great thinkers was a matter of winnowing wheat from chaff, the winnower being the conception of contributions to the progress of political science.

> Then was the iron, the clay, the brass, the silver, and the gold, broken to pieces together, and became like the chaff of the summer threshing-floors.

Faith rather than critical attention has made Blakey's approach serviceable, and even Andrew Hacker, one of the more self-aware of recent political theorists, could happily accept in 1961 that political theory could be, and normally was, equated with the history of political ideas and that the history of political ideas was a series of contributions to a tradition beginning with Plato and (no doubt) ending somewhere in the vicinity of Marx. Moreover, his own chosen ones from this contributory continuum (he starts with Plato and ends with Mill)

> have been selected on the straightfoward ground that out of the hundreds of authors who have sought to write political theory, their ideas continue to have relevance and significance for our time. In the intellectual world there is a survival of the fittest, and fitness may be defined as an understanding of the political life which retains its validity despite the passing of centuries.[52]

In marked contrast, Levin has argued that, if the case of Locke is indicative, classic status is more a matter of luck than fitness.[53] Neither position has much explanatory power, though we should be thankful to the latter as an antidote to Hacker's inherited vulgar Eliotesque Darwinism. But the glimmer of light can hardly brighten until we have examined the more general grounds of qualitative appraisal, until we have descended into the Cave not to watch and applaud the passing shapes, but to identify the source of their illumination.

---

[52] Hacker, *Political Theory*, viii. See also *The Study of Politics: The Western Tradition and Its American Origins* (New York, 1963); the ambiguity in the title I assume to be inadvertent. But, as needs little stressing by now, this sort of sentiment is itself traditional, and read in the context of Sabine, e.g., who also stressed the fitness of ideas, and Blakey, who first mooted the evolutionary organization of political literature, this begins to have an almost Cassian air of protest about it.

[53] M. Levin, "What Makes a Classic in Political Theory: The Case of John Locke," *PSQ* 88 (1973).

PART TWO

It shall be objected that no society was ever any ways civilised before the major part agreed upon some worship or other of an overruling power and consequently that the notions of good and evil and the distinction between virtue and vice were never the contrivance of politicians, but the pure effect of religion.

Bernard de Mandeville, *The Fable of the Bees*

But however we may forget things that are past, let us now oversee that which lies before our eyes; and since the occasion is so very fair, I know not how we can omit the shewing our sense of those Vertues, of which the whole Nation has demonstrated so grateful an acknowledgement by the Body of their Representatives; and never were they more truely their Representatives before.

Anon., A *Dialogue Concerning Women*,
London, 1691

Introduction

The political theory community, if fluid and marginally unstable, has some sense of identity and cohesion; and it is this which has made possible the political and religious metaphor that has been interlaced with the argument. This metaphor may be extended a little further in order to take stock and to suggest the nature and significance of what I now propose to discuss.

In an earlier essay, I suggested that the political thought of distinctive civilizations, such as ancient Greece, Rome, and Medieval Christendom, could be understood in terms of the following general classificatory headings: summation terms, idioms of argument, and ethical structures.[1] By summation terms I referred to those expressions or terms that function as reflexive abridgments of society's sense of political, religious, and temporal identity. They refer not only to geographical locality (if any), formalized institutions, and characteristic economic and social activities, but also, and principally, to an established style of political life. Since political activity is largely verbal, summation terms abridge the given society's established idioms of public discourse and its ethical structures; as political activity changes, so the varying usage of summation terms may act as barometers of changing political identity. By idioms of discourse, I referred to the conventional patterns of accepted political argument through which specific political issues are discussed, the transmission of which constitutes a major aspect of political education. The ethical structures are the sets of abstract *clefs mots* (dim and hazy reflections of Trier's *sprachlichen feldes*) in terms of which political conduct is appraised, particular political problems and possibilities are identified as general issues, and through which the *telos* of the society is understood.

[1] *Three Aspects of Political Theory: On the Confusions and Reformation of an Expression* (Melbourne, 1979), chap. 3.

81

Thus the summation term *polis* referred less to geographical locality and limitation, and to institutional arrangements as slavery, than to a complex of largely verbal activities considered political, and engaged upon by the *politai* of any particular *polis*. Above all, the *bios politikos* referred to how, about what, when, and according to which rules the *politai* spoke. In the archaic and classical *polis*, the dominant idiom of discourse appears to have been a typically aesthetic or poetic one, which was associated with the kudos given to the poet, and was manifested in a goodly quantity of political poetry. More broadly, it involved the employment of aesthetic canons of judgment (*to kairos* and *to prepon*) in political speaking (see Chap. 8, pp. 230–232). The *bios politikos*, then, referred in large measure to how one conducted oneself in the activities thought characteristic of the *polis*, and to how one addressed oneself to the contentious issues of the day. These issues and the propriety of behavior were, in turn, circumscribed by and appraised through a distinctive ethical structure of argument, comprising such terms as *nomos*, *themis*, *eleutheria*, *sophia*, *andreia*, *arche*, to be joined later (if Adkins is broadly right) by the hitherto subordinate notions of *dikaiosyne* and *sophrosune*, all of which could be subsumed by the notion of the *agathon*.[2] It is in this context that we can see the significance of the sophists and rhetoricians: they were the self-appointed heirs of the archaic poets, and insofar as they claimed to teach how to speak well and how to be virtuous, they taught and transmitted the abridged rules of a poetic idiom, thus providing the techniques of an education appropriate to *polis* life, together with an initiation into the possible deployment of its received ethical structure. Similarly, it was this ethical structure and the dominant idiom of discourse with which Plato took issue in *The Republic*, thereby providing a redefinition of the conception of the *polis*.

To compare this with what has gone before: the expression 'political theory' may be seen as the most widely used and serv-

---

[2] A. W. H. Adkins, *Merit and Responsibility: A Study in Greek Values* (Oxford, 1962), passim. The whole set was changed in being augmented, as one would expect linguistically, and as Adkins is at pains to point out.

iceable candidate for the status of an intellectual community's summation term. The manifest looseness of the expression, especially in the context of wider intellectual communities (political science, the social sciences, and the humanities), is an index of the political theory community's unstable and insecure identity. The dominating patterns of convention are analogous to the idioms of political discourse which help characterize distinctive political civilizations. Indeed, as has already been suggested, even the sophist has his academic analogue in the methodologist. In teaching, transmitting, and reformulating appropriate rules of conduct within and for their respective communities, both do something to disturb received identities. There was, in classical Greece, even a sophistic nexus as there is now a methodological one. Characteristically, the thought of the sophists hovered between regulating political discourse and delineating the necessary nature of language and its relationship to the world as a whole. This discursive ambivalence is to be seen in Gorgias, in Socrates' discussion with Thrasymachus, and persistently in the force of Plato's arguments in *The Republic* as a whole (see Chap. 7.vII).

Moreover, the political theory community in the academic world is like the *polis*, in the close-knit world of *poleis*—for the Athenian was also a Hellene; or like a *provincia* or *regnum* of Christendom, or a young nation in a Fichtian universe. It is a distinct identity informed by the notion of a larger legitimizing whole. Thus there are factors which give it a specific identity, and those which maintain it as a part of a larger whole. The political theory community, mainly by virtue of its subject matter, combined with its peculiar conventional structure, has achieved something of a distinctive identity within the *societas academica*, as, for example, England by virtue of a sense of its past, its customs, language, and its enemies established an identity as a part of later Medieval Christendom. But political theory also enjoys the use of a common field of appraisive terms (the analogue of the ethical structure that permeated the political consciousness of Christendom as a whole), and it is to this that I now turn.

II

As has been emphasized before, Part One (Introduction, sec. III), our understandings of the world are controlled and made possible by the use of abstract organizing categories of connection and classification, which may be seen at work even in our most elementary notions. Even the general term 'text' is a classification, dividing the world provisionally into texts and nontexts, and from thereon capable of much refinement, affording detailed patterns of interconnection between items which can be more and more discriminately classified. In the world of political activity and literary artifice alike—there is considerable overlap between them—we begin not with a clear range of political facts and literary texts, but with a diverse and undifferentiated range of material on which are brought to bear organizing conceptions which abridge our concerns and the understandings we seek. Similarly, in both worlds, the understandings we seek are largely appraisive—we come not simply to classify, but to assess qualitatively.

Much of the academic and intellectual life is concerned directly with the appraisal of texts, just as political life is concerned with the qualitative appraisal of actions, actors, and circumstances. The diversity of this world of texts, comprising what Croce called "narration," Laslett "attitudinal evidence,"[3] is indicated by the range of subclassifications into which we constantly divide it: poem, statement, play, thesis, essay, argument, dialogue, note, review, epigram, and epic. The qualitative assessment of this area of experience as a whole requires a very general field of categories which either subsume, or can be translated into, more specific terms appropriate to the subclassifications of 'text' (see Introduction, pp. 3f.).

In a number of respects, the received field of textual appraisal functions in a fashion parallel to the ethical structures of political societies; the one organizes the assessment of the good text, as the other, for example, the ethical structure of Christendom, organized the assessment of and limited the predicates attachable to the good man, prince, action, or policy. As I have suggested in

[3] Peter Laslett, *The World We Have Lost* (London, 1971).

Part One, we are forced to a consideration of this appraisive field because the general conventional structure and the specific orthodoxies of political theory fail to provide distinctive criteria of textual appraisal. The major items in the appraisive field of textual understanding I take to be the terms *originality, contribution, influence, coherence,* and *ambiguity.* The conspectus of this field presented here is schematic. Although these familiar words are intimately and variously related to each other, it must be stressed that each has a subordinate field of terms in its ambit, terms which modify slightly or which are roughly synonymous with what I am in each case taking to be the central item. Insofar as the subordinate terms do not modify the central one (as newness is not significantly different from originality), then they will receive scant attention. What is said of one term can often stand for others, as analyses of *liberty* in English have been able to stand for those of *freedom.* On occasion, however, the words in the train of a major item will modify and complicate. In the case of some of the terms in the ambit of coherence and ambiguity, there is an effective overlap which is apt to entangle the two central terms. In the same way, for example, the terms *power* and *authority* in the ethical structure of the modern state have words in their train which overlap and cause the central items to be drawn together in confusion.

The appraisive organization of any facet of experience has its obvious extension in the specific processes of rhetorical manipulation. The complex ethical structure of Western Christendom, which schematically can be seen to center on such *clefs mots* as *piety, loyalty, justice, tradition,* and *peace,* enjoyed a complex rhetorical manifestation. Items in the structure could function on a directly abstract rhetorical level, furnishing the evocative trappings necessary for persuasion in any given situation. Thus, for example, the Latin translation of Petrarch's lines used with rhetorical emphasis by Machiavelli, "*iustum enim est bellum quibus necessarium, et pia arma ubi nulla nisi in armis spes est.*"[4] The items could function as a means of identification on a constantly available pictorial level, as with Lorenzetti's Sienese

---

[4] *Il Principe* 26.

frescoes of Good and Bad Government. And, most commonly and pervasively, they could be cashed into literary and mythical symbols; Judas, Lucifer, Henry II of England, and Pope John XXII could all represent disloyalty at various levels of cosmic significance, while when Christ was seen as the Prince of Peace, the whole rationale of the history of Christendom could be portrayed as the search for Christ's peace on earth—and the warlike Ludwig of Bavaria could use as a slogan, *"Habeto pacem et per hanc habebis fructos optimos."*[5]

The conceptual field of textual appraisal offers no analogical register as complex or momentous. Even so, at least a one-dimensional rhetorical manifestation is evident. It is as difficult for us to imagine a great book, a classic text, that was not (or should not be) original, coherent, probably influential, and of some contributory significance as it was for the medieval political writer to imagine a good king who was not pious, just, merciful, and loyal, or a legitimate war that was not in the interests of peace and piety. Consequently, in order to make a convincing case about the quality of a book or person, respectively, it is necessary to appropriate the relevant terms; and as the art of overt persuasion is no easier than the art of qualitative appraisal, rhetoric may always be one step away from superfluity of protestation. Thus we may read political sentiment or polemic which in its zeal to manipulate the items of an ethical structure produces a foggy enthusiasm (Machiavelli's use of Petrarch); unconvincing euphemism (Ludwig's and Marsilius' use of Job 22:21); or verbicide (General Westmoreland's Orwellian Newspeak). So, too, we can find in political theory analyses no shortage of empty or obscuring appeals to originality, vague understandings of coherence, and unsubstantiated claims as to influence, all of which tell us more about the commentator's subscription to an activity's appraisive field than about the subject being investigated. Such rhetoric says less about a text than a critic's need to justify his studying and our reading it. Put another way, the specific rhetorics of textual analysis, no less than the richer rhetorics of po-

---

[5] Segall, *Der Defensor Pacis des Marsilius von Padua: Grundfragen der Interpretation* (Wiesbaden, 1959), p. 21.

litical communities, can be regarded as a guide to the structure of an activity rather than a voidable verbiage surrounding a subject matter.

If the ethical structure of Christendom (to persist with a single example) could function at both an organizational and a rhetorical level, it could do so principally because all of its items had an essentially biadic structure. Without a hypothetical negative, no single item could have been used to structure the political world in any clearly discriminating way. Nor would there have been any possibility for sustained manipulation. If the world is totally at peace, and there is no conceptual possibility of war, the conception of peace becomes, if not meaningless, quite redundant. Further, if any biad were modified so that it and its negative could only function on an infinitely sliding scale, categorical power would be diminished accordingly, although leaving a residue of rhetorical possibility. If all actions could be seen by degrees to demonstrate both loyalty and disloyalty, the conception of loyalty would have little organizational power, while both it and its contrary would be rhetorically promiscuous. Similarly, each item in the appraisive field of textual understanding is hypothetically biadic. Each, that is, functions, or *appears* to function, in the context of its negative; each as a distributed predicate has classificatory power and effectiveness as a criterion of quality if, and only if, it excludes its negative. As we will see, however, with several of the items, they fail in these terms, leaving little but a revealing rhetorical slick across the surface of the interpretive page.

Further, just as the ethical structure of Christendom was comprised of a range of terms not all of which had the same logical status, so, too, the much smaller field of terms used in textual appraisal function in different ways and are associated with different sorts of organizational problems. We may see two principal groups: those conceptions that focus on the connections between different texts, from which some conclusions of significance can be drawn (*originality, contribution, influence*), and those that focus upon the intrinsic structure of the text (*ambiguity* and *coherence*), conclusions in terms of which are a necessary prerequisite for the subset of significance conceptions to be employed effectively. Logical relationships between the two groups of terms, however, do not necessarily reflect an individual item's emotional resonance and rhetorical potential. Ambiguity is apparently a fault, but clarity not a greatly praised virtue; originality is a striking quality, and contribution a significant achievement. The items in the field of terms are dealt with in reverse order of logical importance, and roughly in the order of their emotional resonance. The consequence of this is the continuation of a good deal of negative argument before a more positive refinement of a minimal vocabulary of textual appraisal can be outlined (see Part Three) and an explication of the classic status can begin to be developed on the basis of it.

As a loose corollary to the rough distinction between logical importance and communal resonance, it is necessary to consider the members of the appraisive field mainly according to the discursive contexts in which they most commonly operate. As originality, contribution, and influence claims purport to describe the relationships between texts over time, they must be seen broadly in a historical court of appeal. In dealing with these terms, historical conventions of argument will receive a stress perhaps disproportionate to their effective sway in the political theory community as a whole—revealing, as it were, a sort of Harringtonian discrepancy between virtue and power. With respect to coherence, on the other hand, we are confronted with statements whose claims are usually philosophical, and so some philosophical consideration of the term, its meanings, and limitations is required. What discussion of relevance there is will focus on its common status as a marker of ideological discourse in an academic context.

So instinctively do we bring appraisive fields and ethical structures to bear on texts and political activity, respectively, that we are apt, as the children of Pythagoras, to see them primarily as objective characteristics inhering in the worlds around us, rather than as the conceptual means of organizing and appraising those worlds (see Introduction, pp. 3–4; Chap. 2.III). Concomitantly, differently organized understandings are too easily dismissed as empirical error, or too swiftly translated into our own terms—in both cases we fall victim to our own ethical projections. Thus Moerbeke translated Aristotle not only into the language but into the organizational categories of Medieval Christendom. In this light also Freeman was historically correct to criticize Grote for translating *demagogos* (conceptually and linguistically) as "opposition speaker," but equally wrong to discuss the *polis* in terms of *state, sovereignty, nationality,* and *obligation.*[6] Political theorists are right to stress the gulf between medieval and contemporary understandings of politics, but wrong to specify these differences in terms of developing 'realism,' a progression in which Machiavelli is usually the pivotal figure. We do not have a superior grasp of the 'realities' of the political world; we have, rather, a somewhat different ethical structure through which we understand, organize, and appraise the political world.[7] As Freeman's inconsistencies indicate, it is no easy matter to grasp this and its consequences fully. Furthermore, we so naturally appraise the quality of a book in terms of its originality that too rarely are we conscious of the fact that to do this we must first give authority to a binary conception that not all literate civilizations have entertained, and then laud its positive component as many writers have refused to (see Chap. 4). Again we hunt for influences upon a chosen text and search for inner coherence among writers who thought little or nothing of our categories. We should be sensible of this element of contingency, for not to be so is to fall into errors in their way as significant as the issue-orthodoxy, which springs from a parallel source in political understanding (see Chap. 2. III; Chap. 7. IV). Both in political understanding and in the processes of appraising texts, our vocabularies are sufficiently well ingrained for us to see the figures literally struggling to free themselves from the marble rather than their being created by the combined application of conceptual discrimination and practical skill. It is only, I would suggest, in a limited sense the appraisive categories of coherence and ambiguity which may be considered logically necessary in the process of textual appraisal: and to say this (see Part One, Introduction III), is to conjure up the specter of the headless Yoruba and his box of shells.

[6] E. A. Freeman, *Historical Essays,* 2nd ser. (London, 1880), pp. 154–155, on Grote, and pp. 133 and 150 for his own categorically anachronistic translations.

[7] Rescher's general comments, *Conceptual Idealism* (Oxford, 1973), p. 23, are much to the point.

Penultimately, it must be stressed that, as with the items comprising an ethical structure, we are not dealing with isolated terms which can be changed, redefined, or even abandoned without consequences for the terms around them. The ramifications may be slow in making themselves felt, and they may work according to no simple laws, or any clear laws at all, but ultimately they affect all related terms; interrelationship is measured by effects, area of operation by adjacency. Not even Mill could take a single word from a complex political vocabulary, isolate, and analyse it without trading in the currency of related terms, effecting them, and then bequeathing to his society a somewhat changed ethical structure as a whole. As Saussure remarked, with more justification for the sort of abstract field of terms with which we are concerned than for languages *in toto*, to move a single piece is to alter the whole field force.[8] This truth carries with it the practical advantage that not all the terms discussed need to be dealt with at equal length. As contribution is a modification of originality, much that is said of one may stand for the other, and, indeed, much that can be said of either has consequences, in an inverted fashion, for the discussion of influence.

III

Finally, it is because, in part, the appraisive field of textual analysis in political theory is neither an exclusive property nor is its domain restricted to a single inheritance that it was not easy, nor is it now necessary, to define that community precisely as a prelude to exploring the field. Indeed, as some passing footnotes have been designed to intimate, I might as easily have arrived at this point via a discussion of English literature, its discursive character, mandatory subject matter, and methodologically dubious sense of tradition, as I have from the fastness of political

[8] Saussure, *Cours de linguistique générale* (Paris, 1964 ed.), pp. 125-126. Unlike Saussure, however, I would not stretch this analogy to obliterate the importance of inherited connotation.

theory. Thus much that can be said of the employment of an ethical structure of analysis might be evidenced from beyond political theory's shadow. Appropriately, some cross-reference will continue.

The principal focus of attention, however, remains on political theory, partly because its relatively unreflective use of the relevant field of terms is illuminating, and partly because the appraisive field of textual analysis is one of two paramount and clearly related factors which still mitigate against the methodological schismatics and idiomatic tensions now clearly associated with the summation term 'political theory.'

The general parallels I have listed between ethical structures in political activity and a received field of academic textual appraisal have explicated the political metaphor of the essay about as far as I wish. In sum, we may say that if the classic texts themselves provide some topical focus of attention, the ethical structure of terms which informs their analysis provides some residual *religione* of convention in a highly tensile community; the classic names and the deifying qualities complement each other, just as the great human symbols of a political inheritance house the abstract virtues and vices of its ethical structure. But in this respect political theory is in no way unique; it shares, and in sharing, political theory is joined with other activities which have, or have had, a clear sense of tradition of great names, and whose scholarly enterprise is largely geared to the qualitative assessment of classic texts, as well as those works of the present that press their claims to be studied in the future.

There are many groups within the Cave, searching a diversity of shadows, naming them, guessing at interrelationships and qualities, but the light-giving flames are common, and it is their sparks we must chase around the hearth as a prelude to the more difficult task of ascending into the light:

hoc opus, hic labor est.

CHAPTER 4

Originality

Originals shine, like comets; have no peer in their
Path; are rivalled by none, and the gaze of all. Other
compositions (if they shine at all) shine in clusters;
like the stars in the galaxy; where, like bad
neighbours, all suffer from all; each particular being
diminished, and almost lost in the throng.

Edward Young,
Conjectures on Original Composition

When I talked about originality and genius to some
gentlemen whom I met at a supper party given by Mr.
Thims in my honour, and said that original thought
ought to be encouraged, I had to eat my words at
once. Their view evidently was that genius was like
offences—needs must that it come, but woe unto that
man through whom it comes. A man's business, they
hold, is to think as his neighbours do, for Heaven
help him if he thinks good what they count bad. And
really it is hard to see how the Erewhonian theory
differs from our own, for the word "idiot" only means
a person who forms his opinions for himself.

Samuel Butler,
Erewhon, The Colleges of Unreason

I

Edward Young's hyperbole may be taken to stand for the established importance of *originality* as both a rhetorical ornament and a fundamentally important appraisive category in the republic of letters. Its significance seems principally occidental,[1] and it is unnecessary to embark upon a history of the term in order to indicate also that originality has only recently become a crowning virtue.

Medieval writers, if they made any explicit reference to initiation, were apt to ascribe their own work to others, or invent authors to whom their work could be ascribed. Malory 'translated' from the French, and although he certainly did work from existent material, *Le Morte d'Arthur* is, in our terms, more original than he would have us believe. Some of his source material may never have existed outside his work. Chaucer cited an otherwise unknown Lollius as his author for *Troilus and Criseyde*; and an unknown stands behind Barbour's(?) poem *Wallace*; Henryson cited a mysterious extension of Criseyde's life as the basis of his *Testament of Cresseid*.[2] More employs a double fiction of unoriginality in his *Dialogue of Comfort*.[3] Further, when Sidney roundly attacked the poetry of his contemporaries, he nowhere stressed a lack of originality as deadly among their sins.[4] Even so, when he wrote, something approaching originality claims were being made,[5] but the situation was, and remained throughout the sixteenth and seventeenth centuries, more complex and fluid

[1] Joseph Levinson, *Confucian China and Its Modern Fate* (London, 1965), 3:6ff. See also Göran Hermerén, *Influence in Art and Literature* (Princeton, 1975), p. 143.

[2] A. M. Kinghorn, *The Chorus of History* (London, 1971), pp. 140–141 and 207.

[3] *A Dialogue of Comfort Against Tribulation* maintains the fiction of a translation from Hungarian and from French.

[4] *An Apologie for Poésie*, *English Critical Essays*, ed. F. D. Jones (Oxford, 1956 ed.), pp. 41ff.

[5] There is, of course, Machiavelli; yet as Allan Gilbert remarks, *Machiavelli's Prince and Its Forerunners* (Durham, 1939), in the literature *de regimine principum*, such claims were part of the genre.

than it is today. The specific term *originality*, which seems to have come into the vocabulary of criticism from art only in the mid-seventeenth century,[6] was by no means simply taken as the praiseworthy contrary of its lack; less still was it regarded as a reliable index of genius. Rather, originality existed under the auspices of the notion of imitation, which itself could be a proper aim, and an index of artistic achievement when designated *emulatio*. Indeed, to begin with originality could itself be a form of imitation—the imitation of nature.[7] Thus in the eighteenth century Reynolds was able to argue that true greatness was to be found only through imitation,[8] while Johnson in praising the pastoral poets of his age firmly subordinated originality to imitation and, at the same time, in praising Milton could write that "the highest praise of genius is original invention."[9] Such usage reflected uncertainty of status and fluidity of meaning. Shaftesbury in his *Characteristics* (1711) had associated originality in one of its senses with creation,[10] but even so, it is clear that Young was not simply paying somewhat aureate testimony to a

[6] L. P. Smith, "Four Romantic Words," in *Words and Idioms* (London, 1948 ed.), p. 87. He implies that the English must take credit for the invention of the explicit notion of originality, but matters may not be very clear-cut here. In 1644, Milton (*Areopagitica*) associated newness with presumption, a standard ploy in things touching religion, while circa 1671 La Rochefoucault, *Maximes*, 133, refers to originality in a way that seems to indicate familiarity and standardization. The Dominique Secretan edition (Geneva, 1967), p. 56, also lists variant forms of the maxim referring to originality. Young himself helps give this impression of English derivation, relying upon and alluding to Bacon's arguments against authority citation in science (see Richard Foster Jones, "Science and Criticism in the Neo-Classical Age of English Literature," in *The Seventeenth Century* [Stanford, 1969 ed.], pp. 64ff.). Thus it may be that while the image of the original came from art, some of its authority was backed up by Baconian science theory which produced that great original, Newton.

[7] Smith, *Words and Idioms*, p. 88.

[8] Sir Josuah Reynolds, *Fifteen Discourses Delivered in the Royal Academy, Sixth Discourse* (London, n.d., circa 1900 ed.), pp. 78–79.

[9] Samuel Johnson, *Lives of the Poets*, gives a good range of his critical armory. The quotation on Milton is from the edition of S. C. Roberts (London, 1963), p. 144.

[10] Cited in Smith, *Words and Idioms*, p. 93.

traditional and necessary category of appraisal. He had a case to make, and the case made with respect to poetry was part of a larger pattern of change in the shifting appraisive field of literary assessment, including such terms as *wit, fancy, imagination, genius,* and *creativity.* As *originality* ascended, so *plagiarism* became a vice,[11] and the nature of the poet was reconsidered. From being an almost passive interstitial figure, standing between mankind and divine truth (the *makar* Dunbar lamented, who transmitted from muses to men), he became a creator; as Duff had it, creative imagination was "the distinguishing characteristic of true Genius."[12]

The poet, and by extension the writer, was becoming the creator who displayed and declared his genius.[13] The elements of the uncertain change in the appraisive field of criticism, which were brought together by Young, had, as Herder put it, an electrifying effect.[14] By Carlyle's time, the case Young had typified, reinforced, and refined by figures such as Herder, Goethe, and Coleridge had proved largely persuasive. The muses were mere shadows of their former selves, coy metaphors in a world in which the writer, long-haired and mighty-handed, or slender and consumptive, stood alone. Indeed, there is even something about Carlyle's archetypal hero who travels peerless through his time that is reminiscent of Young's comets of originality.

[11] W. K. Wimsatt and C. Brooks, *A Short History of English Literature* (New York, 1957), p. 179—but this may not refer to the vice as we now know it. As early as 1644 Rutherford's *Lex, Rex* is full of accusations of plagiary. It may be that the word refers to an old vice which when removed from the context of old virtue (as was open emulation) could then be used to delineate the new ascending virtue of originality. An awareness of C. S. Lewis's notion of a "dangerous sense" in words is crucial here. *Studies in Words* (Cambridge, 1976 ed.), pp. 12–17.

[12] *Essay on Original Genius* (1767), p. 48, cited in Smith, *Words and Idioms,* pp. 93–94. Vestiges of the older aesthetic attitudes can still be found, not just as one might expect through the heirs of the Oxford movement, but also, e.g., in Paul Klee's image of the tree of art, *On Modern Art,* Introduction, Sir H. Read, trans. Paul Findlay (London, 1962 ed.), p. 15.

[13] M. Murrin, *The Veil of Allegory* (Chicago, 1969), esp. pp. 16–171; Smith, *Words and Idioms,* p. 116.

[14] Smith, *Words and Idioms,* p. 104.

Such a man we call an original man; he comes to us at first
hand. A messenger he, sent from the Infinite Unknown
with tidings for us.[15]

It is, indeed, probably only in the nineteenth century that originality achieves a simple widespread laudatory resonance and a
new unfettered appraisive status which J. S. Mill exemplified
when he wrote that all good things were the fruits of originality,[16]
which similarly Freeman reflects in his claim that in ancient
Greece "everything was fresh and original,"[17] to which Jowett
paid testimony in his belief in the original genius of Plato. Originality had become a rod for the works of the intellect.[18]

Nowadays a glance at most things written about the works of
others will reveal at least passing references to originality: a point
at which an author has moved beyond the discernible 'influences' on him; a point at which he is able to 'anticipate' those
yet to come; a point which constitutes his most likely claim on
our attention. Some brief reference to the originality of a chosen
author is especially common in the proem of a study, where the
reader must be made well disposed and must be encouraged to
continue, or in the conclusion where, regardless of the main
theme of the argument, the general worth or importance of the
author can be reiterated properly. Reference to originality represents at least a vestige of demonstrative rhetoric in academic
life, and is suitably varied by figures of rhetorical excess such as
'a man ahead of his times,' 'totally original,' 'revolutionary de-
parture,' 'striking anticipation,' to say nothing of that most ubiquitous of clichés, the 'original contribution.' An author lacking
originality almost amounts to a commentator in search of justification. Thus we may be told, somewhat defensively, that despite

---

[15] *On Heroes, Hero-worship, and the Heroic in History* (London, 1840), p. 55.

[16] *On Liberty*, ed. A. Lastell (New York, 1947 ed.), line 419.

[17] *Historical Essays*, 2nd ser. (London, 1880), p. 34.

[18] B. Jowett, *Plato: Works* (London, 1892 ed.), 3:iii and ix; and on Swift, p.
ccxxviii; cf. Hodgkin, *The Anglo Saxons* (Oxford, 1935), chap. 20, in which
Alfred the Great fails to achieve true genius because of lack of originality. See
also the revealing "Symposium on the Originality of Roman Poetry," in G. K.
Galinsky, ed., *Perspectives on Roman Poetry* (Austin, 1974).

their lack of originality, the French surrealist political thinkers might still be worth considering; that Nicholas of Cusa, though disappointingly unoriginal, can still be found interesting.[19] If, then, originality commonly seems to function as a simple index of greatness, its absence the mark of failure, it is easy to see how the biad can be pressed easily into the service of overtly political rhetoric.[20]

In this context it would be interesting to explore the correlations between approval or disapproval of Communist China and assessments of Mao's originality.[21] But a specific example may make the point clearly enough:

> The *[Communist] Manifesto* is, in fact, an extract from the thoughts of Helvetius, Rousseau . . . [et al.] on the French side, and from those of Hegel, Heine . . . [et al.] on the German side. Marx is as little the originator of socialism and communism as the chairman of General Motors Corporation is the inventor of the automobile.[22]

[19] R. S. Short, "The Politics of Surrealism, 1926–36," *JCH* 2 (1966):3; Paul E. Sigmund, *Nicholas of Cusa and Medieval Political Theory* (Cambridge, Mass., 1963), p. vii; see also Philip A. Knatchel's Introduction to Marchamont Nedham, *The Case of The Commonwealth Truly Stated* (Charlottesville, 1969), p. xlii.

[20] P. M. Hayes, "Quisling's Political Ideas," *JCH* 1 (1966): 156. Despite the fact that unoriginality is seen to be an intellectual *failure*, the attempt to succeed is often seen as intellectually indecent. Thomas Tompkins read Hobbes' claims to originality as simple perversity, in *The Rebel's Plea* (London, 1660), p. 3, while E. D. Watt, *Authority* (London and Canberra, 1982), remarks generally that striving to be original is thought to be even "narcissistic and out of place" (p. 60). Dead authors might wonder how they can win, doctoral students what they are supposed to do.

[21] Arthur A. Cohen, "How Original Was Maoism?" in W. J. Stankewicz, ed., *Political Thought Since World War Two* (Glencoe, 1964), pp. 226ff., gives an indication of what we might expect.

[22] Stefan T. Possony, quoted with a fitting skepticism in A. Hacker, *Political Theory* (New York, 1962), p. 15. The rhetoric of originality figures similarly in demotional claims made from the anarchist Left. W. Tcherkesoff's *Pages of Socialist History* extensively accuses the *Manifesto* of blatant plagiarism from Victor Considerant, *Principles du socialisme: Manifesto de la démocratie au dix-neuvième siècle* (my thanks to George McIlroy for pointing this out to me.) Or consider T. H. Huxley on his *bête noir*, Rousseau, whose originality is said to

Here patently, originality, in crude opposition to a notion of mere extraction, is used epideictically to undercut the intellectual stature of Marx and thus the authoritative foundations of communism. Conversely, originality may become a valuable mechanism in the processes of ideological promotion. Thus, writes A. Appadorai, although Gandhi was an *ad hoc* writer, from his mind "emerges an integrated view of the individual, society and the state, for his ideas proceeded from an original mind";[23] the obvious *non sequitur* here simply emphasizes the recommendatory rhetoric of originality claims in the process of cranking lineal figures up and down a gradient of greatness.

If, however, as Mill suggested, the best things are the fruits of originality, so, too, we may presume that the worst originate somewhere with someone. In rhetorical terms, however, this is not strictly the case. The political theorist is not required to press an unqualified and laudatory rhetoric of originality into the service of identifying the evil and the erroneous. Instead, the worst things may be seen as the fruits of 'responsibility.' To echo Hobbes' comment on a similarly structured rhetorical compound, responsibility is originality misliked.[24] Thus with respect to downgrading a political thinker, a political theorist can opt for a denial of originality (*à la* Possony), or he can search for a locus of responsibility, *à la* Popper on Plato, Hegel, and Marx, Strauss on Machiavelli, Talmon on Rousseau.[25] With either option, the resonance of originality itself remains unsullied, its significance as a means of organizing an analysis undiminished. Even then at the most superficial rhetorical level, where its usage may pretend to carry little information about a chosen author, originality

be of "the cheap and easy sort which is won by sedulously ignoring those who have been unmannerly enough to anticipate us" (*Method and Results, Essays* [London, 1901] 1:401).

[23] A. Appadorai, "Gandhi's Contribution to Social Theory," *RP* 31 (1969): 313.

[24] Or consider Hobbs, Sir J. B., on the difference between leg theory and body-line, *Fight for the Ashes* (London, 1933), pp. 240ff.

[25] I have discussed a parallel set of rhetorical options made available by the needs/wants and liberty/license distinctions in "The Quest for a Concept of 'Needs,' " in R. Fitzgerald, ed., *Human Needs and Politics* (Oxford and Sydney, 1977), sec. 9.

is shown to be a word of power, one frequently pressed into service, capable of subtle use and amenable to significant qualification through the distribution of an attendant subfield of terms.

Its importance emanates from its underlying role as an appraisive category in the conceptual field through which texts are understood. The rhetoric is, as it were, a fiduciary issue upon the standard; to crib Euripides, originality, like gold, is a currency word-wide. All works are thought to be in principle either original or unoriginal (even if matters of degrees are admitted), and with respect to any work the locus of originality is thought important to establish. It is, it seems, originality which marks the point at which something defies our most refined classifications and tears the tissue of continuity which our principles of connection can impose upon the past. There is a sense in which reliance upon the originality biad makes us all seem like the children of Clio. The academic significance of the search for originality may well have been reinforced by the rise of professional history in the late nineteenth century with its emphasis on change: without change there can be no history; without changes in ideas there can be no sequence of texts having distinctive characters. Yet even if for the moment we grant the legitimacy of the appraisive category as a whole, this itself gives no warrant for the kudos that is so firmly attached to originality per se. As Frye remarks, it may be absurd to make 'unique' a value term, for the world's worst poem is as unique as any other.[26] Yet originality is now seen as a virtue and an index of importance, and it is in no doubt partly because the term seems to signify that residue of a text that sets it aside from others, and thus demands particular attention. That our expectations are so often disappointed simply serves, as is the way with most virtues, to underline its cardinality: the less observed, the more adored. If in practice originality claims, like the protestations of the innocent, are so often contentious, and if in theory, as Frye and many others have remarked, total originality (despite the rhetoric) is either impossible or unintelligible, the term remains fascinatingly sac-

[26] Northrop Frye, *The Critical Path* (Bloomington, 1973 ed.), p. 27; Smith, *Words and Idioms*, p. 116.

rosanct. No formal defense of it has, I believe, been thought necessary in an academic context. J. B. Sanderson's slight discussion is both disarming and revealing. In a passage reminiscent of Acton on the dangers of historical explanation, or a theologian on the necessity of sin, Sanderson advises against too much rigor lest we run the risk "of robbing ourselves of the concept of originality in political thought altogether."[27] Such advice is irresistible.

II

One persistent problem with analysis in terms of originality is the difficulty of substantiating originality claims, for an alleged originality is not just an assessment of the character of a text, it is by negative implication an assessment of all those which have preceded it. Originality claims are thus vulnerable, far reaching, and generative of more dispute than light.[28] It is little wonder that, after prolonged scholarly debate, the originality of a thinker is apt to be elusive. For instance, Ewart Lewis, in the process of attacking the common claim that Marsilius of Padua's legal theory was positivistic and thus in the fourteenth century 'original,' admits that although Marsilius was no doubt strikingly original, it is difficult to say just how.[29] It is indeed. The problem in specifying the originality, however, is less a matter of textual location than one stemming directly from organizing an analysis in terms of a conception which is inherently vulnerable to an infinite regression of counterclaims. Awareness of this difficulty has as a consequence that analysis in terms of originality can be protected only through debasing qualifications: thus the sometimes patronizing (always trivializing) claims that *x* was original within his circle, for his time, if only because of the way he put

[27] J. Sanderson, "The Historian and the Masters of Political Thought," *Pol. Stud.* 21 (1968):45.

[28] Smith, *Words and Idioms*, p. 125; C. S. Lewis, "On Criticism," in W. Hooper, ed., *Of Other Worlds* (London, 1966), p. 47, makes the point about the "concealed negative" in originality claims.

[29] E. Lewis, "The 'Positivism' of Marsiglio of Padua," *Speculum* 38 (1963):541.

existing elements together; or even the echoingly empty x was original within the limits of his language.[30]

Practical difficulties of substantiation apart, originality claims intimate a pattern of argument which is in any case historically questionable. If we are told that x was unique by virtue of ξ, we are encouraged to follow a who-said-it-(ξ)-first paper chase backward in a way that characterizes earlier statements as anticipations or prophecies of later ones. Such a process of characterization depending on a reversal of chronological sequence is in an important sense anachronistic (see Chap. 5, pp. 71ff.). It is difficult to see how we can avoid such a perspective on a range of texts, theories, statements, or ideas if our purpose is to see how far each of them can be characterized in terms of subsequent identities. The terms of argument suggested by originality claims encourage just this sort of procedure: y was not, after all, unique because x had said ξ first, and even he had been anticipated by w. Thus w becomes characterized in terms of what y is eventually to say. Marsilius, for example, who mentions democracy only to dismiss it explicitly, can become by such emphasis on originality and its weaker brother, anticipation, "the Herald of the faceless mass man . . . and . . . of the free-thinking independent democrat."[31] The controversies of the fourteenth century have been left (approximately) six hundred years behind. If we select deftly from an alien fabric of theoretical concern and gloss a little metaphorically, Salutati and Bruni may remind us sufficiently of structuralist and poststructuralist linguistics for them to seem uncannily and strikingly original and anticipatory. But, in the end, who might not? No one, but for a residue of historical convention which remains in tension with the conceptions which appear under its auspices.[32] In short, al-

[30] J. G. A. Pocock, *The Machiavellian Moment*, on the originality of Ludovico Allemanni, p. 153; the other qualifications are dispersed throughout the work. Cf. Carlyle, *On Heroes*, who at one point, p. 149, empties the term of all associations with novelty to protect its association with heroic genius.

[31] A. Gewirth, *Marsilius of Padua* (New York, 1964 ed.), 1:313.

[32] Nancy S. Struever, *The Language of History in the Renaissance: Rhetoric and Historical Consciousness in Florentine Humanism* (Princeton, 1970), where the residue is strong and the work still stimulating.

though originality claims are formulated empirically, they are deceptively unamenable to genuinely historical verification.

A further problem is that, by and large, commentators, especially of a historical disposition, are reluctant to bring *a priori* standards of judgment to bear on a work; yet there is a marked propensity to appraise any species of work automatically in terms of a standard of originality or unoriginality. This itself may be misleading or distorting. There are whole classes of works for which assessment and the consideration of stature in terms of originality or its lack is inappropriate. I do not so much refer here to cases in which a writer has embarked upon a process of *emulatio* or *imitatio*, for clearly in such cases something similar to a recognizable originality biad will be intrinsic to the process of composition—the danger here is that what we may see as originality, the author and his contemporaries might have seen as failure to emulate. I am referring rather to cases in which an author is translating or transmitting or popularizing. Insofar as Boethius or John of Salisbury were transmitting and Fontenelle popularizing what they took to be a body of knowledge, it is arguably irrelevant to consider whether or not their work is original. Similarly, argument through the testimony of established authority involves the persistent strategy of subsuming all one has to say under the prestigious names and words of others. In order to search out originalities, the very conventions in terms of which an argument is structured have to be ignored, just as to comment upon the lack of originality is to have missed the point. Maurice Bloch's comments on formalized oratory in traditional societies are worth noting here. Such oratory is often of great significance, requiring considerable skill and talent, yet it virtually prohibits any originality. Similarly to the point is Margaret Rose's study of parody, a literary form frequently of a highly political nature which, as she suggests, is often difficult to disentangle from, and actually relies for its success upon, plagiarism.[33]

There are, in short, whole classes of theory, and much medieval political theory in particular, the assessment of which is

---

[33] Maurice Bloch, ed., *Political Language and Oratory in Traditional Society* (London, 1975), Introduction; and J. Opland, *Anglo-Saxon Oral Poetry: A Study of the Traditions* (New Haven, 1980), pp. 84–85; M. Rose, *Parody: Meta-fiction* (London, 1979), pp. 41, 175ff., and 180ff.

not unduly aided by asking questions in terms of originality, just as there have been whole generations and are whole societies who have shown systematic indifference or insensibility to the merits of the 'original' mind. Indeed, originality has been most evident in the ancient armory of religious accusation, a point which our faith in the virtue misconstrues. Yet these classes of theory, as well as these generations and societies, have not necessarily been devoid of acceptably 'great' thinkers—a point which suggests that we cannot regard originality as a reliable criterion for measuring classic status. If we have a mind to equate originality with greatness—if we have been beguiled by the familiar rhetoric of *originalgeist*—then we may well run into difficulty when accounting for the established status of many a thinker. Disappointed expectations account for W. M. Southgate's negative conclusion that virtually no one in political theory has been very original,[34] perhaps for Whitehead's comment that we are all footnotes to Plato, certainly for Levin's conclusion (cited in Chap. 3, n. 53) that the unoriginal John Locke was lucky to become a classic of political theory. There are, no doubt, other disappointments in store, and the occasional anomaly. In common parlance and by common consent, Pierre Dubois's *De recuperatione terrae sanctae* is a highly original piece of political theory, but one which remains largely unread and barely within the tradition.[35]

Now the aforementioned problems are those that can be seen to be attendant upon the need to employ a conception of originality, difficulties of which some who nevertheless use the category are aware. The immediate locus of this need, however, has not been elucidated; it is to this, a widely dispersed and seriously inadequate understanding of the history of ideas, that I shall now turn.

[34] Cited in Sanderson, "The Historian," p. 45n.; Andrew Hacker, "Capital and Carbuncles: the Great Books Re-Appraised," *APSR* 48 (1954):779, cites C. J. Friedrich to similar effect.

[35] C. H. McIlwain, *The Growth of Political Thought in the West* (London, 1964 ed.), p. 269; the only modern Latin edition with which I am familiar is that cited by McIlwain (Paris, 1891). The general discrepancy is noted also by Smith, *Words and Idioms*, p. 126, with respect to Rossetti and to P. E. Bach.

III

In this context the work of A. O. Lovejoy has been of seminal importance, and may be taken to represent what has amounted to an intellectual orthodoxy in the academic appraisal of texts and their histories.[36] In order to elucidate the way in which the historian of ideas may work, Lovejoy relied both explicitly and heavily on a distinction between ideas and the minds of men. Indeed, Lovejoy's understanding of the history of ideas looks very much as if it were based on an analogy of ideas to human biography, and is at times, at least superficially, reminiscent of Quintilian's body imagery. According to Lovejoy, ideas, like people, are born, live, form different associations, embark on various careers, become famous and influential, fall into obscurity, and ultimately die. An idea born in Greek philosophy may finally, like the idea of the great chain of being, dwindle and expire in late eighteenth-century poetry and polemics; and during its life it will have exhibited an existence independent of language, distinctive modes of thought, and the thinkers who have in fact articulated it. Ideas, in short, are stable, continuous identities, frequently robust and possessing their own "particular go." Further,

> the history of thought is a bilateral affair—the study of the traffic and the interaction between human nature . . . on the one hand, and on the other, the specific natures and pressures of the ideas which men have, from very various promptings, admitted to their minds.[37]

[36] I am drawing in particular on the essay "Reflections on the History of Ideas," *JHI* 1 (1940), which remains something of a credo for many of the journal's contributors. For additional criticism of Lovejoy see M. Mandlebaum, "The History of Ideas, Intellectual History, and the History of Philosophy," *Hist. & Th.*, Beiheft 5 (1965):34ff., and A. J. Mazzeo, "Some Interpretations of the History of Ideas," *JHI* 43 (1972).

[37] Lovejoy, "Reflections," p. 23, and *The Great Chain of Being* (New York, 1960 ed.), p. 14, for words' "independent action as forces in history." Or consider Claude Lévi-Strauss, *Mythologies* 1, *Le Cru et le cuit* (Paris, 1964), p. 20: "*Nous ne prétendons donc pas montrer comment les hommes pensent dans les mythes mais comment les mythes se pensent dans les hommes, et à leur insu.*"

Put in its simplest form, on the basis of this understanding of ideas, it becomes the task, even perhaps the principal task, of the commentator to search a given text for its more or less adequately realized ideas, and to pinpoint their genesis and their inter-relationships. In so doing, the search for originalities assumes a vital structural significance, either in dealing with a single text, or when the commentator is dealing with a whole sequence of them. For, in a world where ideas are stable yet adaptable and long-lived, originality is going to be proportionately rare and, because of its rarity, significant. Consequently, it is upon such an understanding that *genuine* originality is so often emphasized, so often sought, and so infrequently found with certainty. Equally, in principle genuinely original ideas should be readily identifiable, for we are dealing with mostly complex but stable identities. Notwithstanding the practical difficulties attendant upon the search for originality, a Lovejoyan understanding of the nature of ideas at least predisposes us to believe that in the last analysis either Marx, say, is original or he is not. Having identified an idea of alienation in Marx, we can appraise its originality by searching for the idea in a pre-Marx sequence of texts, the results of which should be (ideally) to confirm or deny that the idea was indeed Marx's, or that he had admitted to his mind an idea originally articulated by Hegel or Rousseau, Heine or Helvétius, or Victor Considerant.

The search for originalities, in the anthropomorphic imagery with which it is so often associated, is like the search in human biography for births, marriages, new careers, falls into obscurity and disfavor, new domiciles, and deaths: namely, it is a quest for the points on which the whole structure of a narrative can be seen to hinge. Originalities, then, appear to provide the reasons for saying that a given text is more than just the collective surfacing of an already available range of ideas; they provide the turning points, the changes in the course of intellectual history which is otherwise one of inevitable continuity.

Jacques Ehrmann cautiously translates this: "We are not claiming to show how men think the myths but rather how the myths think themselves out in men and without men's knowledge" (*Yale French Studies* [1966], p. 56).

What I have called a Lovejoyan notion of ideas further suggests a twofold distinction with respect to the emphasis on originality which is crucial to it, and which seems necessary in order to overcome the commonly acknowledged difficulty of uncovering the incontrovertibly original. Running through Lovejoy's own work was the distinction between the originality of being able to create from available ideas a "unit idea," a conceptual marriage, and that of being able to create the component parts themselves, a much rarer phenomenon. Similarly, Philip Wiener distinguished between the initiation of ideas and their subsequent development, suggesting that among the historian's insufficiently examined problems was that of deciding which mode of originality was the most important.[38] George Kubler, arguing that the history of art is essentially a process of replicating and varying a narrow range of elemental actions, is led also to a similar distinction when dealing with originality. He suggests a typology of initiation between the rare and radical initiation in which an artist invents his own postulates and the more common form in which the work of art is found at the intersection of already existing postulates.[39] Some form of distinction, explicit or implicit, between synthetic and radical originality seems to be both valid and important in the context of a Lovejoyan notion of ideas. Original ideas, if rare, must come from somewhere, yet because of their durability and adaptability, the imaginative combination of ideas may in no less a way be achieved in a unique manner. Painters work with much the same palette to no detriment of their originality. Consequently, when all else fails, recourse to a synthetic originality provides a second-best standard of appraisal and an ever-present means of recommendation. Medieval thinkers may be original not so much because of "their contribution

[38] Philip P. Wiener, "Some Problems and Methods in the History of Ideas," *JHI* 22 (1961): 548.

[39] G. Kubler, *The Shape of Time* (London, 1971 ed.), p. 69; Lovejoy's own work was concerned predominantly with synthetic originality: "Most philosophic systems are original or distinctive rather in their patterns than in their components," *The Great Chain*, p. 3, but the existence of "primary" ideas is conceded, p. 4. See also the characteristic comments of S. Andreski, ed., *Herbert Spenser: Structure, Function and Evolution* (London, 1971), pp. 19–20, assuming that synthetic originality equals greatness.

of new ideas" as because of their systematic "re-creation of old ones" which may be disclosed "as a patient and elaborate patch-work."[40] John of Salisbury's originality may be seen to lie in his "comprehensiveness and systematization, not in particular doc-trines"; Bernard de Mandeville may be held remarkable "not so much for originality of thought, as for the new and . . . startling pattern he made out of the old materials."[41] Might not Possony's Marx equally be credited with achieving a synthetic originality; might not Mandeville, Hooker, Marsilius, and John of Salisbury be deemed extractors, no more originators than mere motor-car moguls? Certainly, it need not be further labored, distinctions between radical and synthetic originality may be employed rhe-torically, not least because the effective denial of a radical orig-inality claim allows a second line of defense for a favored author as synthetically original; and it is sooner or later in such a line of defense that originality claims must be rooted, for if the ideas concerned are intelligible, then they may at least be understood mnemonically, and to admit a previous analogue (ξ is intelligi-ble insofar as it is like some ν) is to undermine strictly radical originality. If, however, we regard radical originality as the only proper originality, then the notion of originality is going to prove singularly irrelevant to the processes of textual appraisal; if we accept the claims of synthetic originality, then it is going to be difficult to find a text, acceptably great or otherwise, that is not in some way arguably 'original.' Although, for convenience, the picture so far drawn is somewhat stereotyped, this much is ap-parent, that even accepting a Lovejoyan notion of ideas, and its emphasis upon originality, we have something more complex and suspect than it might at first appear—an appraisive concep-tion which beneath the rhetoric looks suspiciously unreal or un-workable. There is, however, no obligation to accept such a pic-ture of the history of ideas.

[40] A. P. d'Entrèves, *The Medieval Contribution to Political Thought* (Oxford, 1939), p. 13; Margaret Leslie, "In Defence of Anachronism," *Pol. Stud.* 18 (1970)—a paper peppered with evocations of originality—relies on a related fam-ily of metaphors (kaleidoscopes and *bricoleurs*) to make some nevertheless inter-esting points, pp. 442ff.

[41] C. H. McIlwain, *The Growth of Political Thought*, p. 320. Basil Wiley, *The Eighteenth Century Background* (London, 1939), p. 95.

Now there are noticeable and relevant similarities between what I have called the issue-orthodoxy of political theory (see Chap. 2.III) and the Lovejoyan notion of ideas. Indeed, in the political theory community, a belief in one is likely to be accompanied by a belief in the other. At the most superficial level, the equivocal term 'idea' can plausibly be used as a substitute for 'issue' with respect to the basic, fundamental, enduring issues (ideas) of political theory—hence Glen Tinder: '[perhaps] eight or ten ideas are the lanterns of political civilisation; they enable us to discern and judge the realities of collective life."[42] Further, belief in the issue-orthodoxy may be seen as a specific modification of the more general belief in the existence of stable ideas independent of, but by degrees realized in, language per se. Subscription to a Lovejoyan notion of ideas does not entail faith in the more extravagant issue-orthodoxy, but with both there is a similarly expressed dichotomy which is sufficient for the Lovejoyan notion of ideas to be vulnerable to the same species of criticism as the issue-orthodoxy.[43]

It is one thing to postulate that the specific discourse of a writer must be a reflection of his ideas,[44] but it is another to postulate a realm for these ideas independent of language, let alone independent of the writer. It is yet another to attempt to make the study of these allegedly semi-independent entities the proper subject of historical inquiry. Irrespective of the metaphysical redundancy of resorting to the postulation of a world of ideas independent of language in order to explain language, the Lovejoyan notion of ideas stipulates as the subject matter for historical inquiry that to which the historian can have no access. The historian or the political theorist can specify no ideas beyond language, and those to which he does have access (those articu-

[42] Glen Tinder, *Political Thinking: The Perennial Question* (Boston, 1970), p. 6

[43] Lovejoy in fact uses phrases strongly reminiscent of common expressions of the issue-orthodoxy, referring, e.g., to "the major ideas which appear again and again," *The Great Chain*, p. 17, and "the same old problems" (ideas), p. 4.

[44] Alasdair MacIntyre, "A Mistake About Causality," in Laslett and Runciman, eds., *Politics, Philosophy and Society*, 2nd ser. (Oxford, 1962), pp. 48ff.

lated in discourse) cannot logically be said to provide evidence for, or be reflections of, an ideational reality with which the human world of discourse and action interacts. Again, as with the issue-orthodoxy, we have a species of Pythagorean fallacy: that of mistaking the abstract classifications into which we break up and organize the world of discourse for independent, continuous historical identities. Thus to write the history of an idea in the Lovejoyan sense is systematically to misconstrue the evidence.

Having followed for long enough the convention of discussing intellectual history without specifying the term 'ideas,' I shall now outline an alternative understanding of ideas in intellectual history and its consequences for the appraisive category of originality. Put negatively, a replicated verbal formula does not constitute an idea. Rather, an idea may best be understood generically as an identifiable response in discourse brought about by a distinguishable conventionally circumscribed problem. In Collingwoodian terms, an idea is thus a compound of question and answer.[45] Secondly, as I find the belief in a discrete realm of ideas unacceptable, the history of ideas, being bound by the history of discourse, is the history only of people thinking and writing; it is rather the story of what evidence we have of their varying perceptions, articulations, and responses to problems.[46]

This evidence never speaks entirely for itself, nor can it be said to have disclosed its full repertoire of ideas, or to have displayed an idea entirely to the satisfaction of all readers. Ideas then are both too fragile and too half-apparent to form a structure of continuity for historical writing, and so we cannot ever write a history of ideas. Put another way, 'ideas' are synoptic descriptions, or covering terms, for the interpretive process of bringing together into an intelligible identity parts of a 'text' (to use an uniformative term), for which a hypothetical range of

[45] R. G. Collingwood, *Autobiography* (Oxford, 1967 ed.), chaps. 5–6. In more structuralist terms, ideas are unions of different constitutive planes, as in a somewhat analogous fashion Barthes, *Eléments de Sémiologie* (Paris, 1964), chap. 2, elucidating Saussure, describes the sign as comprising the plane of the signifier (expression) and signified (content).

[46] Levinson, *Confucian China*, vol. 1, Introduction, makes the point elegantly. For further comment see Appendix.

problems forms a completing context. Identifying ξ as an idea within a text is a way of completing that text as a remnant of purposive human activity, although not everyone who reads a text will be interested in completing it in that way. We may see an idea as rather like a glimmer in the sand which we take to be a coin. The marks upon the surface we see as an inscription, an intelligible pattern, but its specification as a coin requires the awareness of an inferred hidden obverse. Not all who see it may be interested in its identity as a coin; they may see it as a perfect circle or a reflective surface (a topic does not determine the convention of discourse through which it is refined). But if we do see the marked disc as a coin, some reference to its hidden face is required and this reference becomes an idiom of explicating what we see. The dangers are that we may picture the hidden face as independent of the surface glimmer in the sand (Lovejoyan reification), or that we may picture our own profiles upon it. Because we cannot see the hidden head we may fall into the error of thinking it pointless to picture any head but our own— which is to say we are not interested in the proper specification of the glimmer as a coin. In either this or the Lovejoyan case, reference to an idea in a text becomes a means of appropriating that text to the present. It is incumbent upon the (misnamed) historian of ideas (though perhaps only upon him) to move between these two accommodating strategies of textual interpretation.[47] His uncertain means of doing so is to keep in mind that the hidden head must be an alien one, that the questions completing the textual answers must putatively be the author's. The author's problems (to adapt Barthes' expression) as "guests in the text" are inferred from a knowledge of the coin in the sand, and

---

[47] In political theory, the term 'idea' is frequently underspecified and is often found floating at the junction of discursive conflict. The historian most reasonably takes exception to other uses of the term when postulated 'ideas' are offered in the idiom of historical explanation— through the evocation of potent names tumbled in the sands of time: modern faces masquerade as the alien dead to give depth and prestige to the living (Chap. 3 of this study). It is when they are revealed to be such that one hears that our own faces have to be on the coins in any case. See Jacques Derrida, "White Mythology: Metaphor in the Text of Philosophy," trans. F. C. T. Moore, *NLH* 6 (1974): 9–17, for an elaboration and examination of this species of imagery.

the markings on its visible reverse. The historian of ideas then trades in explicatory hypotheses which run considerable risks in the hope of considerable specification; and he is never in the imperial position of the genuine archaeologist of a Sutton Hoo burial who can literally examine both sides of the coin and so hazard a date for the entirety of its surroundings.

This will be by no means an unfamiliar conception of ideas, and the reader familiar with the later writings of Collingwood, Joseph Levinson, Thomas Kuhn, and, in some moods, Michel Foucault will be aware of the kind of alternative to a Lovejoyan notion that I have in mind, for all, to different degrees and from varying perspectives, focus upon the hypothetical and fragile nature of ideas and intimate or stress their irrevocably linguistic location and limitations. If Lovejoy's own position is reminiscent of Quintilian on truth and decorum, this, in turn, is reminiscent of that which Quintilian attacked, possibly mooted by Gorgias, and entertained at one time by Cicero—there can be no effective rhetorical distinction between *res* and *verba*.[48] What needs emphasizing here, however, is neither the intellectual lineage of either position nor the gulf between them, but their very different consequences for a conception of originality.

If an idea is a compound of a conventionally circumscribed problem and a verbal response, then a change in either component constitutes a change in the idea. A verbal formula may remain unchanged, but if the problem to which it is addressed is altered, then so is the idea. Thus, as Levinson suggests, the Chinese Confucian thinkers who in the nineteenth century reaffirmed old cultural values in the face of Western technology, rather than in the face of Jesuit evangelizing or Taoist escapism, were not restating old ideas, let alone admitting available ideas to their minds; they were creating new ones. As Foucault remarks, "The sentence 'dreams fulfil desires' may have been repeated throughout the centuries; it is not the same in Plato and Freud."[49]

[48] *De oratore*, Bk. 3.
[49] *The Archaeology of Knowledge*, trans. A. M. Sheridan Smith (London, 1972), p. 103

Indeed, we may say that the conditions necessary for assertions of the continuous identity of ideas are impossibly rarefied. Certainly, if response is changed over time between authors or within the corpus of a single writer, we are confronted with changes of ideas—though we may not regard the changes as particularly significant. But to change the problems to which the response-as-part-of-the-idea is related is also, I have suggested, an eroding factor. Even if we deal with limiting possibilities where one thinker cribs from another or uses an earlier one as an inescapable authority, we have changes imposed upon the identity of the original ideas. An idea becoming authoritative in being 'repeated' is, by virtue of its requiring different predicates, changed from its initial formulation. In describing ideas and their employment, let alone their subsequent 'development,' we are not pinning predicates to independently stable identities, new clothes to old bodies; we are saying something about the immediate problem's preceding linguistic response which is different for initial writer and subsequent user, and as such we are describing a change of ideas. It may well be replied that the differences are trivial, as it may seem if, for example, we call plagiary original; but to designate a change trivial is to accept its reality, and it is with the consequences of change that we are concerned here, not with the promotion of a set of contingent priorities on the basis of a favored perspective held *a priori* to be authoritative. Indeed, our identities are always provisional, our classifications optional. The alleged samenesses of different phenomena are samenesses as somethings and not as others; the continuities of history are those changes that do not concern us. Continuity is the ice on which we stand to watch the setting sun: it is Montaigne's *Ingénieux Mélange de Nature*. As a result of such a line of reasoning, I take it, Levinson can write that it is impossible for an audience which appreciates that Mozart is not Wagner to hear the eighteenth-century *Don Giovanni*; that nineteenth-century Confucians could not (rather than did not choose to) repeat in any strict sense the ideas of the seventeenth-century.[50] Pocock similarly

---

[50] Levinson, *Confucian China*, vol. 1, Introduction. The search for the wheezy consumptive sounds of authentic instrumentation actually enhances the sense of

has related in great detail a similar story of ideational change in the reputation and reiteration of Machiavellian words from Florentine to Atlantic republicanism.[51] Changes in the identity of ideas, however, are not restricted to erosion and augmentation along a line of chronological sequence.

The conventions of argument that define distinctive intellectual activities constitute whole networks of ideas and are partially identifiable in terms of the sort and range of problems that it is proper and even possible to discuss. Ideas which we see as being transferred from one context of argument to another—even within a single work—have their identities changed. Verbal formulas may, in migrating from one discursive unity or conventional complex to another, remain recognizably the same, but the ideas they express are not so resilient. Lovejoy was doubly mistaken when he thought he had identified the same idea of the great chain of being in Aquinas and in Pope.[52] Not only had time played its part in changing the 'idea,' but the problems involved in and the conventions of argument surrounding the creation of a scholastic *questio* and a heroic couplet are palpably of a different order. Again, as Kedourie has brilliantly shown, the principles of Kantian metaphysics were changed radically in being transferred to nationalist ideology; continuity of vocabulary disguised discontinuity in the ideas expressed by Kant and by Fichte.[53]

---

difference between past and present in the attempt to overcome it, so the problem is technological as well as stylistic and part of a larger-scale problem in understanding the past.

[51] *The Machiavellian Moment,* which is mentioned here simply because this sort of sensitivity is at odds with placing much reliance upon originality and may thus explain the oddities of Pocock's use of the term (see n. 30).

[52] Lovejoy, *The Great Chain,* pp. 201ff. on Pope and pp. 15–16 on the same idea cropping up in philosophy and landscape gardening. The objects of historical inquiry must, in both senses of the term, suffer change. Andrew Lockyer, "Traditions as Contexts for the History of Political Theory," *Pol. Stud.* 27 (1979): 215–217, makes a similar point. Lovejoyans could no doubt see Russell and the eighteenth-century Cambridge Newtonians as expressing the same idea that mathematics is a form of logic, despite the fact that Russell's problem was logical, theirs a legal response to the inconveniences of college statutes insisting on logic in the curriculum. I am indebted here to Dr. John Gascoigne's paper, "Politics, Patronage and Newtonianism," *HJ* 27 (1984).

[53] Kedourie, *Nationalism,* chap. 3.

Or when Marsilius made such sustained and copious use of Aristotle (via Moerbeke) as a part of an anticlerical polemic, only an undiscriminating notion of philosophy, or a confusion between the stability of vocabulary and ideas, could lead us to think that Marsilius was expressing the philosophy of Aristotle (see Chap. 7. VI).

In sum, my position can be construed as combining Saussure's relational theory of meaning and linguistic operation with Dilthey's hermeneutic circle: Synchronically, different conventional matrices of intellectual activity are provisionally understood as discriminate wholes of interrelated problems, answers and registers of persuasion, $(A \ldots \Omega)$ in the primary context of which we discern the individual parts (ideas) as discursive items (ξ). Diachronically, the abstraction of continuity fulfills a function directly analogous to any putative synchronous whole; it is a provisional temporal stability requiring a willing suspension of belief in change which enables an intensified focus on a specific mutating item. Thus (and this helps distinguish my position from that of thinkers from Burckhardt to Foucault) the very notion of epistemic breaks punctuated by periods of unoriginal continuity is more a function of the historian's selective sense of suspended animation than a simple matter of objective fact. To misunderstand continuity as some objective absolute is to misunderstand change, whatever the items of historical attention. Above all, ideas exist only at the variable intersections of a spatio-temporal grid of activity (in Fig. 2, S/t), the precise identity of an idea being a function of the character of the intersecting wholes represented along the grid, with our understanding of them being amended by it in turn.

The consequences of this alternative conception of ideas for the predominating emphasis on originality are, I believe, fairly straightforward. The originality biad is important in the context of a Lovejoyan notion of ideas because originality appears as a rare and highly significant phenomenon. Of course, textual commentators of all sorts, including political theorists, who work within the terms of such a notion, accept originality as a matter of degree. It is nevertheless regarded, and on such a conception of ideas understandably so, as sufficiently rare and identifiable,

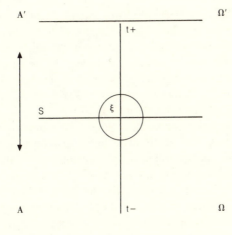

FIGURE 2

(*a*) to organize analysis around it, and (*b*) even to stipulate a distinctive typology of originality. As I have indicated previously, even within the ambit of Lovejoy's conception of ideas, however, there are severe difficulties attendant upon the originality biad, and upon regarding originality itself as an index of worth or importance. On the conception of ideas outlined briefly here, the originality biad is revealed as too indiscriminate a conception around which to organize the analysis and appraisal of the written word; it suffers a Weimarian inflation.

To begin with, as I have already noted, the terms *original* and *originality* seem to have entered the vocabulary of textual appraisal from that of painting in which they referred to the distinction between an original and a copy. Smith quotes Horace Walpole: "It is one of the most engaging pictures I ever saw, I have no qualms about its originality."[54] If this derivation is correct, then it is in fact part of a hallowed pattern of figurative working across the arts. *"La pittura è una poesia muta,"* wrote

[54] Smith, *Words and Idioms*, p. 88n.; and p. 87 quoting Sir William Davenant, *Preface to Gondobert* (1750): "Tis with Originall Pieces of Painters, whose copies abate the excessive price of the first Hand."

115

Leonardo, *"e la poesia è una pittura cieca."* Centuries later, Orwell in "Politics and the English Language" held up to exasperated scorn the habitual and precious use of the palette to describe music, and the clef to appraise paintings.[55] In the case of originality we have every right to be skeptical of the figurative interplay; written ideas turn out to be altogether less stable and have more elusive identities than paintings.

Thus even if the notion of originality is tenable with respect to art (and there may be problems here if paintings are works of 'ideas'), for the plastic and tactile to function as a stabilizing paradigm is subtly distorting and too simplistic for the transference from brushstroke to pen stroke to be successful. That is, the guiding yet too easily forgotten metaphor housed in originality claims makes perseverance with the appraisive category of originality an example of catachresis *manqué*, of what Bruno Lauretano has called the "boomerang effect" of figurative transference[56]—by which he means broadly the counter-productive consequence of persisting with and reifying metaphors in an inappropriate context of intellectual concern. Even if, in one sense of the term, we may have no qualms about the originality of a painting, even if, like Walpole, we may be prepared to stand upon its originality, we cannot stand upon the word in the history of ideas, which is a slippery slope of originality.

The long and the short of it is that all ideas are to some extent original. Thus Sterne can have Tristram Shandy complain about plagiarism in a passage lifted from Burton, and through this create, as Rose notes, something new.[57] If this can be the case— albeit an unusual one—we may say that all texts in which ideas are found, or rather from which they are gathered, are original also. Indeed, when we refer to an idea in a text, because we are drawing together parts of a whole which make sense when com-

---

[55] Cited in Roger Hinks, *Myth and Allegory in Ancient Art* (London, 1939), p. 14, who notes that Leonardo's is a comment on a commonly cited text of Horace. For Orwell, see his essay "Politics and the English Language."

[56] Bruno Lauretano, *Ambiguità e metafora* (Naples, 1964), p. 10, and *preambolo*; chap. 1, passim. The argument is at one with a number of recent studies on the language of philosophy and science. See also Chap. 7, n. 3 of this study.

[57] Rose, *Parody*, p. 157.

pleted by a complementary range of questions, each new ideational explication of a text is, in effect, a partial refashioning of
it. Each is a recognizable reading of the same text not simply
insofar as it shares with others the same contingent starting place
but also as each bears a family resemblance to other readings.
The text is defined through its readings; their subject matter by
their degree of coincidence. If this is so, then the specification
of some texts simply as original and others as not, to say nothing
more of the quest for the genuine originality, seems both misleading and centrally so for the hermeneutic issue of the nature
of texts and their relationships to reading.

The failure of the originality biad is ultimately a classificatory
one, and as has been suggested earlier, the appraisive field employed by political theorists in the analysis of texts must be effective as a set of classifiers in order for it to operate effectively.
Additionally, we need no longer concern ourselves with the claims
to priority and rarity of radical or synthetic originality. This is
not only because (although this reason is in any case sufficient)
radical originality, if found, would be historically unintelligible,
but also because the typology is erected on the dubious foundations of a belief in ideas stable enough to be combined without
having their identities changed. The problem with originality is
similar to the hypothetical attempt to organize historical sequences around the conception of events; because all happenings
are events, reliance on the term 'event' can hardly help us structure a narrative. To take two related and specific parallels, however, one can see a marked similarity between the ineffectiveness
of originality to discriminate between the ideas of texts and the
medieval notion of God as a historical category, or Sir Henry
Spelman's attempt to organize a history around the notion of
sacrilege.[58] In the first case, because all events were ultimately
by the grace of God, the singling out of some events, the unex-
pected death of a prince, for example, as attributable to God was
quite arbitrary and led ultimately to works such as Beard's *The*

[58] Sir Henry Spelman, *The History and Fate of Sacrilege* (1632), with introductory essays and emendations by Two Priests of the Church of England (London, 1853); see chap. 1 for Spelman's definition.

Theatre of God's Judgement—a list of misfortunes by virtue of which God is deemed active, and the unfortunate, sinners. As we are all sick and all must die, the work lacks any genuinely discriminate structure. Spelman's *History of Sacrilege*, which starts by defining sacrilege so that it includes injury to anything that God has created, is saved only from being a morass of arbitrary necrophiliac anecdote by focusing parochially upon England and those in public life who committed sacrilege and who thus came to a (relatively) bad end; or, coming to a bad end, are presumed to have committed sacrilege; or, having committed sacrilege and not having come to a bad end, are presumed punished in the hereafter.

If looked at closely, originality, like the almost original sin of sacrilege, infects us all—and one need not go quite to the extreme of seeing a degree of originality in plagiary (in the absurd way that has fascinated Sterne and Borges)[59] in order to see how once the commodity has flooded the market, its value must fall beneath the requirements of exchange. 'Questionless, there can be nothing more spitefully spoken against the religion of God than to accuse it of novelty, as a new-come-up-matter.'[60]

[59] "He did not want to compose another Quixote—which is easy—but the Quixote itself. Needless to say, he never contemplated a mechanical transcription of the original; he did not propose to copy it. His admirable intention was to produce a few pages which would coincide—word for word and line for line—with those of Miguel de Cervantes" (Jorge Louis Borges, "Pierre Menard, Author of the Quixote," trans. James E. Irby, in *Labyrinthes* [New York, 1964 ed.], p. 39).

[60] John Jewell, *An Apology for the Church of England*, trans. Lady Ann Bacon (1562), ed. J. E. Booty (New York, 1963), p. 83.

CHAPTER 5

Contribution and Influence

People exercise an unconscious selection in being influenced.

T. S. Eliot, *Religion and Literature*

What may be said of jig-sawing need not consume much space here.

J. Richards,
Woodworking Factories, 1873

──────────── I ────────────

Aristotle, we might say, contributed to Greek civilization, Burke to the ferment following the French Revolution, both to our understanding of political theory, the human condition, or the political life. In so saying we use the term 'contribution' in rather different senses, the first two of which are, if trite, unexceptionable insofar as they refer to tangible quantitative phenomena. The third occasion of use is interesting and dubious. For it is not entirely clear how any thinker contributes, in any significant sense of the word, to an abstraction such as the political life. It is, however, by no means uncommon to be provided with lists of thinkers who allegedly do so contribute, and it may seem fair, *prima facie*, to assume that the number or quality of a specific thinker's contributions is a reliable index of his greatness. It is with this sort of contribution claim, located partially in the ambit of the originality biad, with which I am concerned.

Although it is certainly possible to have, within the accepted idioms of political theory, 'originalities' which are not 'contributions,' a contribution is by implication an originality, for a contribution can hardly be deemed that of a given thinker unless it can also be said to originate with him. Ironically, however, although one rarely hears of noncontributory originalities, the clichéic redundancy of the original contribution is a revealing foible.

More significantly, because the vocabulary of contribution presupposes the acceptance of the originality biad, it leaves those who rely upon it open to the same range of strictures as apply to the parent conception. At this point, then, we might pass on, noting only that the devaluation of originality destabilizes neighboring currencies. Contribution, however, must be considered in its own right, for its claims, if taken seriously, are more ambitious than originality claims and its dubiety is suitably augmented. At the least, the term 'contribution' is apt to intensify the normative tone of originality; a contribution is an originality of positive and substantial merit. It is, I take it, in part the desire to underscore the worth of a thinker that provides the rationale for resorting to the stylistic overkill of 'original contributions.' Further, to point to the originality of x is to make a far-reaching statement about thinkers preceding x; but to point to the contributions of x is additionally to imply an overall shape and character of political speculation per se, in which x by virtue of certain writings, has a specifiable place. If an originality is a unique shape, a contribution purports to be a piece in a jigsaw; contributions are not just dramatic changes but individual increments.

II

In practice, however, contribution claims rarely achieve the substance necessary for anything other than rhetorical appeal, and this is readily understandable. In the context of analyzing and appraising a given text, it is possible to do little more than allude to the overall shape of the jigsaw and its residual pieces without leaving the text that is formally under scrutiny a long way behind. In Machiavellian studies, for example, many of Machiavelli's ideas have been claimed to be contributions, but in any serious sense we are obliged to take on faith, or are assumed to know, just what it is that he is contributing to.[1] However, unless we do know of any postulated contribution just how a particular piece fits in a context of equally understood pieces to form part of a clearly discernible whole, then contribution claims are going to be vacuous. And it is precisely this sort of noncontentious knowledge constituting the *telos* of contribution claims that such abstract and porous expressions as 'political science,' 'the political life,' 'political understanding,' and 'the human condition' fail to provide. As abridgments of disputable ideological perspectives, as they frequently appear to be, they convert the subjects of the contribution claims into a desirable political lineage; as nominal entities such expressions provide at best an illusion of substance that sustains contribution claims only in a rhetorical dimension.

The crucial question here, however, is whether what might perhaps be called the jigsaw building or incremental understanding of political theory, which a serious reliance upon a notion of contribution implies, can provide in principle an acceptable framework for the assessment of the canon of great political thinkers. Histories of science have traditionally relied heavily upon an appraisive category of contribution. Since Kuhn's *The Structure of Scientific Revolutions*, however, the historiographical difficulties attendant upon seeing science as a series of contributions to the cosmic (merely latest) textbook have been well canvassed, so the general point I wish to make can be introduced through reference to histories of philosophy.[2]

---

[1] Felix Gilbert's allusions to Machiavelli's many contributions in "The Humanist Convention of the Prince and the Prince of Machiavelli," *JMH* (1939), are representative.

[2] There is a substantial literature on Kuhn and the position from which he later retreated, but in most of the discussions of his work and its applicability, it seems to me the emphasis has been wrongly placed. For his work has been seen almost exclusively as a theory, or philosophy, of scientific explanation rather than as also a framework for writing a history of science. J. Stephens, "The Kuhnian Paradigm and Political Inquiry: An Appraisal," *AJPS* 17 (1973), makes virtually no reference to historical inquiry, while Martin Landau, *Political Theory and Political Science* (Atlantic Highlands, 1979 ed.), p. 71, in the context of an extensive discussion of Kuhn, mentions the word 'history' only to wonder why a "relativist"

Philosophy can be, as I have noted, an extensive and indiscriminate term, one to which all sorts of people have often wanted to make claim. The problems of limiting the scope of philosophical activity, and of stabilizing the area of reference for the term, have provided at the most general level a pronounced motif in the history of philosophy. Understandably, then, specific histories of philosophy, *unless* informed by a discriminate conception of philosophy, would degenerate into formless chronicles of general reasoning with or without a general background attached. This, however, is rarely the case, for such histories are written mainly by philosophers. Russell's rambling work is in fact only sporadically informed by a clear notion of philosophy. When it is not, as is the case in his discussion of Machiavelli, there is little connection to be seen between one thinker and another. Conversely, when the aspects of philosophy dealt with reflect Russell's own abiding interests, the narrative, informed by a conception of philosophy, takes on a more ordered structure. He is

---

like Kuhn should make appeal to the objective facts of history [*sic*]. Richard Rorty, *Philosophy and the Mirror of Nature* (Princeton, 1979), pp. 322ff., is an exception because of his sensitivity to conventional distance. If one accepts a conventional distance between history, philosophy, and science (as Kuhn did in *Structure of Scientific Revolutions*), then the methodological nexus at which his work operated has certainly been oversimplified. As Rorty and the physicist Margaret Masterman have recognized, Kuhn's injunctions were not to the scientific community; neither were they unambiguously to philosophers of science. Rather, on the basis of what he took to be philosophically entailed by adherence to notions of progress and contribution, they were partially to the historian of science, who, unlike the scientist and the philosopher, has *always* to worry about anachronism. Kuhn, in fact, straddles the position of philosopher of science and philosopher of history. The result is an ambivalence in Kuhn between reassessing the philosophical sense in which science can be said to progress and abandoning the vocabulary of progress and development as inappropriate to a history of science.

The nettle has still not been grasped. Iris Sandler, "Some Reflections on the Protean Nature of the Scientific Precursor," *History of Science* 17 (1979): 161–190, is on the one hand aware of the historiographical necessity to avoid the anachronisms entailed by precursive predication, but on the other unwilling to abandon the vocabulary which so Whiggishly structures the narrative form. The almost habitual ambivalence between the commitment to science and historiography has now been seized upon energetically, if a shade naively, by David Stove, *Popper and After: Four Modern Irrationalists* (Sydney and Oxford, 1982).

more precise in his assessments, and the vocabulary of contribution becomes purposeful. The discussions of Ockham, Leibniz, and Kant lead somewhere, namely, to Russell's own conception of the importance of and the interrelationships between logic, mathematics (especially number theory), and philosophy. These, for Russell, are the heartland of philosophy, and it is with a general survey of some modern developments in logic and number theory associated with Leibniz, then directly Cantor, Frege, Carnap, and Russell himself, that the work concludes. The contributory structure of historical philosophy, however, is too widespread and important to be tied exclusively to notions of incremental change. In Hegel's *History of Philosophy* the movement is dialectical, but from the seminal introduction onward it is made quite clear that the work is organized in terms of previous philosophers' contributions to what Hegel regarded as philosophically definitive, in short, to his own understanding of philosophy. To this end the pivotal distinction between form and content is explicated; the one referring to the transitory elements in a philosopher's thought, the other to those elements which, by being recognized as universally true, can be cut loose from a body of thought to take wing through dark time to find rest, transplanted and properly at home, in Hegel's own system. Thus the present becomes an eternity—that is, until the next philosopher comes along to spread himself out anaesthetized upon a table of time.

In both histories of science and philosophy we can see that notions of contribution help structure the narratives and can do so because there is commonly believed to be a discernible end product, a *telos* in terms of which the selective sequence can be organized. In political theory, although there is habitually found the time-stretched sequence of great names, there is no similarly clear substantive or commonly acceptable *telos* of contribution, despite the wish-fulfilling strategies of accommodation (see Chap. 3, p. 71). Were the issue-orthodoxy and the tradition less vulnerable to critique, we might have to think again. Secondly, however, even if we were obliged to think again, on the basis of a neoteric *telos* of contribution, the sequence organized in terms of it would manifest (as do histories of philosophy, science, and, one may add, histories of history) a clear species of anachronism. Phenomena spread over the past are characterized and assessed in terms of a chronologically irrelevant entity, and this is so whether the entity be Hegel's own system of philosophy in the light of which past philosophers either succeed or fail in reminding Hegel of himself, or whether that entity is a currently established scientific orthodoxy laid down as a measure for past scientists (the superstitious not measuring up at all). In both cases, the term 'contribution' signals the appropriation of the past to a specific present: the resulting history, to extend Butterfield's valuable expression, being "whig." It should be emphasized that the form of anachronism characteristic of all whig history is not just a matter of confusing and of mislocating events, of falling into piecemeal chronological confusion; it is a matter of categorical anachronism.[3] Here it makes no logical difference to the process of assessment if the allegedly contributing scientist or philosopher died fifty or five hundred years before the theory to which he is seen as contributing was in fact articulated. What does matter is the chronological irrelevance of that theory acting as an *ex post facto* standard by which he is assessed, in terms of which his activity is characterized, into the terms of which he is more or less dialectically translatable (see Chap. 1, pp. 20–22).

It is now that we can see the full difference between the notion of contribution in political theory with which I have been concerned and the two also commonly found uses of the term which I take to be unexceptionable. If we say that Aristotle contributed to Greek civilization, or that Burke contributed to the debates

[3] I am drawing here on Oakeshott's discussion in "The Activity of Being an Historian," in *Rationalism in Politics* (London, 1962). I have discussed what I have called categorical anachronism with respect to histories of philosophy in "History and Philosophy in the History of Philosophy," *Quadrant* 17 (1973): 24ff.; and with respect to histories of history, in "An Historiographical Paradox," in N. Wright and F. McGregor, eds., *European History and Its Historians* (Adelaide, 1977), pp. 85ff. Skinner's comments on prolepsis, "Meaning and Understanding in the History of Ideas" 8 (1969): 24, and his remark that "the action has to await the future to await its meaning" seem to be of a piece with the argument here. See also Chap. 9, pp. 275ff. for a qualification of the term 'history,' which retains a broad usage here.

concerning the French Revolution, we are in both cases positing a substantial and a historical focus of contribution. Aristotle's works are a major part of our evidence for the Greek civilization which he took to exist around and before him; Burke was participating in the argumentative aftermath of a series of events, the significance of which he explicitly tried to underline. To refer to either thinker's contributions to something like the political life seems to be a very different matter; in practice the *telos* is insubstantial, in theory anachronistic.

In histories of science and philosophy the vocabulary of contribution, whatever else it is, seems to be historically problematic. Hegel was less writing a history than setting down a pedigree; he was engaged in a process of retrospective philosophy. Histories of science (especially educational textbooks) are similar; they are introductions not to the past, but to the established theories and achievements of the present scientific community for which a selective past forms a perspective. The political theory community, by sharing the contributory terminology of science and philosophy, incidentally enjoys a whiff of their prestige or reveals an aspiration to emulate them and, by using the vocabulary of contribution with its intimations of semi-completed universal jigsaws or dialectical transmogrification, has organized a highly selective past as a lineage linked to, and functioning as a general focus of attention for, the present academic study of politics. It matters here not whence the glow of legitimacy emanates, from the lineage itself helping to justify an insecure branch of political studies, or from an authoritative mode of contemporary procedure which is extended backward to cover a selective past that it may bask in our glories. In either case, if we are told that Aristotle was the first behavioral scientist [*sic*];[4] or if we are told of Machiavelli's contributions to something suitably vague and general enough to cover his times and ours, we are being presented with a figure pressed from a pedigree, the contribution

---

[4] Joseph Murphy, *Political Theory: A Conceptual Analysis* (Homewood, 1968), p. 11, refers to Aristotle as the first political scientist. Many make this claim for Machiavelli also, though he seems to have been not very good at being first (cf. B. Mazlish and J. Bronowski, *The Western Intellectual Tradition* [Harmondsworth, 1963], pp. 51–54).

claims being the devices designed to tie us to our lineage, the means of recommending that we pay attention to the past in terms of our own real or imagined achievements and difficulties. Contribution claims, crucial adjuncts to the major articles of faith discussed in Part One, then become mechanisms particularly for dialectic or discursive translation and, insofar as they are serious, at least hamper historical understanding. Although the notion of originality can clearly be used specifically for ideological purposes, contributions allow a clearer shift by bringing the past into a present normally understood through political priorities, just as in science and philosophy the vocabulary of contribution enables the past to be placed respectively in a contemporary scientific or philosophical context. A. P. d'Entrèves seized upon the point well enough.

> The idea of contribution, which is emphasised in the title of these lectures, should . . . by no means be taken as an excuse to arrange the past neatly as a process in which the most significant things are those which are most easily appropriated to the present.[5]

But by tacitly equating political thought with the problem of obligation and by using this as a *telos* of contribution, he turns his chosen thinkers, Aquinas, Marsilius, and Hooker, into significant members of a direct pedigree for twentieth-century philosophical and ideological areas of dispute, in which understanding the issue or problem of obligation has been unquestionably important. His disclaimer is not enough; insofar as the conception of contribution controls the appraisal of his thinkers, his analyses are directed to an anachronistic end. He is, if only in a weak sense, approaching a point where a series of texts are seen as operating outside time, but which can be shown to be used only in the author's present. To paraphrase Eliot on such inadvertent parochialism—we overestimate our own time and mistake it for eternity, falling victim to notions of progress whenever

[5] A. P. d'Entrèves, *The Medieval Contribution to Political Thought* (Oxford, 1939), p. 5.

we confuse the question of what a classic text can do for us with the effort of making it historically intelligible.[6]

Overall one may say that although the vocabulary of contribution is common, even integral to the character of the received tradition (lineage) of the political theory community, without a clear and certain *telos* of contribution such as a tenable issue-orthodoxy might provide, contribution claims cannot help explain how a promiscuous heap of writers became classics in political theory. With such a *telos* we would fall into the same methodological difficulties as are found in histories of science and philosophy. An exploration of the linked notions of originality and contribution indicates that the 'straightforward' approach to the status and appraisal of political texts is but a step in the direction of delusion.

———————— III ————————

As the term *relevance* is frequently found in the attendant train of *contribution*, relevance claims may be similarly dismissed. A relevant writer may be nothing other than one who allegedly has contributed, and contributions (in the sense I have been discussing) are always 'relevant.' Moreover, the term *relevance*, like *contribution*, often functions to make a claim on our ideological attentions. In the eclectic political theory community, the classic texts rarely live for the sake of historical scholarship or philosophical subtlety alone, and to be able to suggest unqualifiedly that such works have also a certain (political) relevance can be seen as an index of the need to ameliorate the different discursive propensities in the activity. So Alan Gewirth suggests that, apart from purely scholarly purposes, works like the *Defensor Pacis* should be translated because their study

---

[6] T. S. Eliot, *Criterion* 12 (1932): 74–75, cited in Kermode, *The Classic* (London, 1975), p. 43.

can help toward a deeper understanding of our political traditions in their relevance for the contemporary world.[7]

There is a sense, however, in which relevance can be rescued
from an existence as part of a diluted rhetoric of contribution,
and in negative terms at least this is a valuable beginning. First,
we may say that the grammar of the two terms is different in
use. To predicate an author a contributor insinuates intention
by placing the author in the active role, his writings in the active
voice. His contributions are both what he did and what remains
worthwhile of his ideas, this surviving contributory residue explaining his importance and thus constituting his achievement.
To call a thinker relevant, however, can be to leave him purely
in the passive role. It might be only to signify currency of reference to him; we need imply nothing about the intrinsic character
of his thought, about the accuracy or validity of understandings
of him. Secondly, in referring to relevance in this way we are in
no way obliged to trade, if only hypothetically, in notions of
cosmic jigsaws of political understandings. The question "relevant to what?" asking for the *telos* of a relevance claim is properly answered simply by pointing to the area of argument in
which the author's name is demonstrably used. Thirdly, because
in speaking of the relevance of a writer one need not be talking
about his putative ideas, notions of relevance, unlike notions of
originality, need not rest on Lovejoyan conceptions of ideas. Relevance claims, in short, may be tantamount to the unexceptionable contribution claims with which we started. In speaking of
Aristotle's or Burke's contributions to Greek civilization or the
French Revolution debates, respectively, we can substitute relevance without difficulty or distortion. Although, then, the two
terms are in practice closely associated, there can be the world

---

[7] Gewirth, *Marsilius of Padua* (New York, 1956), 2:xi, and for similar comments referring to the perennial issues and Marsilius' great contributions thereto,
Marsilius of Padua (New York, 1964 ed.), 2:ix. For brief but pointed comment
on some of the historical difficulties to be overcome in making a thinker 'relevant,' see Duncan Forbes, *Hume's Philosophical Politics* (Cambridge, 1975), pp.
vii–ix.

of difference between referring to x's relevance and to x's contributions, because relevance claims carry with them altogether less presuppositional baggage, and given the character of that baggage, this is something of a virtue. But in virtue can lie the seeds of boredom, for relevance in a minimal sense may convey nothing very interesting; the statement "x is relevant" may express no more than the *de facto* importance of a name. In this sense we all know that Marx is relevant as we all know that Burke contributed to the French Revolution debates, or that Vico was not relevant until the nineteenth century. But how does this help us organize an account of the relevant authors? It does nothing to explain why or how Vico became relevant. In terms of a minimal notion of relevance we may say that all the classic texts are and have been relevant; the notion pays testimony to usage and currency, and it is this that needs explaining. But, it may be added, it is precisely this need that a reliance upon the more edifying appraisive category of contribution obscures.

IV

A vocabulary of influence is common to several areas of theoretical dispute concerning historical change and social structure. As a principle of connection it is found in the controversies surrounding causative history, which have proved to be one of the more marked continuities in the twentieth-century philosophy of history. In another context, reliance on the term *influence* may indicate commitment to some doctrine of the sociology of knowledge. Again the term may be used as a category central to charting the significance of individual action and its repercussions in complex social situations, suggesting stories of the noses of Egyptian queens. In another rather limited sense, the term *influence* is frequently found as a category of textual appraisal, and it is only with this textual influence that I am directly concerned; that is, with claims radiating from statements with the structure "x

influenced *y*." These claims include statements of simple positive or negative influence (*x* did, did not influence *y*); they include assertions of pervasive influence, where we might be told that, despite antipathy, there remains a residual influence of *x* upon *y*; conversely, they include statements of reactive influence, where we might be told that *y*'s reaction against *x* (say, Bentham's against Blackstone) was so strong that it influenced the ideas he developed in a purely negative fashion. Finally, at the very perimeters of radiation, we may find claims of indirect, disguised, putative, pervasive, and spurious influence: *w* influenced *y* through the medium of *x*; *y* wishes us to think that *x* influenced him, although it was really *w*; perhaps *x* influenced *y*; there seems to be a general presence of *x* (*grise* or ghostly) in the writings of *y*; it seems that *x* influenced *y*, but the relationship is not a genuine one.

Because reliance on a category of textual influence forms part of a wider network of the term's currency, a thorough analysis would be altogether more extensive than the general comments that follow. At the same time, however, in the appraisal of the classic texts and their interrelationships in political theory and in related areas of textual interpretation, influence claims do not at all points rely directly on covering law models of history,[8] nor need they necessarily confront the apparent problems of locating and measuring the generation and significance of ideas in human history per se. We may treat textual influence in relative isolation; it has problems enough to make it worthwhile.

---

[8] *Contra* Skinner, "The Limits of Historical Explanation," *Philosophy* 61 (1966): 199ff. His position is modified, however, in "Meaning and Understanding"; see esp. pp. 25–27. See also Göran Hermerén, *Influence in Art and Literature* (Princeton, 1975), pp. 105ff. and 306. Hermerén's study, which has come to my notice too late to deal with properly, is the most painstaking analysis of the notion of influence of which I am aware, and the drift of his arguments is very much at one with my own. However, unlike Hermerén, I see no necessity to rescue the vocabulary of influence despite its disadvantages; and I believe that he does not see the full implications of his own position for the notion of originality.

V

Influence with an attendant field of terms, *effect, reliance, debt, derivation,* and, at the perimeter, *usage,* is one of the principal tools with which the significance of a text is thought to be calculable. The hunt for the influences in the analysis of a work is the endeavor to apportion that work between a range of intellectual creditors (*y* was influenced by *x, w, v . . . a*), and as such the influence hunt purports to be a means of defining an immediate context for understanding the relevant text. In reverse it is this status of intellectual creditor which is commonly regarded as a prime indicator of greatness, for the more influential a writer, the more he has a claim on our attention. The more his work can be apportioned among intellectual creditors, however, the more they are apt to attract attention away from him, and *ipso facto,* the more other reasons have to be found to justify studying him for designating him a 'classic'. The significance of a writer, in short, may be seen to lie in the balance between the influences upon him and his influences upon the work of others.

There is an image of Western art from Giotto to Picasso which illustrates the significance of the category of influence by picturing the relationships between artists and schools in terms of a confluence of rivers and tributaries, with each noteworthy artist as a two-dimensional island withstanding the floods of time— color marking school, size marking influence. At the very head stands Giotto well diked from the fickle ravages of time, fortune, and obscurity by the implication of his almost immeasurble influence upon all who stand downstream: a sort of lone Scrovegni chapel in a flooding Venetian plain.[9] With such figures there is no need to justify the processes of continual reassessment and exploration. Such a conspectus is at least simplistic, but it could be adapted to fit the history of political theory wherever the category of influence is employed, saving that the delineation of schools would perforce be far more tenuous and subjective. But

[9] Eric Newton, *European Painting and Sculpture* (London, 1960 ed.), p. 238. See also the remarks of J. M. E. Moravesik, *Aristotle: A Collection of Critical Essays* (Notre Dame, 1968), p. 6, where the claims made for Aristotle's influence would make him analogous to Newton's Giotto.

131

even less than the alleged currents of artistic influence do the claims of textual influence bear close inspection; they deserve a Keatsian epitaph.

At the most superficial level, influence claims may be little more than stereotyping shorthand expressions. Under the auspices of alleged influence a work may be abridged and distributed between a series of prestigious creditors whose names themselves might be little more than emblems for complex arguments. Similarly, the hunt for influences might be little more than a euphemistic hunt for a suitable lineage or, as Skinner remarks, a series of reminders.[10] Equally, a writer's own claims to have been influenced by others may be seen as a claim on an appropriate pedigree.[11] I am not directly concerned with such loose and rhetorical usages of influence, although they may in some respects be revealing. As some of Marx's less sympathetic commentators illustrate, the more significant the putative influences upon him, the more his classic status is thrown into doubt. It is perhaps partially in such a climate of analysis that Althusser's *Pour Marx* can be seen. In attempting to sever the mature Marx from an entanglement of Hegelian ethical and enlightenment 'influences,' he was attempting to forestall his master's diminution. Would it be unfair to attribute his silence concerning the *Grundrisse* to the importance of separating the real (uninfluenced) scientific Marx from the Hegelian apprentice? Irrespective of this particular possibility, what is clear, even in the context of rhetorical usage, is the complex interplay between originality and influence. The two terms and fields are supplementary. It is true, of course, that an acceptable influential writer need not in the common parlance be highly original. He may be like Voltaire, or Fontenelle, principally a popularizer. Nor need an 'original' writer be influential—he may, like Dubois, or, for so long, Vico, be shrouded in obscurity.[12] Nevertheless, the 'originality' of a

[10] Skinner, "The Limits," p. 212.

[11] Ibid., p. 206. Conversely, as Hermerén correctly stresses, *Influence*, p. 134ff., the reluctance to admit 'influence' is often among artists a reluctance to fall victim to the prejudicial connotations surrounding 'debts' and 'borrowings'. To accept these economic metaphors is to admit insufficient originality.

[12] It is worth noting also a discrepancy between the allegedly influential and

writer is undermined by the catalog of his debts; as these are uncovered, so his originality withers. Conversely, the absence of influence upon a writer shifts us back into the province of positive originality claims. Indeed, reliance upon one category is apt to activate counterclaims under the auspices of the other. Originality claims may always be countered by recourse to an influence hunt, and the more successful it is, the more the originality of the luckless author must be reassessed. As the objectionable Professor Smedley Force asks,

> Where did Milne borrow from tradition; where was he "original" (i.e. where did he draw from sources that cannot be identified); and where, by the magic of his art, did he transmute traditional elements in the alembic of his imagination?[13]

Where indeed?

The reciprocity between originality and influence claims can result in the process of textual appraisal being reduced to something approaching a perpetual oscillation between their poles, and this possibility is sufficient to warn us of a related pattern of difficulties in the use of the two categories. In conventional terms, just as there is a difficulty in establishing originality claims, so, too, the conditions necessary for establishing influence claims would, if taken seriously, greatly restrict the use of the category, especially after the print explosion of the early modern period. Skinner sets down three simple conditions necessary for asserting an influential relationship between thinkers: (1) that there should be a "genuine similarity between the doctrines" of the writers; (2) that the influenced writer could only have got the relevant

---

the acceptedly important which parallels the discrepancy between importance and originality (Chap. 4, p. 119). George Buchanan whose *De jure regni* was almost a grammar school textbook when the major seventeenth-century English political thinkers were growing up is hardly mentioned in the political theory textbooks. As late as 1680, writes William Lamont, *Richard Baxter and the Millennium* (London, 1979), p. 246, Baxter felt the need to assure his readers that Buchanan and the even more obscure Christopher Goodman were not "seminal influences on nonconformist political theory."

[13] Smedley Force, "Prolegomena to Any Future Study of *Winnie-the-Pooh*," in F. Crews, ed., *The Pooh Perplex* (London, 1972 ed.), p. 144.

doctrines from his alleged creditor; (3) that there should be a low probability of the similarities being coincidental.[14] These conditions suggest a rudimentary definition of textual influence as the discernible effect of x on y through specific characteristic items (ξ, ν, η) common to both. This, in turn, emphasizes the importance of being able to establish stable and continuous items that can be transmitted from x to y as a necessary condition for any acceptable influence claim. Insofar as y alters the items said to be taken from x, then direct evidence of the influence of x is concomitantly diminished, and y within the confines of this closed model appears on the evidence more original. The plausibility of evidencing influence claims—of making them historically credible—depends at the least upon the degree to which y can be seen to have taken over ξ from x unaltered. As influence claims most usually and centrally concern the influence of ideas, we must recall the modifying factors affecting the transmission of ideas in political theory. If my final criticism of the category of originality holds, it has a residual importance for the category of influence. Vocabulary can certainly be transferred from one writer to another and manifest remarkable continuity over time. But the words writers use are seldom private property, and the use of even peculiar terms and expressions is rarely enough to characterize a text sufficiently to enable us to point to an influential relationship between two writers (say, between Wittgenstein and Schopenhauer with respect to *family resemblance*) without ignoring Skinner's second and third conditions. More importantly, however, the ideas, specific concepts, and more extensive arguments that the words are used to express are, as I have suggested, always modified in transmission. It is with these that historians of ideas and political theorists are concerned when assessing the influence of one writer upon another. Ideas are modified by being reiterated in a different context of argument, restated in association with newly perceived problems or being given new applications, as well as by being misunderstood or refuted, or given the status of authoritative dicta. They are mod-

---

[14] Skinner, "Meaning and Understanding," p. 26. See also Hermerén, *Influence*, chap. 2.

ified over time (and all influence claims presuppose a lapse of time) and through intellectual space. The result of this inevitable process of modification of ideas between thinkers is to diminish the effective scope of the category of influence. With both originality and influence we are presented with such a wide and infinitely varied continuum of applicability that neither has any clear classificatory purchase in the characterization of a text—hence the unsatisfactory propensity to categorical oscillation. In order to put weight upon the classificatory power of originality, we have to be prepared to simplify the changing complexities of ideas from one thinker to another. If we do not so simplify the processes of historical change, all ideas may be seen to rest on a gradient of originality.

By this same token, the ideational influence of x on y must be also continually qualified. It is perhaps some partial awareness of this classificatory failing, together with a reluctance to abandon a traditional category of appraisal, that leads to emptying qualifications such as 'possible,' 'pervasive,' 'marginal,' and 'indirect' influence, which mirror the emptying qualifications that buttress originality claims. By virtue of these, almost any work composed prior to another might possibly be marginally an indirect or pervasive influence on any other, just as any ξ might be original within the language of its time or because of its combination of existing ideas.

If, then, ideas cannot adequately remain sufficiently stable in transference for them to be clear-cut items of influence, the historian of ideas generally, or of political theory in particular, is left relying heavily upon the public scaffolding of language in which he is not primarily interested. To make ideational influence claims, on which the reputations and characters of the classic texts have appeared to depend, he is obliged to confuse the discontinuities of ideas with the stability of vocabulary. A further difficulty found with influence claims parallels the grammatical voice confusion mentioned with respect to the category of contribution. Influence claims grammatically put x in the active role (x influenced y; y was influenced by x). As it stands this may seem a trivial point, but there is nothing to be gained by the reversal and something may be lost. Once we have reversed the active and the passive roles, we have formally misconstrued the relationship between two thinkers, and have done so in a way that makes questions of evidence easy to overlook.

If we replace influence with usage, at least the formal confusion is avoided, and usage by being a general term covering a multitude of possibilities also invites immediate specification— how and in what way and to what extent did *y* in fact use *x*? Influence, by connoting a firm imprint, and the expectation of characteristics transferred, makes it all too easy to overlook just what in fact was done by the active partner (*y*) cast in the passive role. If when dealing with the possible relationships between Hobbes and Machiavelli, inquiries had been organized around a category of usage rather than influence, it is difficult to see how the fact that Hobbes gives no evidence of using Machiavelli could have been so often overlooked. But in the absence of any evidence of usage Machiavelli is still credited with influence, direct, indirect, or pervasive, so much so that for one commentator influence without evidence can only be explained by calling Hobbes ungrateful.[15] So, too, for another commentator when Marsilius' highly controlled and eristic usage of Augustine is misconstrued as Augustine's influence upon him, the manifest discrepancies of argument, which reference to Marsilius' use of others would lead us to expect, is seen as the Paduan's *failure* to be genuinely influenced.[16] It is almost as if the point of his writing should have been to be influenced by another.

Finally, adherence to the vocabulary of influence structures historical processes in a hypothetical and unnecessarily arbitrary fashion. To posit that *y* is influenced by *x* too easily gives way to the fiction of a (natural) train of thought in *y* which is effected by the outside by *x*. As Oakeshott remarks in a broader context

[15] Conor Cruise O'Brien, "Imagination and Order: Machiavelli," *T. S. Eliot Memorial Lecture*, University of Kent, printed in *Times Literary Supplement*, 13 November 1969, is a clear example; see also Giuliano Procacci, *Studi sulla fortuna del Machiavelli* (Rome, 1965), pp. 227–228, who seems to run together Machiavelli's *anticipation* of Hobbes and Harrington with his influence on them, for which evidence is adduced only from Harrington.

[16] D. G. Mulcahy, "The Voice of Augustine but the Hands of Marsilius," *Augustiniana* 21 (1971): 457ff.

of argument, a figure's intervention in a historical situation does not effect, or influence, the course of events; it is a part of the course of events.[17] Again we avoid a species of the miscontruction Oakeshott has in mind by abandoning the vocabulary of influence altogether and speaking more simply and properly of *y*'s use of *x*.

It is at this point that the problems of textual influence touch on some of the problems of causative history and the relationship between ideas and events. There is a marked similarity between the way in which textual influence claims, a belief in causative history, and a concern with the relative roles of ideas and events in the understanding of a given historical situation all require a process of classification which raises purely hypothetical questions about artificial identities. In trying to ascertain in general what role ideas played in the French Revolution, we have to abstract from the historical situation (a compound of events, writings, speeches, their dissemination and transmission) a situation in which some components that define the whole are absent—we have to picture a French Revolution without *its* 'ideas' in order to see how the 'ideas' influenced *it*, what role they played, whether they can be numbered among *its* causes. This, as Pocock remarks, is rather like asking whether 3 or 5 is the more important part of $3 \times 5 = 15$.[18] Indeed, this is arguably to

---

[17] Michael Oakeshott, "The Activity of Being an Historian," p. 154. This remains the case even, e.g., concerning the style of Joseph Glanville, as discussed by Richard Foster Jones, "Science and English Prose Style in the Third Quarter of the Seventeenth Century," in *The Seventeenth Century* (Stanford, 1969 ed.), pp. 89ff. Jones discusses two versions of Glanville's *The Vanity of Dogmatizing* (1661 and 1676) in order to prove the distinct influence of the Royal Society on prose style. The changes are significant, and the case argued is plausible, but even so, other admitted factors (more or less related to scientific plain style which Jones takes on the face value of its promoters) have to be abstracted from the argument. These include the fashionableness of the plainer antique authors (Seneca, Lucan, Tacitus) and the fact that Glanville was also conceptually simplifying his work. Thus the model may in part have been the plain style promoted by the early Stuart puritan lecturers. My thanks to David Oldroyd for drawing this case to my attention.

[18] J. G. A. Pocock, "The History of Political Thought: A Methodological Enquiry," in P. Laslett and W. G. Runciman, eds. *Politics, Philosophy and Society*, 2nd ser., (Oxford, 1962), pp. 191–192.

understate the case because all numbers have a conceptual independence of their possible sums, whereas the French Revolution *sans* its 'ideas' as parts of a whole is both nonexistent and conceptually absurd.

Such *questions mal posées* seem important only because of our reliance on the vocabulary of influence, a vocabulary which raises problems that recourse to historical evidence cannot adequately answer. The difficulties attendant upon the search for textual influences may well seem less momentous than those of grappling with the influence of ideas in human history. This is so, however, because the search for textual influences is frequently little more than a marginally misleading, restrictive, or euphemistic way of cataloging usage, and consequently a recourse to vocabulary usage seems infinitely preferable. It constitutes a workable residuum, standing to influence as relevance does to contribution.

VI

Like relevance, usage indicates a relationship between writers without carrying the presuppositional infections of more portentous terms. But, as has already been indicated, usage is an unspecific term, referring not so much to a distinctive relationship (the purport of influence), but virtually to any evidential relationship between writers. It is not so much a category of appraisal as an abridgment of the various things that writers may in fact be doing when they show explicit awareness of the works of others. It is possible thus to catalog a number of distinctions under the auspices of the general term.

The most fundamental distinction concerns the discursive context in which usage appears. Most simply, the use of x by y may be within the ambit of a common conventional context of argument, or, alternatively, the usage may itself involve discursive translation of x by y. From an understanding of the putative context of discourse will flow understanding of the purpose of use, and the structural role that the used author is made to play. So also it may furnish grounds for explaining y's attitude to the used author (approval, disapproval, distrust, exasperation, indifference), provide a standard for distinguishing use from misuse, and even a means of explicating style of usage; for some stylistic idioms (e.g. parody and emulation) are more appropriate to some discursive modes than to others. The extent of usage, however, is quite another matter and of uniform relevance, running the gamut from passing allusion at the limits of detectable usage to systematic incorporation, which in confused circumstances may even blur the identities of the writers concerned. Thus usage unpacked reveals a number of headings for discussing that relationship between y and the used writers w, x, v, comprising purpose and role, attitude and style—all standing in supplementary relationship to each other under the general auspices of the extent and discursive context of the putative use. The result, methodologically, if not always in practice, is to furnish sufficiently fine distinctions to enable the precise characterization of the relationships between different thinkers; to misuse an old song, anything influence can do, use can do better. Indeed, use marks the fact, rationalizing the category of influence in whose associational field it normally exists, that one writer has found another germane to his own enterprises. This, like relevance, pays testimony to the *de facto* significance of a text and presses upon us immediately the need to explain it in other terms. The connection is in fact closer, for the relevance of a writer is revealed only in a species of use, or rather we can draw conclusions as to relevance from an exploration of usage. This, however, should not lead us to believe that 'relevance' provides a distinct means toward the explanation of qualitative status, any more than the widespread nature of usage, which enables us to speak hyperbolically of a writer as 'universal,' should mislead us into thinking that universality is itself some sort of magic quality explaining classic status. Universality claims, too, are conclusions drawn from explorations of usage; and it is what facilitates usage that we need to know—the greater and more widespread, the more difficult the task. At the same time, the acceptable forms of both terms, *relevance* and *usage*, are not of the same order as the

139

appraisive categories *originality, contribution,* and *influence,* which, as they are used, purport to isolate the qualities in terms of which (allegedly) all textual analysis and appraisal can be organized, different texts compared, and their classic status (or lack of it) explained.

But, as has been labored long enough, this pack of appraisive categories, used to hunt the cause of greatness, can ground no such quarry. As a basis for any explanation of textual significance they have no more purchase than Byron thought Coleridge had on German idealism:

> And Coleridge, too, has lately taken wing,
> But like a hawk encumber'd with his hood,—
> Explaining metaphysics to the nation—
> I wish he would explain his explanation.

Nevertheless, the argument is beginning to be developed in a more constructive and less curmudgeonly fashion, just as it will soon focus on members of the appraisive field more concerned with intrinsic textual structure than with relationships between texts and authors. There can, however, be no sudden transformation scene, not least because the items in the appraisive field are not neatly limited in the ways they function, nor are their interrelationships necessarily clear-cut. The point can be illustrated with reference to the notion of comprehensiveness—a quality sometimes mentioned as a mark of important political theory, and a conception which flows uncertainly between notions of usage, relevance, and coherence. Sanderson associates comprehensiveness with coherence, stating simply that the great thinker needs to provide "a single comprehensive document stating his political philosophy."[19] There is some plausibility in this if only because what I shall have to say about the misuse of the category of coherence applies directly to it. However, as a statement about the comprehensive, the assertion is not so straightfoward. Insofar as the term *comprehensive* is used to refer to *what* is taken into account rather than *how* one argues, it is at least partially to

---

[19] J. Sanderson, "The Historian and the Masters of Political Thought," *Pol. Stud.* 21 (1968): 44.

one side of the questions concerning textual structure which we normally associate with coherence claims and is, in any case, more likely to be associated with incoherence than the biad's positive component. Petrus of Candia (Pope Alexander V) apparently liked to write on all sorts of things for readers with various and changing tastes—an aspiration to comprehensiveness, perhaps, but hardly a propensity which would augur well for the achievement of coherence. Moreover, if like Sanderson, we regard comprehensiveness as a means of distinguishing the greater from the lesser thinker, we find only the vicarious correlation between the relatively comprehensive and the relatively important—as we find with respect to 'original' and 'influential' thinkers. The Leveller *Manifestoes* have received a good deal more attention than Baxter's *Holy Commonwealth*, and they hardly compare with his comprehensiveness. At the same time, some of the more 'comprehensive' masters (Hobbes, whom Sanderson cites, or Augustine) are apt to have large portions of their "single comprehensive documents" singularly put to one side in political theory analyses. By exploring the interrelationships between political, linguistic, theological, ecclesiastical, and eschatological problems, are they perhaps a little too comprehensive for us? It is not unreasonable to conclude that comprehensiveness is largely a euphemism for a thinker's covering (or our being able to cut him down to) most of the things we regard as important—shades of the latitudinarian notion of "adequacy." In short, comprehensiveness is in some respects closer to items such as relevance, usage, and universality than it is to coherence. In effect, what more might be said of it as an appraisive expectation could well be distributed between those notions already discussed and that of coherence, to the use and abuse of which we can now turn, as we crawl from the fire to the gloom.

CHAPTER 6

Coherence

Combinations are wholes and not wholes,
Drawn together and torn asunder.
Heraclitus, *Fragment 59*

However, with each part, irrespective of the amount
of study which it may itself require, we must not lose
sight of the fact that it is only a part of the whole.
Otherwise our courage may fail us when we find
ourselves faced with a new part leading in a
completely different direction, into new dimensions,
perhaps into a remoteness where the recollection of
previously explored dimensions may easily fade. . . .
What the so called spatial arts have long achieved in
expressing, what even the time-bound art of music has·
gloriously achieved in the harmonies of polyphony,
this phenomenon of many simultaneous dimensions
which helps drama to its climax does not,
unfortunately, occur in the world of verbal didactic
expression.
Paul Klee, *On Modern Art*, 1924, trans. Paul Findlay

————————— I —————————

I shall take *coherence* as existing at the center of a network of
terms (principally *unity, precision, oneness, consistency, validity*), and as representing an unavoidable and persistent genus of
concern in textual analysis. No matter what else we may wish to
say about a given text, to some extent we are logically obliged to
trade in the currency of *coherence*. At one extreme a cursory

statement about an author's central concern or an indication of what a book is about represents some minimal coherence claim. At another, detailed analysis will frequently go much further by trying to elicit to what extent a work can be comprehended within a single net, even if the commentator's primary concern is with the work's originalities, contributions, its influences, or the influences upon it. For, whereas terms such as originality are concerned with the significance of a text, analysis in terms of coherence focuses upon the problems of determining the structure of a stable identity which can then be predicated original, non-original, contributory, or noncontributory; that is, the mere designation of a phenomenon as *a* work, *a* text, or *an* argument signifies a certain oneness, by specifying a singular entity to be talked about. Even the designation that a work is a miscellany concludes a search for coherence.

In short, a *coherence/incoherence* biad is ubiquitous and logically prior to the categories of textual analysis so far discussed; its use is a condition for their plausible deployment. There is a sense, then, in which W. H. Greenleaf is perfectly correct to insist on the centrality of coherence in textual appraisal;[1] a sense also in which Skinner's valuable attack on "mythologies of coherence" (to which I take Greenleaf to be alluding) blurs the distinction between the misuse of a category and its redundancy.[2]

But misuse is common enough. Sometimes, coherence becomes a vehicle for significance claims by being extended to connote far more than simply the way in which a text hangs together as a whole.[3] More significant is the metaphorical pro-

[1] W. H. Greenleaf, "Hume, Burke and the General Will," *Pol. Stud.* 20 (1972): 139–140.

[2] Q. Skinner, "Meaning and Understanding in the History of Ideas," *Hist. & Th.* 8 (1969): 16–22.

[3] Thus Arthur McGrade, maintaining that Hooker's arguments in the final books of *Ecclesiastical Polity* are coherent, concludes that *therefore* Hooker may be of some relevance and significance for our problems, "The Coherence of Hooker's Polity: The Books on Power," *JHI* 24 (1963): 163. See also D. Lowenthal's Introduction to Montesquieu, *Considerations on . . . the Greatness of the Romans* (New York, 1968 ed.), p. 19. But again, as with notions of originality and influence, there are discrepancies between attributions of a specific quality

pensity to sustain coherence claims only at the level of hack-neyed but dubious imagery, or the logical one to equate coher-ence with consistency. These propensities need further elucidation.

The most common metaphors for coherence are biological and architectonic, and the fact that they are resorted to so often perhaps indicates the difficulty of employing the category of co-herence. Whenever the world becomes difficult, we are apt to reach for familiar metaphor. Be this as it may, it is no exagger-ation to say that biological and architectonic images permeate textual analysis, constituting a form in which coherence claims are most readily available and to which they are frequently re-stricted. Werner Jaeger employs both when writing of Plato's continuing concern with *paideia*, shifting from writing of an ar-chitectonic awareness to picturing Plato's work as being like a tree. R. B. Levinson, directly attempting to rebut claims that Plato's thought is incoherent, sees fit to use a somewhat mixed architectonic metaphor of roads and buildings;[4] and familiar pyr-amidical, mechanistic, and labyrinthine images have been used of Hobbes. More broadly, we need only refer to the standard, general small change of coherence claims, of 'buttressed argu-ments,' 'shaky foundations,' works as 'edifices,' and concepts as 'capstones' to indicate the currency of such imagery.

Now even if such images are found in a context of argument which makes it literally more clear what is being meant by co-herence, they may at least be arguably unhelpful. Written texts are not like buildings, machines, or biological phenomena in a way that is directly relevant to any coherence claim. Assump-tions, for example, are not like foundations which have a simple and uniform relationship to the manifest structure and the proc-ess of its creation. They do not have to be laid down first; they may be implicit, explicit, they may be revealed at the beginning, the middle, or the end of a work. Whereas in a building, a plant,

---

and established significance. It has not been explained how the coherence of a work is historically related to accepted greatness; see Stephen Toulmin, *Human Understanding* (Oxford, 1972), 1:225ff.

[4] Werner Jaeger, *Paideia*, trans. G. Highet (Oxford, 1944), 2:96; R. B. Lev-inson, *In Defence of Plato* (Cambridge, Mass., 1953), p. 34.

or a machine, we know clearly what functions a root, a capstone, or a lever have, their precise and *exclusive* textual analogues are not so certain. And, if and when they seem so, it is because the physical imagery is apt to blur the essential categorical variability of coherence claims. An item may look like a buttress, a root, a cog, if we are looking for, say, an aesthetic coherence, but if we are not, then appearance will be confounded. The moving pen moves on, and back, and on again often with hesitations and striking changes of purpose, and what will disappoint some expectations may well satisfy others. That is, the understanding of any text as propositional, poetic, or argumentative, in short, as a work of ideas, places it in a different realm from physical phenomena which are, by and large, more easily classified. Yet it is perhaps because terms like 'book' or 'text' can function in both an intellectual realm and a physical one that physical analogues are facilitated when one is interested in intellectual structure. The analogical flow from the tactile (as with originality), however, runs a constant risk of oversimplification and intimates a categorically inappropriate understanding of all intellectual phenomena.

> Choose a paragraph of *Pooh* that superlatively illustrates Professor Penwiper's useful definition of poetry: whole meaningful structures composed of the building blocks of language and the glue of experience. In order to capture the very essence of Milne's creative method, make two lists indicating which elements in the paragraph are the blocks and which the glue.[5]

This is not to denigrate the importance of metaphor as such. What Ortega y Gasset once beautifully called the "high algebra of art" provides perhaps more widely the set theory from which so much of our understanding develops and on which it is ini-

---

[5] F. Crews, ed., in *The Pooh Perplex* (London, 1972 ed.), p. 99. One is reminded of Herbert Spencer's aggregational theory of society, *The Study of Sociology* (1899 ed.), reprinted in S. Andreski, ed., *Herbert Spencer: Structure, Function and Evolution* (London, 1971), pp. 35ff.; and of Lévi-Strauss' notion of *bricolage*—see e.g. *The Savage Mind* (London, 1967 ed.), chap. 1.

tially predicated. It is precisely because metaphorical understanding is so important that metaphorical decorum is so necessary. Once we are aware of the metaphorical nature of much of the vocabulary attendant upon coherence claims, it is possible to suggest two conditions under which physical imagery in particular need not be harmful in the realms of discourse: (*a*) when its use is so well established that it has (catachrestically) taken on meaning independent of its initial physical genesis, that is, it has ceased to be an active metaphor; or, (*b*) when it is a mere abridgment of what can be explicated in other terms, being suggestive but negotiable.

What we see, however, when such metaphors can be cashed in, or when we are presented immediately with a more literal, rather, standard or lexicalized, understanding of coherence,[6] is the constant almost subliminal equation of coherence with logical consistency,[7] although from the logical necessity of some form of coherence claim, it does not follow that all coherence is a matter of logic. When a writer is deemed coherent or incoherent, the standards that guide the commentator are those he takes to mark the conventions of the informal, or sometimes formal, logic characteristic of much contemporary philosophy. Incoherences become equated with logical blunders; the revelation of an inner or underlying coherence frequently amounts to a logical restructuring of a text—a salvage operation for a thinker believed to be in error, or who has been held guilty of fallacious reasoning. Thus where Sachs sees a radical incoherence in *The Republic*, taking the form of a fallacy of irrelevance—a failure to answer the question first posed in Book 1—Vlastos sees an elliptical argument and, by a consideration of the term *pleonexia*, makes a claim for the underlying coherence (and merit)

[6] Despite its ugliness, *lexicalization* (favored by French linguists) is to be preferred to literality, which carries metaphysical expectations and difficulties best avoided here. On metaphor and lexicalization see Jean Cohen, *Stucture du Langage poétique* (Paris, 1966), especially on science as a lexicalized realm acting as a standard for metaphorical deviation; and Michael Le Guern, *Sémantique de la métaphore et de la métonymie* (Paris, 1972), pp. 82ff.

[7] See e.g. the recent discussion on Michael Oakeshott's political thought in *Pol. Stud.* 30 (1982): 178, 179, 185, and 187 for belated explication.

of Plato's understanding of justice.[8] It is here perhaps that it is possible to hazard a reason why coherence as a noticeable characteristic in a work is taken to be an index of great intellectual virtue. In an intellectual community, such as that of political theory, where the conventions of philosophical argument act as norms for legitimate conduct, works of the past appearing to reflect them will seem *ipso facto* praiseworthy examples of the theorist's own activity. Such works, then, can take their places as part of the lineage. Or conversely (and more frequently), given that a range of works is part of an inherited lineage, it is expected to mirror contemporary conventions of argument, and is judged by them. Recalling the somewhat miscellaneous cluster of works which in fact comprise the classic and near-classic works of political theory, however, the equation of coherence and logical consistency is both inadequate and misleading.

And this is so even where there is an awareness of the dubiousness of so many coherence claims. This equation underpins Skinner's attack on "mythologies of coherence" and leads him to believe that because the search for logical consistency is often historically irrelevant or anachronistic, concern with textual coherence is greatly exaggerated.[9] Although he remains correct in pointing to the contingent errors that may be attendant upon the search for coherence (as consistency), it is the philosophical unsoundness of the equation per se with which I am concerned.

II

For the moment, accepting the common belief in the effective identity of philosophy and logic, we may say that the persistent association of coherence with consistency constitutes a form of philosophical reductionism which represents an insensitivity to

---

[8] David Sachs, "A Fallacy in Plato's Republic"; and Gregory Vlastos, "Justice and Happiness in *The Republic*," in G. Vlastos, ed., *Plato: A Collection of Critical Essays* (London, 1972), 2: 35–51 and 66–95, respectively.

[9] Skinner, "Meaning and Understanding," pp. 16–22.

the limits of philosophical speculation, and hence an insufficient awareness of any overall discriminate character of philosophical argument. *In extremis* it can result in a random irrelevance that characterized Richard Bentley's philosophical bowdlerizing of *Paradise Lost.*[10]

To elucidate the main point: at its most general level, coherence refers to the ways in which parts are interconnected to form a whole; and at a similar level of generality, the appraisive category of coherence is an abridgment of the range of questions one asks of a text in terms of its parts and the closeness of their interrelationships. These concern the ways in which the work can be divided into components, the kinds of relationships which are sought, and the kinds of relationships which subsume the various parts. What is vital here is that none of the questions have to be answered in terms of logical propositions (or even ideas)—answered in the coinage of consistency (entailment, contradiction, implication, and so forth), with the parts being subsumed under the 'whole' of philosophical argument. When we are told that ξ is a coherent text, we should ask, to echo David Wiggins, coherent as a what? (See Chap. 2. II.) Further, the weight we can put upon the answer will depend not only or even primarily upon the specific analysis of ξ, but upon the stability, character, and availability of the covering term under which it is being subsumed.

Our understanding of a range of covering terms $\bar{A}$, $\bar{B}$, $\bar{C}$ . . . (in this context of argument, *coherence categories*) will itself provide us with the initial expectations varying in specificity and character. At a very general level ξ may be deemed coherent/incoherent as an argument. This is by no means entirely indis-

---

[10] Richard Bentley, possibly suffering from the afterglow of Ramist methodological reforms, changed Milton's "Thither came Uriel gliding through the Eeven" (*Paradise Lost*, Bk. 4, line 555) to gliding through "Heaven" on the grounds that evening was not a division of space. A related tactic as Skinner has catalogued (ibid.) is to construct a philosophy from scattered fragments. A. Rapaczynski, "Locke's Conception of Property and the Principle of Sufficient Reason," *JHI* 42 (1981): 305, does this and then has it both ways by discounting as question-begging that which he doesn't fit in (p. 308). Whose question is begged by whom is another matter, as the theory paraded is said to be Locke's property, just as Paradise "logicked" was peddled as Milton's poetry.

criminate, but the notion of an argument is nevertheless a broad and flexible one. Certainly, it subsumes logical argument and thus (to beg the question of logical plurality) covers canons of logical coherence—that is, principles of interconnection between propositions in the light of which the structure of ξ can be appraised. But argument subsumes also, for example (and again to simplify), legal, historical, and, in one sense of the term, rhetorical argument, as well as their differing canons of coherence. Although these may at points overlap, none of them are coextensive with each other or with logic, and some may be joined under the general auspices of 'argument' more by shared vocabulary (terms such as *reason, conclusion*) than by shared principles of interconnection. Although from the standpoint of a given discursive form we might have to translate into the terms it recognizes (see pp. 13–14, 20–22, and 183–184), strictly speaking we cannot assume (to refer to Toulmin's related point) that canons of coherence are really invariant.[11] In short, to say that ξ is coherent as an argument (X) is no more than a beginning. It needs refining, either explicitly or through reliance on the context in which the analysis of ξ proceeds. Thus we may predicate it further: ξ is coherent/incoherent as a logical argument (X'). Such statements as this are considerably more informative, though they, too, may require further refinement, for a principal means through which forms of logic (Aristotelian, Boolian, dialectical, deviant) are distinguished is provided by the propositional interconnection sanctioned under their auspices; and a subsidiary way is through the various systems of notation which can alter the tolerance of logical allowance.

Again we may be told that ξ is coherent as a piece of literature (the expectations of coherence being aesthetic), or more precisely that it is coherent as a poem. But there are here also different canons of coherence appropriate to different poetic forms, not all of which are entirely stable, not all of which are found universally—the point of saying which is to stress that coherence claims are a function of available coherence categories. With respect to the same work, genre disputes in one language may

---

[11] Toulmin, *Human Understanding*, p. 44.

be nonexistent in another.[12] In short, to be informative (and this is obviously not a question of whether any specific claim is right or wrong), coherence claims require precise, discriminating coherence categories. It is probably the failure to ask and, above all, to pursue the question 'coherent as a what?' that has been responsible for so much trouble with coherence claims and can result in interpretive injustice, as well as argument at cross-purposes. As a corollary, insofar as a covering term functioning as a coherence category is indiscriminate or unstable, coherence claims made in terms of it are uninformative. Both the categories of, say, Menippean satire and Aristotelian logic provide relatively clear and informative criteria for assessing coherence claims made under their auspices; thus without confusion or contradiction we can say that ξ is coherent as one, incoherent as the other. As No Good Boyo remarked on landing a corset, "Bloody funny fish."

In contrast, we can rely very little on a coherence claim made under the auspices of political theory. As has been labored sufficiently in this study, the expression does not have an entirely settled usage, and as it is frequently found, it subsumes quite different species of discourse about a variable subject matter: fish, flesh, corsets, and good red herrings. Thus ξ may appear both coherent and incoherent as a piece of political theory, and in appearing so can generate much wasted dispute. Many discriminations are necessary before the statement ξ is coherent as a piece of political theory becomes unequivocal and informative, in which process the general coherence category itself might well be abandoned without regret. Insofar as 'philosophy' is certainly a marginally variable covering term, its use as a coherence category may be similarly uninformative. We may even run into trouble with such a valuable term as 'logic.' When, for example, Ernst Cassirer tells us that Machiavelli's logic is impeccable—that if

---

[12] Consider the problem of genre dispute with respect to Tolkien's *The Lord of the Rings*, which caused problems in English, but none in Italian, it being an example of *epopea*. See Averil Condren, "Leaf-Mould and Tower: A Study in the Connections Between the Writings of J. R. R. Tolkien" (M.A. thesis, University of Sydney, 1979), p. 5; or the genre problems generated by a poem such as *Beowulf*.

we accept his assumptions we must accept his conclusions[13]—
the term 'logic' is being used as a coherence category, in terms
of which a specific coherence claim is being made. But to see *Il
Principe* as logically coherent requires that we expand the notion
of logic (not refine it) to an almost meaningless extreme. If we
do not accept the expansion, then the coherence claim is untenable, for Machiavelli never defines, nor does he attempt any
argument through entailment, nor in any logical sense does he
prove, or provide, what he takes to be formally inescapable conclusions. In fact, he proceeds less through syllogism than through
a series of diversely illustrated enthymemes of often unstable
components, which is hardly 'logical' under the generous auspices of Aristotelianism.

If, however, we do accept the expansion sufficiently to include
Machiavelli's style of argument under the auspices of logic, the
coherence claim is strikingly indiscriminate. It is, I suspect, only
the common equation of coherence with logical consistency which
makes Cassirer's convolutions intelligible. This returns us to an
earlier point. Insofar as philosophical, or for that matter logical,
arguments are accepted as having distinctive forms, then a coherence category such as philosophy, by being discriminate, implicitly recognizes *de facto* alternatives to philosophical argument—that the intellectual world is not divided simply into good
and bad philosophers—that all theories do not aspire to being
philosophy. It recognizes, in short, alternative coherence categories in terms of which ξ may always be reappraised. To recall
a dictum of Strawson's, that which can be predicated can always
be repredicated. "Does the artist concern himself with micros-
copy? History? Paleontology?" asked Klee. "Only for the purposes of comparison . . . and not to provide a scientific check
on the truth of nature."

---

[13] Ernst Cassirer, *The Myth of State* (New Haven, 1950 ed.), pp. 140 and 144;
see also Roberto Ridolfi, *Vita di Niccolò Machiavelli* (Rome, 1954 ed.), p. 224,
for an unexceptionably colloquial reference to the logic of Machiavelli's thought
prior to the hyperbole of reference to *"una logica ferrea"* and *"la stessa inesorabile
logica"* (p. 226); and even the sober Gennaro Sasso, *Nicolò Machiavelli: Storia
de suo pensiero politico* (Naples, 1958), p. 186, for references to Machiavelli's
rigorous coherence and the rigor of his conclusions.

If, then, we accept the variety of intellectual life, however we specify and delineate it—accept that there are different discursive unities fleshed out into differing complexes of conventional activity (see pp. 11ff.)—the appraisive category of coherence, as a genus, has a concomitant number of species, which the equation of coherence and (logical) consistency overlooks or denies. In either case, the error is a philosophical one, a cousin to the *ignoratio elenchi*. It is ironic that such coherence claims, *pars pro toto*, mistake the part (a species of coherence) for the genus. The point here is not merely of formal significance, nor relevant only when a Richard Bentley tries to remove the logical incoherences from a *Paradise Lost*. The equation is apt to reduce even acceptedly philosophical works to a monochrome which does their complexity less than justice.

With Hobbes' *Leviathan* there has been a persistent, and almost exclusive, hunt for logical coherence and incoherence in the name of coherence per se, which has left in partial obscurity the cohering power of his language. Syntactically, Hobbes' characteristically well-marshaled legions of baroque sentences, frequently ending with a short striking or discordant phrase ("nasty, brutish and short"), virtually a rhythmic bob and wheel, lend his work a coherence independent of the logical structure of his arguments. More significantly, the work has an aesthetic coherence which may be explored through Hobbes' imagery, economical and evocative of his arguments, but independent of the logical validity they may have.

Leaving aside Leviathan himself, the mailed man made of many men, and the distinctive coloring given to the familiar *topos* of the state of nature, there is the imagery of hunting, evoking an aura of competitive movement, fear, aggression, danger, and death, even when Hobbes is writing not of peace and war but of reasoning;[14] and there is the imagery of mathematics

---

[14] Consider the cumulative tone of *Leviathan* 1. 3. A specific reference is made to the Civil War when Hobbes considers unguided trains of thought "this wild ranging of the mind." Ordered trains of thought he calls "seeking" and "a hunting out" of causes. "Sometimes a man seeks what he hath lost . . . his mind runs back, from place to place, and from time to time. . . ." Again the urgency of the running mind is used, "His thoughts run over the same places and times."

and money. These last two patterns of imagery are supplementary and they carry claims concerning his own work which are of central importance. Further, a brief consideration of them will lead us to yet another species of coherence which has been largely overlooked in the analysis of *Leviathan*.

Hobbes' association of reasoning with mathematics functions both complexly and uniformly. By making the association Hobbes is not simply, or perhaps even mainly, making a logical point about the universal structure of right reason; he is drawing on the established authority of mathematics, intimating that a similar authority should attend all good reasoning. More interestingly, the deliberate simplicity of his chosen mathematical analogues (*sum, addition, subtraction*) is a means by which he is able to connote the virtually laughable idiocy of those he considers to be in error. Essentially, reasoning is as simple as $1 + 1 = 2$, and the discrepancy between the complex language and terminology of his opponents and their inability to do simple arithmetic is there for us to laugh at.[15] And when we laugh, we share the joke with Hobbes, we flatter ourselves,[16] and are half-persuaded irrespective of argument that Hobbes' understanding of reasoning and his exemplification of it are one and correct.

Then the thinking man is likened to the spaniel ranging the field "till he find a scent." And then prudence is presented through a simile of crime and the gallows. The next chapter takes up an image of the trapped creature. As an example of joining names in consequence Hobbes uses "a man is a living creature" (1.4). In the next paragraph the necessity of definition is urged through the image of the bird trapped in lime twigs, "the more he struggles the more belimed." The virtual tenor of panic is sustained by reference to those who build upon errors being like birds trapped in a room and who "flutter at the false light of a glasse window."

[15] This is again much of the general force of *Leviathan* 1. 3–5. But in particular consider numbers 1 and 7 of the causes of "absurd conclusions" listed in chapter 5: "The first . . . I ascribe to the want of Method; in that they begin not their Ratiocination from Definitions; that is, from settled significations of their words: as if they could cast account, without knowing the value of the numeral words, *one, two,* and *three.* . . . The seventh, to names that signifie nothing; but are taken up, and learned by rote from the Schooles, as *hypostatical, transubstantiate, consubstantiate, eternal-now,* and the like canting of Schoolemen." See also ibid., his comments on the "priviledge" of absurdity enjoyed only by man, and mostly by philosophers; and 1. 8.

[16] *Leviathan* 1. 6.

Since antiquity, money has provided a field of metaphorical expansion for reasoning.[17] and Hobbes' use of it complements his use of arithmetical imagery. Whereas the former is concerned to convey the simplicity and the normative authority of reason, the latter is used to convey the public significance of reason and its dependence upon stable social relationships. If the scholastics cannot add up, their authorities are the money of fools.[18] Money can function only in a context of stable social relationships (there can be no commerce in the state of nature),[19] and it depends for its effectiveness on its being accepted universally, and being understood in the same way by all in the community; so, too, for Hobbes, right reasoning. Equally for Hobbes reasoning, like money, has important social consequences—the Civil War was explicable in terms of the currency of ill-founded opinions;[20] and currency and reasoning alike can be debased, thus requiring skepticism and vigilance in their handling; and both need the imprimatur, or at least the sanction of a sovereign who guarantees, limits, and even issues them. Moreover, there is a certain arbitrariness attached to both; money does not have to be gold as long as a given community shares a currency with specified and accepted values, while also for Hobbes our definitions are similarly nominalistic. The arguments that Hobbes is conveying, in part through his imagery, may or may not be logically coherent, but the imagery is certainly aesthetically so, even

[17] *Repuplic* Bk. 1, provides a sustained metaphorical motif of money, interest, gold for reason. See also, e.g., Horace, *Ars poetica* 2. 58, and more directly, Bacon, *Advancement of Learning*: "Words are the tokens current and accepted for conceits, as moneys are for values," cited in Ullmann, *Semantics*, pp. 13 and 36.

[18] *Leviathan* 1. 4–5, where counting becomes accounting, and not considering each bill but only the sum is little use to him who has to pay as he must take on trust the honesty and competence of the accountant. It is this which is to take up "conclusions on the trust of authors," He who does so does not know anything, "but only believeth."

[19] *Leviathan* 1. 13.

[20] *Behemoth, Dialogue* 1. *Leviathan* 1. 3, explicitly makes a fleeting association between the war, a Roman penny, and the thirty pieces of silver. In the context of its commonplace nature and classical connotations, we should not regard such imagery as a reflection of or evidence for the rise of the market economy.

to the extent that one is a metaphorical modification of the other. Our diurnal monetary transactions require the arithmetical skills of simple addition and subtraction that Hobbes uses as a synecdoche of all sure mathematical and scientific reasoning; indeed, the existence of any currency requires (logically) the acceptance of a system of simple numbers. Yet there is a vital reflexive force to Hobbes' arguments which is not conveyed by any attempt at sustained logical reasoning. Hobbes is at pains to persuade us first that he argues correctly according to the philosophical understanding of reasoning he has felt obliged to set down because of the accumulated blunders of the past; and secondly, that because of the public significance of reasoning good and bad, it is necessary for society's sake that his own right reasoning attain public authority, that his definitions and proofs become an official currency in the universities.[21] It is the burden of his arithmetical and monetary imagery to carry the weight of these two bold claims that help structure *Leviathan*, sustaining his analogical claim to be reason's own Leviathan.[22]

It is at this point that we can identify a rhetorical dimension to Hobbes' argument. Despite the common equation of logic and philosophy, philosophical arguments rarely, if ever, live by logic alone. As J. L. Austin once remarked, philosophy is largely a matter of finding the right illustration—and for centuries, it may be added, rhetorical theory has proceeded on the same assumption. If, more precisely, logic may be seen as a certain sort of structure that an argument may have, or be reduced to, as well as being more specifically a vital tool of philosophical discussion, then rhetoric (as I indicated at the outset, Introduction, n. 7) may be seen in a similarly dual light, as referring to a specifically and discretely organized set of techniques of persuasion, and as referring to the persuasive structure to which any argument may be reduced. Indeed, rather than being seen simply as logic, philosophy itself may more adequately be seen as a variable coin-

[21] *Leviathan* is framed, as it were, by references to the universities; the errors they perpetuate are mentioned in pt. 1. 1, Hobbes' own claim that his works might be taught therein is found also in the Review and Conclusion.

[22] Sheldon Wolin, *Politics and Vision* (Boston, 1960), chap. 8, gives a fine account of *Leviathan* as an image of the philosopher.

cidence of rhetoric and logic (in both senses of each term) in which, for example, appeal to logical cogency has a (specific) rhetorical authority. Certainly, since philosophers seek to persuade—at least other philosophers—(see Chap. 1, pp. 23–24) it is not unreasonable to seek a rhetorical structure even in philosophical argument, marked by specific rhetorical devices and maneuvers which philosophers consider legitimate to employ and which may be seen to constitute a sense of philosophical decorum.

It may be in large measure changes in the sense of philosophical decorum as much as changes in logic that divide philosophy over its whole history into different schools and phases. Hobbes' sense of decorum was one that fitted a combative speculative spirit. Less an owl of Minerva than an eagle swooping in the sun, he saw the world of philosophy populated largely by moles, rabbits, and twittering birds scurrying about in confusion. Much of his imagery, as I have already indicated, carries such a rhetorical force. But it is supplemented also by his sense of mock confusion about the arguments of others—a tactic of philosophical rhetoric since Plato—and by his persistent use of philosophical expletives such as "absurdity." All of this is simply to suggest that insofar as there is a rhetorical dimension to Hobbes' work, *Leviathan* may be judged in terms of rhetorical coherence, as it may be judged in terms of syntactical or aesthetic or logical coherence: although there may well be some effective agreement between different species of coherence claim, no one can be reduced to the other without similarly reducing the whole work to one of its discursive dimensions.

I have attacked the common equation of coherence and consistency through reference to Hobbes, precisely because Hobbes' logical claims are striking and because we can no doubt expect political theorists to remain preoccupied with the logical consistency of his work. But having emphasized the varieties of coherence which necessitate our always asking of a coherence claim, "coherent/incoherent as a what?," it is important to distinguish the potential variety of coherence claims from degrees of coherence. If coherence were like originality a matter of infinite degree, then we would be presented with a difficult situation, the existence of a necessary appraisive category which is too porous to act as an effective classifier. This, *prima facie*, may appear to be the case, for there is a sense in which the totally coherent work and the totally incoherent work are in fact as nonexistent as the totally unoriginal one. All coherence claims are located on a vector terminated by these hypothetical absolutes: thus such expressions as "ξ is a relatively coherent work." But this may be misleading, for whereas when we think we have detected *a* distinctive originality we have isolated an area on an unbroken continuum, when we speak of a degree of coherence, we are, or should be, referring more precisely to *n* number of incoherences (according to a specific principle of interconnection found under the aegis of a specific coherence category), and this is not to suggest an infinitely sliding scale. If an argument or theory is incoherent *qua* inconsistent, it is so because it is marked by certain unqualified and specific inconsistencies. So, too, if an argument or theory is aesthetically incoherent, we should be able to point specifically to mixed metaphors, uncontrolled images, or a breakdown in meter. In either case, we are enumerating specific items in terms of a potentially clear and discriminating classification, and in doing so we have reached the point where we must consider the specific cohering principles in terms of which we must back up any coherence claims.

III

Once we have dispensed with the persistent connection between coherence and consistency, we must also accept that cohering principles may be infinitely various. By a cohering principle, I refer to no more than any textual item or phenomenon that may have some special claim to be holding the text together as a whole under the auspices of a coherence category. Candidates for such a status may be specific concepts, distinctive vocabularies, restrictive argumentive procedures, potent images, controlling purposes, to any of which it may be argued a work is bound—

for example, even Skinner's notion of intention-in-doing provides a class of cohering principle.[23]

Here three main classes of cohering principle may be distinguished, and it is important to do so as the confusion between them can give rise to unnecessary interpretive difficulties. First, there are imposed cohering principles such as the three dramatic unities which preoccupied early Shakespearean criticism and which consist of principles of unity not elaborated by the author of the text, but by his commentator, who then proceeds to see how far the text may be held together in terms of them. Popper's reading of Plato and ancient Greek society in terms of the abstract categories of "open" and "closed" societies is a familiar example.[24] Orr's reading of Machiavelli with reference to an overarching conception of time is another.[25] Since the conventions of the political theory community are not coextensive with those of intellectual history, there is much scope for the elaboration of such principles, which may in strictly historical terms be regarded as redundant or anachronistic. Their elaboration and use corresponds to what Lumiansky called "critical unity,"[26] and they are strategies of accommodation.

In contrast to such principles there are inherent principles, in Lumiansky's phrase, principles limited to "historical unity." These are too many and too familiar to require much enumeration, and they are equally too various to be reduced to a catalog. I have in mind here, for example, Augustine's image of the two cities, Burke's of the French Revolution, Marsilius' of the original Christian Church; Aristotle's conception of teleology; Plato's

---

[23] Skinner, "Meaning and Understanding," pp. 45ff.

[24] Karl Popper, *The Open Society and Its Enemies: The Spell of Plato* (London, 1966 ed.), vol. 1, passim.

[25] R. Orr, "The Time Motif in Machiavelli," *Pol. Stud.* 17 (1969): 146ff.

[26] For Lumiansky's distinction between critical and historical unity, see e.g. "The Question of Unity in Malory's *Morte d'Arthur*," *Tulane Studies in English* 5 (1955); for an elaboration and application which is particularly revealing with respect to problems of coherence, see Elizabeth Pochoda, *Arthurian Propaganda: Le Morte d'Arthur as an Historical Ideal of Life* (Chapel Hill, 1971); for a general critique of the Lumiansky school, see S. Knight, *The Structure of Sir Thomas Malory's Arthuriad* (Sydney, 1974 ed.), pp. 13ff. See also Chap. 3 of this study on synthetic traditions.

theory of forms; Machiavelli's dichotomy between *virtù* and *fortuna*; Marx's conception of the dialectic of class; Hegel's of reason. Thirdly, there is a compound or bridging group of cohering principles which may be called hypothetical or contextual. This group consists of those putative purposes and circumstances which lie beyond the text and are not explicated within it but in terms of which the text may be arguably held together. I have in mind here such phenomena as concealed purposes, pervasive habits of mind; extratextual historical situations; authorial intentions specified beyond the text. This class of potential cohering principles greatly facilitates the shift between the first two, for it exhibits some of the marks of both. On the one hand, such principles purport to be judged by historical standards and may frequently be taken to supplement or explicate inherent cohering principles. On the other, they are by their nature extratextual and hypothetical, and often require the sort of critical imagination and association of usually discrete phenomena that can take an analysis beyond direct textual confirmation. C. B. Macpherson sees *Leviathan* and the *Two Treatises* each as cohered by *their* persistent reflection of and relationship to emerging capitalist society and its attendant ideological conception of possessive individualism. In his analysis of these works, "possessive individualism" and "the market economy" provide contextual cohering principles. It is, however, a moot point whether these principles, to which the works are supposed historically to be bound, have any firm grounding in seventeenth-century political awareness, or whether their elaboration and imposition on the thought of Hobbes and Locke is dependent upon post-Marxist perceptions of society. In short, the principles are not inherent, and are only ambiguously historically verifiable or imposed through an imaginative restructuring of the texts.[27]

---

[27] More convincingly, see Vlastos' brilliant discussion of *pleonexia*, "Justice and Happiness," where it is argued that the term was taken much for granted by Plato and provided an assumed background against which he expected his understanding of justice to be understood. Contextual cohering principles, such as Vlastos' *pleonexia*, may be thought only appropriate to what Skinner has called relatively heteronomous texts, "Hermeneutics and the Role of History," *NLH* 7 (1975): esp. 221ff., but in the light of this chapter it may be suggested that even

The propensity to conflate different types of cohering principle under the rubric of coherence is important since it can easily lead to confusion as to what a commentator is attempting, as well as doubt as to the relevant standards of critical appraisal. Although Orr is careful not to attribute his imposed conception of time to Machiavelli's own argument, Popper writes as if it were Plato's explicit and persistent purpose to defend the conception of a "closed society" (an example of Sir Karl's not claiming originality of conception); and because he does so, he is apt to be misunderstood as attempting and failing to provide an historical account of Plato's thought. In cases such as this we are, I suspect, not confronted with a simple intellectual confusion, but again with a manifestation of the oft-felt need among political theorists to coalesce or assimilate the differing conventional demands of their composite activity. In the guise of an account of Plato's thought and society, Popper effectively mounted an ideological attack on what he saw as a threat to his own society, and the cohering principle of the closed society was a vital mechanism to this end.

A similar tactic has been characteristic of the writing of Leo Strauss, especially through his interpretation of Machiavelli, whose thought is allegedly cohered by a governing conception abridged by Strauss as modernity (see Chap. 3, p. 59). The existence, let alone the status, of this cohering principle in Machiavelli is arguable to say the least, but it may certainly be regarded as an inherent cohering principle in Strauss' own work, which holds together his ideological position. When attributed to Machiavelli this principle enables Strauss to pursue historical scholarship through ideological disquisition.[28]

Now clearly, imposed principles of coherence may be as many and as various as there are commentors ingenious enough to elaborate and explore them, and the interest of such principles will probably lie more in their reflection of the commentator's

---

a rough or graded distinction between heteronomous and autonomous texts as Skinner draws is a function first of the interpreter's chosen coherence principles, ultimately the sort of interpretive activity in which the reader is engaged (see Appendix).

[28] John Gunnell, "The Myth of the Tradition," *APSR* 72 (1978): passim.

own arguments than as textual analyses. But neither can we expect either contextual or inherent candidates for the status of cohering principle to come in anything but variety, or with respect to any given text, to stand necessarily unopposed. Concepts, images, and vocabulary may clearly be revealed in a text, a range of extratextual phenomena may be historically certain and relevant to its understanding as a whole, but the elevation of any of these things to the standing of a cohering principle is a matter of complex and sometimes controversial interpretation. Thus in the understanding of Aristotle's *Politics*, the golden mean may vie with the conception of teleology as an inherent cohering principle; Hobbes' *Leviathan* may be seen as held together as a unity against the background of the Civil War, the French Wars of Religion, or the methodology of Paduan medicine. In one respect this is simply to pay testimony to the difficulty of employing any appraisive category. Penwiper notwithstanding, methodology cannot determine everything.

But in another sense, once we ask the methodologically central question "coherent as a what?" the variety of potential cohering principles is to be expected. For the question may frequently be answered in terms of quite different conventional patterns of discourse and thus is likely to intimate the existence of different cohering principles appropriate to their specific textual manifestations. This much is relatively simple; if we read *Leviathan* as a work of philosophy, a conception of philosophy is likely to thread through the whole, and a background of nominalism, and/or Paduan science, is likely to loom large. Conversely, the shadow of the Civil War, as well as an explicit commitment to monarchical government, will recede. More difficult, and more significant, in explaining the variety of coherence claims is the situation in which textual items can function in different intellectual contexts, can be used to answer the question "coherent as a what?" in different ways.

Rousseau's notion of the General Will may illustrate the point. As Cameron has pointed out, the General Will functions as a philosophical criterion for appraising the quality of public decisions, and as an (ideological) method by which decisions are reached—a dualism which he also suggests leads to an incoherence in the notion and function of the lawgiver.[29] Further, a concept such as the General Will seems both to be philosophically required in Rousseau, but also rhetorically promiscuous in an ideological context of argument. It may be seen on the one hand as a cohering abridgment of Rousseau's faith in the altruistic propensities of humanity; it is a remembrance of that hypothetical contract which marks the rudimentary awareness of the "I" in the "thou," and it is an improvement upon it as it replaces a single legitimizing act (a dubious purchase upon the future) with a perpetual process.[30] Yet for Rousseau humanity remains unevenly and uncertainly altruistic, hence his acceptance of more Hobbist propensities requires a parallel social abstraction, most succinctly—the will of all. Thus Rousseau is able to encompass society as Hell as well as Heaven on Earth. The result, however, greatly facilitated by Rousseau's style, is also a rhetorical compound which may be used subjectively and defensively by any group or single person. In short, the General Will can be seen in the context of both a rhetorical and a philosophical context of argument, and it has enriched our philosophical and ideological vocabularies.[31]

Similarly, Plato may be seen to use his theory of forms in a diversity of discursive enterprises. It is used to explain the nature of reality and knowledge; to order the interrelationships between different forms of mathematical inquiry; to differentiate between the processes of definition and illustration. It is used also as a

[29] David Cameron, *The Social Thought of Rousseau and Burke* (London, 1973), pp. 175–177.

[30] Ibid., p. 159. Thus also the General Will may be seen as an answer to the philosophically tenuous obligation arising from the logic of contract.

[31] It is something of a commonplace that the General Will is highly abstract, and that it was misread and vulgarized through the rhetoric of the French revolutionary ideologues. Both views are too simple. Insofar as the General Will functions in a philosophical context it is indeed abstract, and the Robespierres of the world are indeed vulgarizers. But Rousseau was no pure and single-minded philosopher; his own work set the tone, manifested in the Revolution. This is not to say *à la* Huxley, Talmon, and Russell that Rousseau is in some way 'responsible' for phenomena such as *The Terror*, but simply that Rousseau set the precedent for both rhetorical use and philosophical exploration of the notion of *la volonté générale*.

means of undermining the established authority of poets and poetry (as a mode of discourse) in Attic society, and as a means of legitimizing a certain sort of political rule. Put another way, we may say that the vocabulary of *eide* exhibits semantic and aesthetic economy, but probably at the expense of logical coherence. In this light the potential status of both the General Will and the theory of forms as inherent cohering principles in the works of Rousseau and Plato, respectively, is equivocal. When seen as the specific parts of a whole, are they best understood as concepts capable of different or even conflicting uses, or as suggestive images? Again, are their elaborations and applications to be read as exercises in metaphysics, poetry, or rhetoric? Do they hold their respective works together as one thing, or beguilingly disguise their incoherences as something else?

Now when such questions are raised, they are in these cases, and many others, amenable to no simple answers. But what is common to all such questions is that they touch on underlying issues of identity; the discursive identity of the text, and the identity of the specific items which may be taken to have a cohering function. Questions of identity have to be settled or put aside before we can answer questions concerning coherence. Any coherence claim (ξ is coherent, incoherent as an $\bar{X}$) is predicated upon the clear identity ξ, $\bar{X}$, and the specific part of ξ in terms of which we are concerned to sustain our coherence claim (inherent cohering principle); or the specific phenomenon to which ξ is tied as a whole (contextual cohering principle); or the specific item through which it is possible to impose unity on the whole (imposed cohering principle). Above all, coherence claims are thrown into doubt by uncertain identities. This, in turn, is to suggest that, important as it is, the currency of coherence that necessarily circulates in the process of textual analysis remains on its own something of a fiduciary issue. For texts are not simple wholes and not wholes, brought together and torn asunder, interconnected and connected as unities to other things, for the very entailed vocabulary of coherence (parts, wholes, and interconnections) presupposes sets of clear identities, which in any given case may or may not exist. Crucially the existence of such identities can be determined only through the use of another category of appraisal: the biad of ambiguity and nonambiguity. To hazard a dangerous but well worn species of metaphor, beneath the stratum of coherence lies the bedrock of ambiguity, on an implicit or explicit acceptance of which all textual appraisal stands.

PART THREE

In Religion the egg is a symbol of the natural source of all things, of the ἀρχὴ γενέσεως. . . .
We may conclude that eggs stand in an intimate relation to circus games.
J. J. Bachofen,
Myth, Religion, and Mother Right,
trans. R. Manheim

. . . nessuna cosa sì trista che non abbia del buono, nessuna sì buona che non abbia del tristo. . . .
Guicciardini, *Ricordi*

Introduction

So far, although incomplete, my argument has shown sufficiently the difficulties of taking the major items of the received
appraisive field of political theory seriously as a means of organizing the qualitative analysis of a text and of using the accepted
virtues of this field as a means of explaining classic status. "A
very wholesome and comfortable doctrine" perhaps, as Fielding
wrote of something quite different, "and to which we have but
one objection, namely, that it is not true." Analytical categories
easily become a pattern of historical expectation (see pp. 3–4),
and it is as unsatisfactory to see our classic texts as a set of originals whose contributions and coherence have elevated them to
the status of guiding models in eternity as it is to search any text
for the requisite originalities, contributions, coherence, and subsequent influences which might rectify or reinforce its qualitative
standing.

Although they provide little more than a superficial rhetoric
of rationalizations, the principal items in the appraisive field of
political theory analysis do at least point to the relationships between appraising a work and explaining its status. For, as has
been suggested to me, the status of a text is, in a sense, the sum
of its different appraisals. Concomitantly, the less illuminating
our appraisive field, the more important becomes the task of
exploring the means by which some texts seem to defy time by
the very fact that they are constantly traipsed before us in the
firelight.

A transitional chapter immediately behind us, then, my first
more constructive purpose is to go further up from the Cave by
refining and illustrating the application of a rudimentary appraisive vocabulary on the basis of which we must develop the anal-

ysis of a text as a work of ideas. This is not a matter of seeking precision for its own sake, let alone of rectifying what Penwiper would regard in principle as a *"distressing scarcity of terminology"*; what I have to offer is far too schematic for that. It is rather an exercise undertaken for the sake of revealing and being able to chart more adequately and self-consciously the approximations and contingencies of our world.

Alas, the problems of the physical world do not vaporize at the conjuring of a natty neologism, or at the invocation of a metaphorical locution; but the intellectual world of texts, arguments, poems, theses, and the analyses of political theories is largely a matter of words and conventional restrictions governing their use. But for expressions such as 'political theory' or 'political philosophy,' the texts of Plato, Machiavelli, Rousseau, and the rest might well be blown to the earth's four imagined corners to be regrouped and reconsidered as anything but great texts of political thought. The processes of naming, renaming, and re-classifying have, if sufficiently thorough, a potentially magic and creative function just as a failure to be aware of this has a marvelously stultifying one. So we command words, conjure, exorcise, or expel them, or get entangled in the spells and problems of their often long-dead users and inventors. Broadly, this is a point recognized with all its occult ramifications by the Greek rhetoricians,[1] and with its logical ones by philosophers as distinct as Hobbes, Nietzsche, Ryle, and Quine and Rescher. Word-mongering is, of course, an attendant risk and E. S. Dallas had a point applicable well beyond the cauldron when he wrote of the "wildest confusions, distinctions without difference and endless repetitions—the result of stupidity [and] of vanity."[2] Nevertheless, the attempt at altering and refining a vocabulary which is undertaken in this study is the sort of thing which, by itself, may be a means of restructuring as well as seeing afresh and more clearly that which lies inchoately and problematically before us. "People being as they are," wrote Nietzsche, with direct and

---

[1] Jacqueline de Romilly, *Magic and Rhetoric in Ancient Greece* (Cambridge, Mass., 1975), passim.

[2] E. S. Dallas, *Kettner's Book of the Table* (London, 1968 ed.), p. 1.

synecdochic simplicity, "it is the name that first makes things truly visible to them."[3] This in principle can be shown to be so of an appraisive field of textual analysis as it has been demonstrated to be true of such phenomena as the courtly vocabulary of Middle High German, the (rudimentary) grammatical terminology of Classical Greek; the scientific nomenclature of seventeenth-century Europe; the delineations of the chromatic spectrum; and the ethical structures of political communities. As a corollary, my second task, when the basis of a reformed vocabulary of textual appraisal has been outlined, will be to suggest a framework in terms of which the 'classic' status of some political theory texts which lie before us might be more plausibly and clearly explained. In doing so, I shall return in an *ad hoc* way to the misleading expectations engendered by the accepted virtues of the received (unreformed) appraisive field.

To hark back to the beginning, in considering the terms through which we can both begin to shape an understanding of texts and explain the classic status of some of them, we are dealing in a special sense with the problems of the written word in time, more specifically with the use of the past in the present—problems which clearly hover around the consideration of classicism and its rhetorical penumbra of eternity. In approaching these problems, however, I shall not be concerned with any qualities which require a supporting metaphysic of timelessness, rather only with that loose family of mechanisms facilitating the varied use of past texts in a series of differently restrictive presents—not least, but last, with the present of the modern political theorist. Thus I shall turn again to the conventional structure of political theory, to the character of methodology, and to the genesis and role of the historian who (as Caesar's sexton more than his encomiast) is a potential danger wherever the aeonian classic is an intellectual prop. The argument returns, in short, to the beginning. It offers no *eucatastrophe* as a prelude to a happy ending—

---

[3] Nietzsche, *Die Fröhliche Wissenschaft*, Werke 2 (Munich, 1963 ed.), p. 158, par. 261. *"Wie die Menschen gewöhnlich sind, macht ihnen erst der Name ein Ding überhaupt sichtbar."* He continues, *"Die Originalen sind zumeist auch die Namengeber gewesen,"* which is not to put *originalität* on any sounder footing than it already has.

that is, for a virtuous world and our intellectual virtues have failed us; it offers a new beginning only in the re-evaluation of intellectual sin. But this is something, for if recognition of sin is the mark of a redeemable society, its appreciation is a sign of civilization.

CHAPTER 7

Ambiguity:
Delineation and Typology

Am I afraid to say, that holy writ,
Which for its style and phrase puts down all wit,
Is everywhere so full of all these things—
Dark figures, allegories? Yet there springs
From that same book that lustre, and those rays
Of light, that turn our darkest nights to days.
Bunyan, Author's Apology to
The Pilgrim's Progress

The rest is silence.
Shakespeare,
Hamlet 5. 2

I

Ambiguity has long been recognized as a significant phenomenon of discourse, if too frequently as only an undesirable one. In these respects, and in terms of its logical significance, ambiguity provides a strong contrast to originality, the category with which I started. Yet if ambiguity has been commonly regarded as a fault, the nonambiguous has acquired neither proportionately laudatory connotations nor even adequately discrete delineation. The area of the unambiguous is one of virtue but not of cardinal virtue. In England, the doctrine of the clear, simple prose style initially propagated by puritan lecturers, institutionally associated with the Royal Society, and bequeathed to the eighteenth and nineteenth centuries as a philosophy of write, had its *raison d'être* in the communication of scientific theories and universal truths, while similar motivations underlay the work of the Port Royal Grammarians and the Académie Française. Clarity was a virtue insofar as it enabled the greater intellectual virtues to be displayed. Theoretically, good style was for a long time a simple one, free from ambiguity and, *in extremis*, free from figure and metaphor, 'forms' which could too easily obscure 'content,' and in which ambiguity could be so easily rooted. Metaphors, as Bunyan's poetic demon put it, "make us blind."[1] But if metaphor was pushed into an ornamental and poetic backwater by the powerful currents of scientific and philosophical reason, which ran over the sands of a simple Quintilianesque faith in the distinction between linguistic form and content, more recently, as the currents have eddied and the sands have been eroded, metaphor has flowed back into the mainstream of intellectual interest. In its wake has come the possibility of ambiguity as a discursive virtue. Nowadays, even where the distinction between form and content is accepted as an empirical fact, it is severely qualified.[2] For the most part, however, the distinction is not mistaken for a factual separation, but is recognized to be an abstraction from the mutually informing aspects of discourse, to be an abridgment of perspective convenience. With this has come the recognition that metaphor is not simply an ornament, but is potentially a means of structuring and augmenting discourse.[3] With this, in turn, has come reconsideration of ambiguity above all with respect to metaphor, poetics, and rhetoric.

---

[1] Bunyan, *The Pilgrim's Progress*, Author's Apology.

[2] E.g. W. O. Hendricks, *Grammars of Style and Styles of Grammar* (New York, 1976), pp. 4ff. and 19ff.; Claude Lévi-Strauss, *The Savage Mind* (London, 1976 ed.), chap.1, and pp. 35–36.

[3] The literature on this role of metaphor is now enormous, as Warren Shibbles' valuable but already out of date bibliography demonstrates, *Metaphor* (Wisconsin, 1971). Among important recent studies, Paul Ricoeur's discussion of catachrestic metaphor, *La métaphore vive* (Paris, 1975), trans. as *The Rule of Metaphor*, Robert Czery et al. (London, 1977), is invaluable. See also Max Black, *Models and Metaphors* (Ithaca, 1962), for the legitimate, logical role of metaphor in philosophy; W. Leatherdale, *The Role of Analogy and Metaphor in Science* (New York, 1974), for its necessity in science; C. M. Turbayne, *The Myth of Metaphor* (New Haven, 1962); Bruno Lauretano, *Ambiguità e Metafora*

Thus I. A. Richards stated that ambiguity is a means of expressing our most important statements concerning poetry and religion;[4] and Empson, it might be argued, virtually restructured the agenda of poetic analysis through reference to ambiguity.[5] So much has contemporary linguistics focused upon the putatively ambiguous that Turner has recently warned against the overuse and the misuse of a now fashionable term.[6] There are, then, powerful exceptions to the propensity to deprecate ambiguity. It is my impression, however, that the study of the classic political theorists is not foremost among them. Given the fact that so many of the classic texts of political theory are recognized to be literary (even metaphor-laden) masterpieces, and given the positive vibrations concerning ambiguity that have emanated for some time from the literary and linguistic corners of the academic world, the still common status of the ambiguous in the political theory community as a simple fault requires a note of explanation.

II

Although McDonald and Rosenau warn correctly that the activity of political theory is sufficiently eclectic for almost any generalization about it to be given credence,[7] my impression here is strong and by no means idiosyncratic.[8] An ambiguity found is a thinker faulted, and the fault either gets exploited and emphasized, or converted depending on whether the commentator wishes

(Naples, 1964), for explorations of the dangers attendant upon its logical significance. Jean Cohen, *Structure du language poétique* (Paris, 1966), is an antidote to the impressionistic and emotive uses which accompany the term's fashionableness.

[4] I. A. Richards, *The Philosophy of Rhetoric* (New York, 1976 ed.), p. 40.

[5] W. Empson, *Seven Types of Ambiguity* (London, 1965 ed. cited).

[6] G. W. Turner, *Stylistics* (London, 1975 ed.), p. 101.

[7] N. A. McDonald and J. N. Rosenau, "Political Theory as Academic Field and Intellectual Activity," *JP* 30 (1968): 311.

[8] John Dunn made the point a few years ago with specific reference to Locke, "Consent in the Political Theory of John Locke," *HJ* 10 (1967): 153ff.

to bury or praise the offending Caesar. The tone, perhaps, was first set by Artistotle, who in *The Rhetoric* remarked that the chief use of ambiguity was to enable speakers to mislead their audiences.[9] In the fourteenth century, as Alan Gewirth noted, Marsilius, drawing on the inheritance of antiquity, used *ambiguitas* as a term of abuse intended to discredit his opponents.[10] In the late seventeenth century, Farquhar echoes Hobbes and what is tantamount to a whole encumbrance of received wisdom when he wrote dismissively of Greek oracular utterance, "The more ambiguous, still the more believed."[11] Ambiguity, then, may be more than just blunder, or confusion, a failure of the intellect, like an incoherence or a failure to be original (and these we have been taught are bad enough); it may well leave a suspicion of sharp practice. So much do we assume an ideal of clear, monovocal expression that to be able to explain an apparent ambiguity in terms of putative intention threatens to carry us into the whiggish futility of castigating the dead. Ambiguity is a means of dissembling (Bunyan's demon again), and if we suspect a theorist of playing the chameleon too well, our indignation can be matched only by moral and interpretive frustration. So we find that it is Vico's very (dissembling) ambiguity which makes it difficult to make an effective case against him as being one of those responsible for modernity.[12] The emotional effect of none of the other appraisive categories I have considered is quite like this.

In general terms I suspect that the tainted reputation of ambiguity in the appraisive field of political theory is explicable in terms of the established importance of ideological and philosophical conventions of argument. These share, albeit for differing reasons, a low tolerance of the ambiguous, and often exhibit a

[9] Aristotle, *Rhetoric* 1407a, 33–1407b5. As he cites Empedocles, it is clear that he does not just have speakers in mind. See also *The Topics*, and *De Sophisticis Elenchus*, esp. 4. 1, 165b23f. Aristotle's attitude was typical among the ancients. According to W. B. Stanford, *Ambiguity in Greek Literature* (New York, 1972 ed.), only Cicero, Isocrates, and Plutarch were prepared to defend ambiguity; see pp. 13, 20 and 123.

[10] A. Gewirth, *Marsilius of Padua* (New York, 1956), 2:lxviii.

[11] *A Letter from Gray's Inn.*

[12] F. Vaughan, *The Political Philosophy of Giambattista Vico* (The Hague, 1972), p. 33.

heavy reliance upon form/content distinctions. As in political activity one of the most important of practical distinctions is that between friends and foes, prudence requires that those who cannot be counted among the former are for safety's sake clustered with the latter. "He," wrote Matthew, providing the quintessential political *topos*, "that is not with me is against me."[13] And any who are resistant to such starkly crude classifications are apt to be treated with the utmost suspicion. It is precisely because he is apt to insure his own room to maneuver through the ambiguous (Matthew also contains the story of the Pharisees and the tribute money—23:15–22) that the political animal is unhappy with the ambiguity of others. Consequently, if we survey the lineage of the political theory community, or any of its individual texts, from an ideological perspective (searching for a certain sort of 'content' in a variety of 'forms'), then, we expect the voices of the past essentially to be with us or against us. In this way Elliott and McDonald, on academic sentry duty near the dawn of the Cold War, manage their confident discriminations for the whole passing troop of major political theorists from Plato on, friend or foe, constitutional or totalitarian (see Chap. 3. III, n. 36); well and good, well and bad. Insofar as any figure is unambiguously neither friend nor foe, then he seems to be at serious fault, and is a challenge to further critical ingenuity, which if it fails may cause the figure to be dismissed as irrelevant, lest he become an emblem of our own parochialism.

Similarly, the conventional philosophical stress on clarity, consistency, and certainty of argument, which renders any hint of equivocation a sin, is carried over into the analysis of political theory texts, which are frequently read, sometimes *in toto*, as being, or aspiring to be, works of philosophy (a different sort of 'content' among the 'forms'). Here, too, then, ambiguity revealed within or with respect to the delineation of philosophical content is a blemish uncovered, and any process of rescuing or shoring up a philosophical reputation in political theory is apt to involve the removal of such.

Irrespective of the precise intellectual motivations, however,

---

[13] *Matthew* 12:30.

philosophical or ideological, insofar as ambiguity is still seen as a fault, a failing, even a mark of moral turpitude, it is difficult for us to appreciate the logical importance of the appraisive category *ambiguity* as such, and to appreciate the potential significance of the ambiguous as a principal determinant of classic status. In the analysis and appraisal of texts, we more naturally prefer the vocabularies of *influence, originality, contribution,* and *coherence.* We still repair to received virtues in order to explain the established greatness of the received texts, when we would do better, like Mandeville, to seek clues in established vice. But before the logical importance and the historical significance of the ambiguous can be assessed, it is first necessary to untangle it from other terms and other less revealing sins, in which process it will help to make some reference to ambiguity to begin with, more as a revealed characteristic than as an appraisive category.

III

First, a word to stabilize the area of the nonambiguous covered principally by the terms 'clarity' and 'certainty.' In some specific contexts we will deny an ambiguity claim with an assertion of clarity (ξ is not ambiguous, it is perfectly clear); and in some cases, such a claim will be denied with reference to certainty. Conversely, when we deny ambiguity by an assertion of clarity, we may also implicitly evoke the term 'obscurity' as an effective alternative for ambiguity. There may be occasions, however, when obscurity suggesting opacity does not express the diversity of distinct interpretive options entailed by an ambiguity claim. Similarly, when we deny ambiguity with an assertion of certainty, we implicitly evoke an association of ambiguity with vagueness. Here, too, the words may commonly be virtual synonyms, and with any ambiguity claim there must be distinct elements of uncertainty; with respect to choosing any one of the delineated interpretive options vagueness, a matter of degree, is not enough. Despite, then, a largely shared domain, the terms 'clarity' and 'certainty' are not in all cases and contexts synonymous, and insofar as this is the case, ambiguity itself is given soft edges; it may extend in differing directions. On occasions, then, 'ambiguity,' without a specific contrary acting as a safeguard, is capable of ambiguous usage.

To put the matter another way, the ambiguous ξ suggests distinct interpretive options which we do not find with vagueness and obscurity when these terms are understood strictly. Yet the contraries of the vague and obscure themselves constitute the domain of the unambiguous. Ambiguity, then, appears initially as squeezed between vagueness and obscurity, but its literal contrary is distributed between certainty and clarity. Abstracting from common usage we have, as it were, a crude pentangle as depicted in Figure 3. It is this schematic situation which helps give

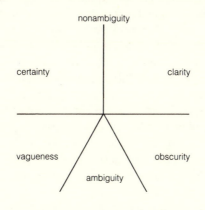

FIGURE 3

ambiguity soft edges, extending it in different directions. As it stands, however, this identification is adequate for my purposes, partly because there is more disentanglement ahead, and partly because much of what I shall argue concerning the shady area of ambiguity proper stands for the marginally vague and obscure.

We may now at least begin to unravel the ambiguous from some of the other immediate elements in its associational field, namely, complexity, dissimulation, suggestiveness, equivocation, and inconsistency. When we call a provisional discursive identity ξ ambiguous, we are not least pointing to a certain complexity. We are, however, doing more than this. In the terms of transformational grammar, as Turner has it, the ambiguous is a surface structure which can be derived from alternative deep structures.[14] The point from which the different possibilities emerge we may call the *équivoque*. According to the scale of analysis and the type of discourse, what may function as an *équivoque* may vary considerably from single word to elaborate concept. A polysemous word may thus provide an *équivoque* if it is surrounded by insufficient safeguards against its different meanings becoming interpretive possibilities in a single situation.[15]

On a larger, discursive scale, allegory may similarly lead to ambiguity through the complex interplay of tenor and vehicle. Empson is probably right in suggesting that most allegories only pretend to be ambiguous—the story (vehicle) being clear and rudimentary, and the moral (tenor) to which it is tied, and for which it exists, being certain and obviously signposted.[16] There may occur points, however (and it has been argued that these are the hallmarks of good allegory), when both tenor and vehicle may be inextricably fused by, or may, as it were, be seen to flow through, a single device which in different ways is crucial to the development of both.[17] As Wimsatt remarks with respect to metaphor, "We are often required to consider not how B (vehicle) explains A (tenor), but what meanings are generated when A and B are confronted or seen in the light of each other."[18] Once we have called something an allegory, we have indicated an intention on the part of the author, an intention to say one thing in order to convey something else of a different order as well. If there is more than a pretense of ambiguity, this may be very

---

[14] Turner, *Stylistics*, p. 102.

[15] Stephen Ullmann, *Semantics: An Introduction to the Science of Meaning* (Oxford, 1972), pp. 167ff.; for a pictorial representation see e.g. the ears/beak of Jastrow's duck/rabbit, cited in Wittgenstein, *Philosophical Investigations*, 2 xi.

[16] Empson, *Seven Types*, p. 128.

[17] E. Honig, *The Dark Conceit* (London, 1959), e.g. p. 141.

[18] Wimsatt, *The Verbal Icon* (London, 1970 ed.), p. 127; Max Black, *Models and Metaphors*, makes a similar point, but is unhappy about the use of *tenor* or *vehicle*, p. 47; in this context the terms are adequate.

close to dissimulation, but dissimulation refers to motive, not textual structure, and not all purposive ambiguity (on which see Chap. 8. III) has its end in dissimulation. The ambiguities of allegory, like the ambiguities associated with certain puns at the microcosmic level of polysemy, are invitations to hold distinct possibilities in tension at the same time. It is at this point that we can begin to isolate ambiguity from suggestiveness. In several ways, and at all levels, the terms are closely associated. In one sense, if it is possible to postulate purposive ambiguity as providing a series of options open to a writer, then we might expect the tone of his writing to be suggestive and indirect, rather than direct and explicit. In another sense, however, all ambiguities are suggestive, inasmuch as they provide interpretive options for the reader. Such possibilities provide, in David Worcester's metaphor, a "time lag"[19] in which there is a certain freedom of intellectual movement, an element of interpretive choice. Even so, we should not regard suggestiveness and ambiguity as equivalents; we may properly call something suggestive without implying an ambiguity—for we may mean by the former term nothing more than stimulating, interesting, or incomplete. Frequently, it may refer more to our ability and willingness to use a text, to play variations on a theme, than to any discernible ambiguity.

Equivocation and ambiguity, however, are terms that are frequently used synonymously, although, again, it is worthwhile drawing a distinction between them. When two or more interpretive options flowing from a given *équivoque* are possible at the same point in a text, we have an ambiguity, whereas when they are manifested in succession, we have an equivocation. An *équivoque* may be common to both. Thus ambiguity may emerge from an *équivoque* at a given point in a text, and at later points there may be equivocations between the possibilities earlier held in tension. Ambiguity is a condition for equivocation, and may now be defined as a plurality of simultaneously available interpretive options arising from a single locus. See Figure 4. Later,

---

[19] Cited in Leyburn, *Satiric Allegory, Mirror of Man* (Westport, 1969), p. 10. The association of ambiguity with the virtuous suggestiveness (fertility) indicates that one half recognizes the underlying importance of ambiguity in discourse.

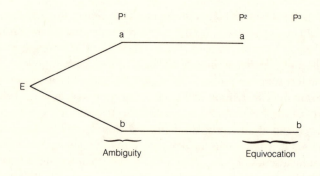

FIGURE 4

it will be possible to provide a detailed illustration of just this diagram and the exploitative shift which defines the difference between ambiguity and equivocation (see sec. VI of this chapter).

IV

The close associations of ambiguity and inconsistency lead us back into the net of terms radiating from coherence. The various possibilities flowing from an *équivoque* may well reveal logically incompatible interpretive options. Thus an *équivoque*, in disguising or in giving rise to a specific sort of incoherence, may be of central importance in the context of the operation of the different appraisive categories of coherence and ambiguity. Conversely, different interpretive options may well be translatable in terms of each other, or may be capable of subsumption, without there resulting any formal inconsistency within the context of discourse. Underlying these contingent relationships between inconsistency and ambiguity is the fact that the designation of any discursive item as consistent or inconsistent requires analysis also in terms of the appraisive category of ambiguity. This is so whether the relevant item is deemed clearly inconsistent (e.g. a simple

180

contradiction) or whether in contrast it arises from, or is related to, an ambiguity.

As was suggested previously, the vocabulary of wholes, parts, and their interrelationships, to which all analysis in terms of coherence can be reduced, also presupposes the identification of the parts and the interrelationships in terms of ambiguity and nonambiguity. This is the case irrespective of the scale of analysis. If the minimal items under scrutiny are deemed ambiguous, the character of any postulated whole is thrown into doubt. By virtue of the recognition of differing possibilities held in tension, the crucial question "coherent as a what?" has its answer converted into the adjacent vocabulary of ambiguity; conversely, we may say that insofar as any ambiguity claim implies the presence of an irreducible plurality of interpretive options, then a specific kind of negative coherence claim also becomes possible (ξ/x is incoherent). Revealed ambiguities always place specific limits on coherence. Concomitantly, the denial of ambiguity removes such limit, and in either case the conclusion may then take its place in a discussion of coherence. Hence a process of appraisive oscillation is always possible between the categories of coherence and ambiguity. But the relationships between them are asymmetrical and supplementary rather than symmetrical and vicarious. For, whereas ambiguity implies a mode of incoherence, and coherence implies nonambiguity, incoherence is not coextensive with ambiguity, nor is the unambiguous necessarily coherent.

Indeed, we may go further and state that, within the realms of the intelligible, the category of ambiguity is never entirely avoidable; it is always implicitly a point of appraisive oscillation. However else we may wish to predicate a range of given discursive items (good, bad, original, unoriginal, coherent, incoherent), we must also do so in terms of the ambiguity biad—for it is through this category that we establish or fail to establish a discernible *it* to be talked about and specified further. Everything may be seen, in the last analysis, as ambiguous or unambiguous; it is the appraisive rock on which we build.

Even where we might be uncertain of the ambiguity of a given item, we are obliged to persist with the category itself (supplement it as we will), rather than abandon it entirely: ξ/x may be (1) ambiguous or (2) unambiguous; here there are no problems. But if it seems to be neither (1) nor (2), then we are obliged to designate it ambiguous as being clearly, certainly, neither ambiguous nor unambiguous, the possibilities (1) and (2) being the interpretive options held in tension and located in the initial item. The general principle of reflexive application holds even on a more discriminate scale of analysis: thus to resort to the pentangle (Fig. 3) ξ may be ambiguous if located at any of the diagram's points as well as when it is located in the base area. This is to say that a larger pentangle has been imposed upon the first. The more discriminations we have, the more opportunities we have for refinements of ambiguity. Thus although the notion of ambiguity may in principle be used *ad infinitum*, the essentially biadic structure of any ambiguity claim removes the middle ground which weakens the classificatory power of other appraisive categories, on whose functioning the ambiguity biad can usefully be brought to bear. The discriminatory power of conceptions such as originality and influence is measurable by the area of ambiguity lying between the concept's defining poles, that is, by a given appraisive category's range of unambiguous applicability. So (as I argued) originality claims are inadequately discriminate with respect to ideas insofar as there are infinite gradations of originality and unoriginality. The status of any item located along that particular scale is ambiguous, and in this lies the source of the rhetorical vitality of the notion of originality— the condition, that is, for the inconclusive claims and counterclaims made under its auspices. Here we have almost a microcosm of the problem of classicism itself (see Chap. 9. II). The singular importance that the category of ambiguity has within the field of textual appraisal is also indicated by the fact that its use leads directly to the very reassessment of the covering concepts that structure the world of discourse by providing us with its provisional identities—concepts, books, texts, ideas, doctrines, theories, theses, and arguments.

If under the auspices of covering concept $\bar{X}$ identities are persistently ambiguous, we may fairly doubt the classificatory power of X̄. In less extreme and more likely terms, if too many items must be seen as ambiguous, we may at least question the relevancy of the covering term, but there is no certain rule here.[20] If political theories only ambiguously fit into our doctrinal classifications, we have to consider the possibility not only that they may indeed be ambiguous, but also that our doctrinal classifications are only partially appropriate and improperly formed. Certain rule or not, however, the point is important well beyond the formal confines of political theory. It is central to the question of historical understanding itself, for it describes the most general manifestation of what is commonly called the hermeneutic circle—the problem of minimizing the distorting, simplifying, and anachronistically assimilating propensities of our language when used to describe a temporally alien one. The point at which our historical language appears to throw ambiguities in an alien world may always be the point at which we should deconstruct our own vocabulary (see also Chap. 8. I and II); if it may be said that deconstruction is an essential means of maintaining historiographical momentum, ambiguity is a marker of its periodic necessity.

Similarly, the point is central to what might be called the hermeneutics of cultural assimilation and translation. Events, as Marshall Sahlins has remarked, enter cultures as examples of established categories; and, certainly, these usually show a considerable capacity for accommodating the alien. But on occasion such categories may only uneasily or ambiguously accommodate certain events (which thus seem extraordinary). Apparent dislocation may then require the use of additional strategies to reduce the alien to manageable terms; or new categories may be developed to cope with the ambiguities and other related difficulties now manifest in the world.[21] Even the miracle is domesticated a little by our having a concept of the miraculous.

[20] See Denis Foreman's remarks in *Mozart's Concerto Form* (New York, 1971), p. 17.

[21] Marshall Sahlins, *Historical Metaphors and Mythical Realities: Structure in the Early History of the Sandwich Islands Kingdom* (Ann Arbor, 1981), p. 7. Sahlins provides a fascinating account of the fate of James Cook in these terms.

Ambiguity invites us to restructure the world. In fine, ambiguity functions at all levels of analysis, having a singular role with respect to the predicates we use in order to refine the character of items provisionally placed under the auspices of the general covering terms, and to the efficacy of those covering terms themselves. Whatever we wish to say of anything within the broad universe of human discourse, the conception of the ambiguous provides us, as it were, with our most elemental range of predicates, and the conditions of their further elaboration. The conception may be seen as setting down the perimeters of intelligibility, within which the ethical structure of textual analysis in fact operates. Ignorance or disregard for ambiguity's role is apt to make us beg questions and misconstrue the terms of textual understanding.

To emphasize the singular and necessary importance of a conception of ambiguity is not, or course, to argue that there are ambiguities under every textual stone, or that any discursive item has to be ambiguous. To repeat, as with any other category of analysis, negative claims come as much under its auspices as positive ones. Neither is the emphasis on the conception of ambiguity to be read as an insistence that anything deemed ambiguous is incontestably, or pathologically, so. Questions as to ambiguity are one thing, the designation of specific ambiguities is another, being contingent upon the classifiers in terms of which the relevant items of discourse are provisionally identified (see sec. v of this chapter). An item may be ambiguous if seen under

---

Perchance Cook arrived at Hawaii at a moment in a ritual to which he could easily be assimilated as a God-King, *Lono.* As befitted his ritual status he left Hawaii and returned, virtually and unwittingly to play out his part in the rituals through which he was seen. But on his return his own behavior (and that of his sailors) only ambiguously fitted his ritual status and became mythically—conceptually—disruptive, as indeed Hawaiian behavior seemed erratic to the British. He died literally not just ritually as *Lono* should have, as it were, at the confused and mutually confusing interfacings of different understandings of the world. Immediately, Hawaiian mythology set about assimilating him *sans* the ambiguities of the final phase of his story so that the categories of their world were reinforced, a process, Sahlins suggests, which also helps explain what in Western economic categories seems to have been the disproportionate importance of Britain in nineteenth-century Hawaii.

the auspices of $\bar{Y}$, not so under the auspices of $\bar{Y}'$; the question "ambiguous as a what?" is as important as the earlier question "coherent as a what?" It is only if the human brain is so structured that certain classifiers *have* to be employed in the processes of understanding the world that we can have the conditions for pathological ambiguity in any absolute sense.

In fact, the efficient causes of what we normally designate ambiguities are various. Insofar as we can assume a relevant and relatively stable range of general classifiers, ambiguity may emerge as a direct result of a simple ellipsis. If $\bar{X}$, in the immediate context of argument, is untroublesome and pertinent, and if a given item appears ambiguous under its auspices, it will be because the item provides, or is surrounded by, insufficient evidence to control interpretive response, and to prevent our filling the ellipses in a variety of ways. Thus Ullmann's listed safeguards against polysemous ambiguity (gender, inflexion, word order, addition, and form modification) all are means of filling in or overriding ellipses so that our interpretive options are cut down beyond the threshold of ambiguity. Or again, as Turner illustrates at the syntactic level, prepositional ellipsis may compress a statement to the point of ambiguity—the expression "student expulsions" referring potentially to expulsions of or by students.[22] In principle, insofar as we cannot eliminate options, any item will drift toward unintelligibility as anything in particular; insofar as we can do so, it achieves a sufficiently firm identity for us to be able to specify it further. At any stage, however, through any item functioning as an *équivoque*, we may find ambiguity placing a limit on certain understanding, and the more complex the overarching conception under which we classify phenomena, the more scope there is for such ambiguity. Ambiguities may thus be seen as skeletons of sense which may be fleshed out to form alternative species and genera of creature. We have a skeleton, an item as such unambiguous, but we wish to specify it further. We are able, still without invoking a relevantly porous classifier, to identify it as mammalian, but in pursuit of a more refined understanding we run into difficulty; we have a sufficient and

---

[22] Ullmann, *Semantics*, pp. 167ff.; and Turner, *Stylistics*, pp. 87ff.

normally adequate battery of classifiers, but only elliptical evidence suggesting alternative possibilities; that is, bones are missing, fragmented, and tumbled in soil that has been disturbed. Our identity has been pursued to the point of ambiguity, and until the ellipses can be filled (the remaining fragments found) or overridden (the development of carbon fourteen dating), the identity remains ambiguous.

——————————— V ———————————

In its simplest terms, with respect to any putative ambiguity, we are presented with one of two possibilities: either the ambiguity appears in the context of a single discursive form (A/A), or else a plurality of generally quite distinctive forms (A, D/A, Δ) is directly relevant to understanding the item as ambiguous. The first species of ambiguity I shall call ambiguity of ellipsis, the second ambiguity of coalescence. Perhaps the most general classifier we can use is the notion of discourse as such; but this is far too broad and indiscriminate to be of any help in the analysis of a specific text or argument. As I suggested at the outset, the most general level at which effective discriminations can be made concerns what I have called discursive unities. These abstractions are in practice reflected in the established, concrete, and complex patterns of intellectual convention to which people subscribe or have subscribed in writing. Writing is not simply about something, but is writing in a discernible way, employing certain types of classification, pursuing certain principles of connection (see pp. 11ff., 148ff.). The abstract symbols (the series A, B, C, D,) may thus be cashed in as discursive unities or less abstractly as established conventions of argument (A B Γ Δ). However we choose to translate the symbols, ambiguity of ellipsis refers to that sort of ambiguity which we see under the auspices of a single set of conventions of argument. Interpretive options are left open, but they are options of a single species. The skeleton may be *homo sapiens*, but it may or may not be my missing grandmother

Hera (and to isolate the ambiguity we are not required to define the category *homo sapiens*). Again, we may be in no doubt that an argument is an exercise in formal logic, but insofar as it is marked by an ambiguity, it is marked by ambiguity of ellipsis. The Latin term *malum* may have functioned only within the realm of ethical discourse, but as Kant pointed out, within that realm it could function ambiguously to mean either harm or evil.[23]

Cashing the symbolic series *A, B, C, D*, А В Г Δ will not always result in the full potential of discursive items fitting neatly into our classifications (if it did, language would be altogether less interesting and problematic than it is). Items will appear to lie at the intersections of discursive unities and established activities, even at the edges of our least porous ones. The difficulties that result from our failure to achieve a stable, certain identification may indeed signify the inadequacy, or the irrelevancy, of a particular attempt to delineate and use a discursive unity, or a pattern of established intellectual conventions. Equally, however, these difficulties may signify the irreducible Heraclitean instability of the world which as we order it leaves us with cobwebs upon our fingers. There may be no better discursive classifiers than the ones we are using (see Chap. 8. II). In either case, the ambiguities that presage the limits of our understanding of the particular, or equally which suggest the abandonment of a concept of the general, can be called ambiguities of coalescence. Our options are multidimensional; our difficulties are not limited by a single perceived class or species of discourse; differing conventions of discourse radiate from the *équivoque*. When thinking in terms of mammal, we can be confronted not only with a possible grandmother, but with a duckbill platypus, a duck/rabbit, or with a piltdown man. On the semantic level, we may, by close analogy, classify words under the primary conceptions

---

[23] Cited in Ullmann, *Semantics*, p. 172. Again, the Anglo-Saxon *dom* covered the shame culture phenomenon of honor bestowers (analogous to the Greek *time*) and the theological notion of God's judgment. For a discussion of this and its interpretive consequences for reading *Beowulf*, see A. J. Bliss, "*Beowulf*, Lines 3074–3075" on *Soðfæstra dom*, in M. Salu and R. Farrell, eds., *J. R. R. Tolkien, Scholar and Storyteller* (Ithaca, 1979), pp. 49–51.

of verbs and nouns, and under the modifying conceptions of adverbs and adjectives.[24] It is possible to find elliptical ambiguity within one of these classes, or to find a word which, because it may function in more than one, if not all, of these word classes,[25] can give rise to the sort of coalescent ambiguity which potentially blurs our apparently clear distinctions between word classes. A word like 'diet,' for example, can function ambiguously between and within specified word classes. Again, we may have a term such as *kakon*, which in ancient Greece could function equally in what we see as the distinct realms of morals and aesthetics; that is, *kakon* could function as an *équivoque*, which, referring to Socrates' ugliness, could suggest his badness. At the level of sustained discourse, we may be uncertain as to whether St. Anselm's ontological argument should be properly classed as an attempted logical proof of the existence of God or as a prayer to his God in the idiom of logic, or whether (as I suspect to be the case) it was intended to be both *fides* and *ratio*, and thus ambiguously exhibits the differing conventions of logical argument and affirmation of religious belief. In short, coalescent ambiguity is a function of the conventional distance (see Chap. 1, pp. 20ff.) between the possibilities of an *équivoque*, its existence being prefigured in the delineation of the methodological nexus (see Chap. 1, pp. 20 and 23).

To reiterate and then illustrate: assuming that we can discriminate within the broad realm of human discourse between different discursive unities and established patterns of intellectual activity, and assuming also that this is necessary in order to achieve a precise and specific understanding of any statement, idea, theory, or argument, then irrespective of the manner in which we subdivide this realm, we have now a practical working typology of ambiguity which can be employed to describe the limits of

[24] The closer we move toward the microcosmic level of ambiguity, where assuming A, A, we can see an item under the auspices of a specific covering term $\overline{A}$, then the more ambiguities will be seen as coalescent. The less coverage $\overline{A}$ has, the less room for ambiguity under its auspices. Conversely, increasing generality in terminology and extensive coverage means more scope for ambiguity, seen as ellipsis rather than as coalescence.

[25] Ullmann, *Semantics*, p. 159, cites 'double.'

understanding at the level of discursive analysis. Elliptical ambiguity is that which may be seen under the auspices of a single discursive mode; coalescent ambiguity is that in which the interpretive options span a plurality of modes. Thus insofar as we are able to work within and assume a single style of discourse, it is sufficient to consider any putative ambiguities as elliptical. Insofar as we consider it necessary to shift between what we might regard as major discursive discriminations, we must trade in the vocabulary of coalescent ambiguity. In particular, we have a typology of ambiguity which can be brought to bear upon the analysis of political theory texts, for as has been argued, these texts, subsumed under the umbrella term of 'political theory,' do not conform to any single conventional pattern of discourse.

VI

Ambiguity of Ellipsis

To illustrate the typology of ambiguity at work in the textual family lineage of political theory, it is then necessary to cash the symbols of discursive unities for some specific conventions of argument. Here I shall continue to accept and work within the generous and familiar ambit of the notions of philosophical and ideological discourse, which I have already identified sufficiently for my present purposes. Elliptical ambiguity may be illustrated with reference to Marsilius of Padua's conception of the *legislator humanus*.

The *Defensor Pacis* is, as I have argued elsewhere, although a discursively coherent work, not a work of political philosophy.[26] To use again Dante's apposite Aristotelian expression, the *Defensor Pacis* manifests theory for the sake of action, and it is, moreover, never significantly diverted into the realms of theory for

---

[26] "Marsilius of Padua's Argument from Authority: A Survey of Its Significance in the *Defensor Pacis*," *Pol. Th.* 5 (1977): 205ff. See also the opening comments of Hermann Segall, *Der Defensor Pacis des Marsilius von Padua: Grundfragen der Interpretation* (Wiesbaden, 1959).

the sake of further contemplation. It was a theory intrinsic to the politics and religion of fourteenth-century Christendom in that its genesis lies principally in matters of direct political and religious controversy; its avowed purpose is to affect the political and religious structure of that society; and the conventions of argument employed are those of ideological and polemical discourse, not of politically disinterested and systematic philosophical reasoning. None of this is to say, of course, that it is impossible to translate the work discursively into philosophical terms, or that it is unsuggestive to those who read it with the sort of philosophical question in mind that Marsilius was (at most) prepared to allude to, or sketch, in a rudimentary fashion.

The stated purpose of the work is what we would clearly identify as ideological: it is to isolate and explore a form of political disruption or religious corruption peculiar to Christendom. Its publication was received accordingly. It was condemned by Pope John XXII, and its author fled to the protection of John's enemy, Ludwig of Bavaria. It was replied to by the official papal apologists, and Marsilius appears to have achieved the position of court apologist for Ludwig, in whose train he marched to Rome in 1327. The work was condemned again by Pope Clement VI, who found in it two hundred and fifty heresies, but it was translated into the vernacular wherever there were strong centers of anticlericalism.[27] On its own, this information is inconclusive. Even so, there is more than enough evidence here to suggest that ideology provides the most promising intellectual context for the work, and this is borne out by its structure and tone.

The bulk of the work is concerned with cataloging and dis-

---

[27] For the early history of *Defensor*, and for the sparse details of Marsilius' life, I have drawn on: A. Gewirth, *Marsilius of Padua*, vol. 1 (still the most valuable study in English), chap. 1; N. Valois, "Jean de Jandun et Marsile de Padoue, auteurs de *Defensor Pacis*," *Histoire littéraire de la France* 33 (1906): 528ff.; C. K. Brampton, "Marsiglio of Padua, Life," *EHR* 37 (1922): 501ff.; J. Sullivan, "Marsiglio of Padua and William of Ockham," *AHR* 2 (1896–1897): 409ff. and 593ff.

On the immediate reception of the work, see most recently Angel Sanchez de la Torre, "Quelques arguments contre Marsile selon Alvaro Pelayo," *Medioevo* 6 (1980): 467f.; and Louise Handelman, "*Ecclesia primitiva*: Alvarus Pelagius and Marsilius of Padua," ibid., pp. 431ff.

playing the misdemeanors of the established Church, from the Papacy and the Curia to its apologists and the more lowly priesthood. Thus, understandably, foremost among his anticipated opponents, Marsilius lists not differing schools of philosophy, but priests, bishops, and their toadies.[28] To the end of attacking the claims made by the Church to political power, legal jurisdiction, material wealth, and its biblically derived right to a clear hierarchical structure (on the effectiveness of which its other claims depended), Marsilius rehearsed and extended the polemical religious apologetics of the different parties involved in the fourteenth-century poverty controversy.[29] His mode of argument is through the very complex citation of established political and religious authorities, which prohibits rather than requires the development of any self-contained philosophical reasoning. Now it is true that in *Dictio* 1 Marsilius develops an argument that is not tied exclusively, or even in many chapters directly, to the ideological dispute with Rome. It is true also that if we take Aristotle to be a philosopher rather than an ideologue, at first glance *Dictio* 1 looks philosophical in its concern with and citation of Aristotelian argument. But the first glance is misleading. Aristotle is used explicitly as an authority, a secular supplement to *Dictio* 2. Both in Paris and northern Italy Aristotle's prestige was great indeed, and therefore not only was he likely to prove immensely suggestive, but his was a name well worth co-opting in the interests of eristics. Thus for Marsilius a point may be proved because the philosopher had made it;[30] argument may be redundant if the philosopher has discussed it.[31] Generally, Aristotle's vocabulary is used to characterize a civil society that

[28] *Defensor Pacis*, ed. H. Kutsch (Berlin, 1958), II. i. 1.

[29] On which, see Kerry Spiers, "The Ecclesiastical Poverty Theory of Marsilius of Padua: Sources and Significance," *IPP* 10 (1977): 3ff.; and G. Leff, *Heresy in the Late Middle Ages* (Manchester, 1967), 2: 411ff.; Jeannine Quillet, *La philosophie politique de Marsile de Padoue* (Paris, 1970) pp. 230ff.; Marino Damiata, "Funzione e concetto della povertà evangelica in Marsilio da Padova," *Medioevo* 6 (1980): 411f; C. Condren, "Rhetoric, Historiography and Political Theory: Some Aspects of the Poverty Controversy Reconsidered," *Journal of Religious History* (1984), forthcoming.

[30] *Defensor* iv. 1–2.

[31] Ibid., I. viii. 2.

does not require, indeed cannot tolerate, the Church (priestly organization) as it is presently structured. So pervasively important was the Church to the very fabric of Western Christendom, however, that any wholesale attack on it and its theoretical claims demanded ideologically, at least, some image of a practical alternative. Thus the force of Marsilius' statement that he is going beyond the analyses of Aristotle[32] should not be read as either a theoretical extension, modification, or rejection of Aristotle's categories of analysis, but as an attempt to subsume his own world under them. It is an attempt to subsume the Church under Aristotle's discussions of the causes of civil disruption and *stasis*, as the specific cause of *intranquilitas* of which Aristotle could know nothing.[33] In the last analysis, however we label the sort of discourse to be found in Aristotle, it is of a different order, exhibiting different conventions of argument (procedures and criteria of judgment, though in this case not conceptual vocabulary) from that found in the *Defensor Pacis*. But adhering to the discursive categories of philosophy and ideology, we may say that just as Marsilius has since had his arguments translated into the terms of a more philosophical discourse, so he translated Aristotle's philosophy into an ideological weapon.

It is within this general discursive context that we must see, and can isolate, the ambiguity of Marsilius' conception of the *legislator humanus*. If the established Church's claims to direct or indirect authority in the secular community cannot be allowed, what is the source of legitimate secular authority? This is a question which can easily raise a host of speculatively far-reaching possibilities. It is interesting that Marsilius pursues none of them. He is satisfied with circumscribing a symbol and bequeathing it to the rhetorical armory of his world, and, as such, its quality hinges precisely on its ambiguity.

Having discussed in a relatively cursory fashion the importance and nature of law in civil society, Marsilius outlines its ultimate source—the only legitimate authority in society. This

[32] Ibid., I. i. 7.
[33] Ibid.

prime and proper effective cause of law he calls the *legislator humanus*, and it consists of

> the people or the whole citizen body, or its weightier part
> . . . (*esse populum seu civium universitatem aut eius va-
> lenciorem partem*).[34]

By the expression "the weightier part" (reminiscent of Aristotle's expression *kreitton meros* and translated by Moerbeke as *pars valentior*),[35] Marsilius states that he means to take into consideration both the quality and quantity of persons in the law-governed community (*quantitate personarum et qualitate in communitate illa super quam lex fertur*).[36] By "citizen" he means those who participate according to rank, in principate, council, or jury (*participat in communitate civile principatu aut consiliativo vel iudicativo secundum gradum suum*).[37] Having then explicitly excluded women, children, aliens, and slaves, he finally states that the *valentior pars* should be viewed acording to custom (*policiarum consuetudinem honestam*), or alternatively (*vel hanc*), according to Aristotle, *Politics* 6. 2.[38] Now clearly, the *legislator* stands in formal opposition to the claims of Rome, either to sanction directly or to veto or modify the laws and policies of political communities. As such its compositional character would be a matter of considerable interest to his readers, be they members of an aristocratic court, a princely administration, or a relatively popular mercantile commune. It is precisely with respect to its composition, however, that the *legislator* is inherently and sustainedly ambiguous.

"The people," as Gewirth points out, is used by Marsilius in an inclusive Roman sense rather than in an exclusive (Greek) sense;[39] it subsumes both the few and the many in an unspecified

[34] Ibid., I. xii. 3.

[35] Gewirth, *Marsilius*, 1: 191.

[36] *Defensor* I. xii. 3. The following reading is further developed in Condren, "Democracy and the *Defensor Pacis*: On the English Language Tradition of Marsilian Interpretation," *IPP* 13 (1980): 301ff.

[37] *Defensor* I. xii. 4.

[38] Ibid.

[39] Gewirth, *Marsilius*, 1: 180–182.

balance of authority. Consequently, it is potentially ambiguous, but rather than adding safeguards against, Marsilius actualizes and reinforces the ambiguity. This is done first by stating that the *valentior pars* may be taken as the whole citizen body.[40] This is no passing thought, as the *valentior pars* is mentioned nine out of the eleven times Marsilius names the *legislator* as *universitas civium* in the short chapter devoted to the *legislator's* definition. It is significant, also, that when Marsilius uses the maxim that the whole is always greater than its parts (the judgment of the former being sounder than the latter), it is made clear that the *valentior pars* represents the *universitas civium* (*que totum universitatem representat*), and that it is taken to be the same thing as the citizen body (*quod pro eodem de cetero supponatur*).[41] The *valentior pars*, then, can be the whole, that is, the *legislator* itself and is not one of the parts of society (the Aristotelian six classes including the priestly) into which society is divided.

Secondly, the ambiguous character of the *legislator* is reinforced insofar as the composition of the *valentior pars* is itself to be determined according to quality and quantity, the balance between which is to be determined according to the authoritative counsel of Aristotle, or else according to honorable custom—the vocabulary of which was equally, if not more, authoritative and variously exploitable. In short, the character of the *legislator* pivots on the conception of the *valentior pars*, which functions to make manifest the potential ambiguity of the Romanesque conception of *populus*, and which is, in turn, specified in such a way that the ambiguity can be sustained. Marsilius' locus of authority is a locus of ambiguity, both possibilities of which Marsilius himself is prepared to outline as his argument proceeds. At *Dictio* 1. xiii. 4 Marsilius explicitly includes farmers, artisans, and others of that kind as members of the *legislator humanus*, and further emphasizes the importance of quantity by using *plures* and *plurimi* as synonyms for *valentior*.[42] Here, although Marsi-

---

[40] *Defensor* I. xii. 3.
[41] Ibid., I. xii. 5.
[42] Gewirth, *Marsilius*, 1: 185.

lius is clearly pointing to the relatively populist possibilities of his definition of the *legislator*, it is also important to note that the context of argument is that of the claims of the educated (ecclesiastical) few to judge on behalf of the ignorant (secular) many. To balance, however, the 'democratic' exploitation of his ambiguity, at *Dictio* 2. xxvi. 3, 5, and 9 Marsilius refers to the *legislator* in a distinctly aristocratic context, where he comes close to equating the Holy Roman Emperor with the *pars principans*, and his electors (great in quality but few in quantity) with the *legislator*. His arguments are cross-referenced directly to *Dictio* 1. xii and xiii.

It is possible also that Marsilius is alluding to the aristocratic possibilities of the *legislator* at *Dictio* 2. xxvi. 9, where he argues that there is less chance of the electors electing a heretic emperor than there is of the Pope choosing one, for there are a number of electors (including some churchmen), and only one Pope, and the judgment of them all (i.e. a whole?) will be more certain than the judgment of one (a part?). In his later work, which he considers to be a modification of his too idealistic *Defensor Pacis*, he equates the *legislator* with the emperor, and only here does he ignore the dual criteria of quality and quantity upon which the *Defensor pacis* insists. In short, having set up an ambiguity, Marsilius equivocates between its options. One could virtually gloss Fig. 4 (see sec. III) with chapter numbers, replacing P1, P2, and P3 with D. 1. xii, xiii, and D. 2. xxvi, respectively.

Having looked at the conception of the *legislator* in terms of a conception of elliptical ambiguity, we are now in a position to indicate its *de facto*, if not its specifically intended, force. Once it has been defined, the *legislator* is mentioned always in a context of argument directed against the coercive pretensions of the established Church. Whatever else it is, it is the legitimate alternative to the secular claims of the Church. Here there is no equivocation. Marsilius furnishes detailed defense and elaboration of the powers of the *legislator contra* both Church and even the *pars principans*, which are clearly available for any political society feeling itself most at odds with the clergy. But in order to utilize the full battery of Marsilius' arguments, any society must be able to associate itself first with the authoritative *legis-*

lator. This potentially institutional Duke of Omnium maximizes Marsilius' audience. The Church was a universal institution, defining the limits of Christendom; an attack on it that was anything less than universal started off at a disadvantage and was likely to founder in parochialism. Conversely, a universal appeal with potentially a universal institutional backing was extremely difficult to achieve. Marsilius' conception of the *legislator* achieves, and appears to be designed to achieve, just this. He takes the rhetorical common denominators of the widespread authority of Aristotle, and the vocabulary of custom, and says that explicitly, in terms of these, the *legislator* may be tailored as specific communities think fit. Insofar as it could identify with the *legislator*, any *regnum, provincia,* or *patria* of Christendom, from Padua to Paris, from Flanders to Florence, is provided with an off-the-peg suit of armor in the battle against a corrupt Church. Thus rather than seeing the *legislator* as an anticipation of democratic ideology, or as a guarded defense of aristocracy, or even worse (because philosophy is strictly speaking an irrelevant world of discourse) as an inadequate or embryonic philosophical theory of sovereignty, the *legislator humanus* should be seen as a polemical device within a clear but alien world of ideological commitment.[43] The *legislator*, indiscriminately embracing so much on which we are apt to regard clear commitment as mandatory, may seem to be something of a conceptual harlot—an affront to the commandments of the basic issues. But a harlot may fulfill a role that a faithful Parisian, Paduan, or philosophic wife could find beyond her. Even so, there are limits to the *legislator*'s conceptual promiscuity.

Marsilius requires that his readers stand firm and at one upon the matter of the Church in Christendom, and to this end the important and always divisive issue as to whom, the few or the many, should rule in its stead is cloaked and subordinated in a studied ambiguity. This is not, as Aristotle suspected the ambiguities of practical discourse always tend to be, designed to mis-

---

[43] These three positions are the most common. I have cataloged the representative claims in "Marsilius of Padua's Argument from Authority" (see esp. p. 215, n. 11; p. 218, nn. 41–42) and "Democracy and the *Defensor.*"

lead his audience; it was designed to give interpretive maneuver where it was most needed and to stabilize a distinct agenda of debate. Inhabiting a world of ambiguity, the politicians who inherited Marsilius' conceptions were, as we shall see (Chap 9. III), altogether more aware of this than his modern academic commentators, who insist upon a single acceptable meaning to be elicited through the established field of textual appraisal.

VII

Ambiguity of Coalescence

Because of its discursive complexity we may expect coalescent ambiguity from *The Republic*; it is a work woven from several different strands of discourse, wherein "a single string speaks for a whole crown of voices." Of these strands we may mention three which become ambiguously entangled in the Cave.

First, there is the philosophic, focusing upon the exploration of problems of definition and language, the question of what there is, the supplementary question of how, and in what ways, we might understand it, the relationship of universals and particulars, and the examination of the philosophical credentials of established modes of discourse such as poetry, rhetoric, astronomy, and the different branches of mathematics.

Secondly, there is the ideological, that which has caused so much passionate discussion of *The Republic*. It is concerned directly with diagnosing Athenian—even Hellenic—moral and political corruption, with suggesting reforms in education and law, with outlining something approaching an ideal *polis*, and with redefining the ethical vocabulary through which the *bios politikos* should be appraised.

Thirdly, there is the aesthetic impulse manifested in the dramatic structure of the work (especially in Book 1), in the allusive use of poetry (as opposed to criticisms of poets), in the characteristic numerical ordering of the work (irrespective of the dictates of argument), in the threads of related imagery, and finally, and above all, in the punctuation of the whole by metaphorical set pieces, such as the images of the shepherd, the nearsighted man, the ship of state, the myth of Er, the myth of Gyges, the Sun, Line, and Cave.

Much, if not all, of *The Republic* can be effectively understood in terms of these much explored discursive propensities, each providing, in turn, effective contexts in terms of which passages, arguments, dialogue, and monologue can be understood. If conceived in sufficiently broad terms, or rather in terms controlled by the evidence of Greek intellectual life, none need involve unduly what Derrida has called an orchestrated violence to the text—the anachronistic and procrustean imposition of alien categories, arguments, and sensibilities. If we proceed with care we can minimize some of the rigors of the hermeneutic circle (p. 183). Yet, although we may say that Plato was manifestly a philosopher in both a loose and a recognizably strict sense of the term (a serious epistemologist and ontologist), more roughly that he was something of an ideologue (a political rhetorician, a moral polemicist, and a rationalistic programmer), as well as among the most careful of literary craftsmen (a poet among philosophers), he was also a writer whose discursive dexterity was apt on occasion to result in ambiguity. The awareness of conventional diversity without which *The Republic* is drained to a dry doctrine (crude, unqualified, and un-Platonic) itself suggests the limitations of clarity in Plato and the possibility of significant ambiguity.

The image of Sun, Line, and Cave form a complex central section of *The Republic*, through which the philosophic and ideological strands of discourse pass, to get entangled in the Cave and unravelled again as Plato approaches Er, restating the themes of Book 1. It is my purpose here to do no more than outline the ambiguity in which the *Simile of Light* culminates.

No section of the *Simile of Light* is without its difficulties of interpretation, but we may initially survey the Line, less because it provides us arguably with an elliptical ambiguity than because the Cave is introduced to supplement it. As a whole, the *Simile of Light* is introduced to elucidate the posited relationship between the forms and the Good.[44] The tone of the argument is guarded and tentative, but the style is unquestionably philosophic. The Good, we are told, is to the world of forms in the realm of reality that which the Sun is to the visible world—the principle on which both sight and life depend. But before Plato had adequately elicited or specified more precisely the relationships between the Sun and the Good, that is, by locating the form of the Sun in the intelligible world, he complicated his metaphor by adding Line to light.

We are told to take a line divided into two unequal sections, these, in turn, are to be divided in the same proportion (a necessary consequence of which is the equality of the two middle sections).[45] The upper line stands for the intelligible world, the forms of understanding proper to which are *dianoia* and *noesis*. The lower part refers to the visible (*to horomenon*), the forms of understanding proper to which are *eikasia* and *pistis*.[46] There are two principal sources of difficulty: first, the implications to be drawn from the image of linear dissection; secondly, the significance of the continuing imagery of light, from which, at 510A, Plato shifts to belief (*to doxaston*). We have the following principal possibilities: the line represents a continuum of understanding, what Nettleship called "the four stages of intelligence."[47] Understood as such, the line fills some of the ellipses of the Sun section of the total simile, suggesting the unbroken intellectual processes by which it is possible to move from an understanding of this world (a matter of belief only) to the principles of reality on which it depends, and from there to the one principle on which the *eide* themselves depend, thus reaching the ultimate stage of understanding, *noesis*. This familiar, indeed traditional,[48] understanding is supported by the image of an unbroken

[44] *Republic*, ed. P. Shorey, Loeb (Cambridge, Mass., 1969 ed.), 509C–D.

[45] R. C. Cross and A. D. Woozley, *Plato's Republic: A Philosophical Commentary* (London, 1964), p. 204.

[46] *Republic* 509D–511E.

[47] R. L. Nettleship, *Lectures on the Republic of Plato* (London, 1963 ed.), pp. 238ff.

[48] The designation of such an interpretation as orthodox is Cross and Woozley's *Plato's Republic*, p. 209.

line, by the continued use of images of light, and by the explicit
shift from *to horomenon* to *to doxaston* at 510A. But this understanding is not entirely satisfactory. Thus it has been argued that
the Line is intended as only an illustrative ratio, not a single
ongoing progression, and that it is intended to illustrate the relationship between philosophy and mathematics (being a prelude
to explicit discussion) and, of course, constitutes a most appropriate form of image.[49] The Line then looks less like a mixed
metaphor tacked onto the image of the Sun than a parallel image
introduced to make a new, though related, point. The manner
in which Plato explicitly tells us to divide the Line supports such
an interpretation, as might his casual treatment of the lower sections of the Line once they have been introduced. Although then
there are serious disagreements as to the significance of the Line
image and its mode of division, and as to precisely what philosophical weight the lower sections are meant to carry, the following point at least is clear: the different possibilities emanating
from the Line are of a single species. Whatever its precise role
in the simile and in Plato's thought as a whole, the answers are
to be sought in the context of his metaphysical preoccupations.
If there is an ambiguity here, it is one of ellipsis.

It is also clear that the Line is not and cannot be self-explan-
atory; for enlightment we are forced, ironically, down into the
Cave.[50] There is no doubt that the Cave is concerned to elucidate the Line in some way, but how, how far, at what points,
and whether or not exclusively is another matter. One principal
received interpretation posits a relationship of map to journey,
and indeed, if the Line is to be read as a single continuum, a
story of ascent and descent fits it plausibly enough. The Cave
story may be seen then as elaborating in dramatic terms the four
stages of intelligence, suggesting an archetypal educational experience, harking back to the image of the Sun, which is finally
realized by the released prisoner to be the ultimate source of
light, as well as prefiguring the literal and detailed educational

[49] A. S. Ferguson, "Plato's Simile of Light," pt. 1, *CQ* 15 (1921): esp. 133ff.
[50] *Republic* 514–517C.

prospect for the philosopher kings.[51] Thus when Plato tells us to see the Cave in the light of what has gone before, we can properly read *prosarteion* as meaning apply the Cave to the Line. Similarly, when Plato tells us to consider the fire with respect to the Sun, we should read *aphomoioun* as corresponding to the image of the Sun. So, too, when we are told the prisoners are 'like ourselves,'[52] they are like ourselves living in the world of *pistis* and *eikasia*, a limitation of self-awareness that restricts Socrates to only a metaphorical elaboration of knowledge. In short, the allegory of the Cave can be seen as expressing in dramatic and poetic terms the epistemological theories of the Line and the Sun. Again, however, this is contentious. The four stages of the Line do not in any precise or unambiguous way correspond to the release and ascent of the prisoner, neither within the Cave nor when he has achieved the upper world. The prisoner is first able to move his head, his chains are released, and he discovers that what he thought was reality is only a series of shadows dependent upon the fire and the figures who traipse with objects across it. He then discovers the tunnel to the upper world, and after a long and difficult ascent he reaches the surface. At first he can look only at shadows and reflections until his eyes become accustomed to the light sufficiently for him to see the objects themselves; he is able to turn his head to the night sky and see the light from the moon and the stars. Finally, he is able to contemplate the Sun, realizing the dependence of all else upon it. He then descends into the Cave. Now not all these stages are philosophically significant, certainly not all of them fit in with the Line, and it is difficult to say with any confidence which are the four stages as represented in the story. The interaction of tenor and vehicle is giving rise to ambiguity. Thus within the ambit of traditional interpretations—that is, those which seek to relate the Cave principally to Line and which see both as continuing the thread of specifically philosophical discourse in *The Republic*, there is considerable room for interpretive maneuver.

[51] See e.g. F. M. Cornford's translation, Oxford, 1941 (the 1961 ed. is here referred to), or Nettleship, *Lectures*. The general relationship is outlined with utmost clarity by Cross and Woozley, *Plato's Republic*, chap. 9.

[52] *Republic* 515A.

The principal philosophical distinctions may be reduced to three or increased well beyond that.[53] But such modifications are in principle inadequate because they ignore a further discursive dimension, which, absent from the Line and Sun, qualitatively complicates the allegory of the Cave. The detailed and evocative description of the Cave, where a series of objects are manipulated to fool others; where the prisoner's understanding (and clearly not everyone in the Cave itself is a prisoner) is restricted to blinkered guesswork rewarded by prizes; into which the released sun and stargazing prisoner returns, isolated in his knowledge and at risk of ridicule and destruction—all suggest that the vehicle is conveying an ideological tenor. It suggests a contingent world of corrupt *doxai* rather than the necessary category of *to doxaston*; "the puppet-show rather suggests Vanity Fair than the cosmos."[54] Ferguson argues that the Cave itself is something that exists below the Line, the Sun and Line imagery being picked up again only when the prisoner has escaped from the tunnel and the contrived world beneath it. On this reading the allusion to the death of Socrates takes on a central significance; the stated connection between the Cave and what has gone before embraces the ship of state of Athenian democracy; we are required to attach, not *apply*, the Cave to the Line; "like ourselves" refers not to the human but the Athenian condition; and *aphomoioun* means we should contrast the fire with the Sun.[55]

Rooted in the allegory, then, are both philosophical and epistemological possibilities, and explicitly ideological ones. The vehicle conveys both discursive threads, but we are not in a position to attach the story elements to them each in turn. This is so, however, because the vehicle itself is the culmination of a complex and developing pattern of imagery, and has an aesthetic integrity of its own. In short, it is necessary to take the allegory of the Cave seriously as allegory, if we are to be able to define

[53] For the threefold argument, see N. R. Murphy, "The Simile of Light in Plato's Republic," *CQ* 26 (1932), and "Back to the Cave," *CQ* 28 (1934); for a good range of other views as to the number of significant stages, see Cross and Woozley, *Plato's Republic*, who differ themselves on the question.

[54] A. S. Ferguson, "Plato's Simile of Light," pt. 2, *CQ* 16 (1922): 16.

[55] Ibid., e.g. pp. 15–16.

and explain the dimensions of the Cave's ambiguity, rather than fruitlessly insisting on a single unambiguous meaning.

The images that structure the Cave are extensions in part of the imagery of the Sun and light, which are prefigured in the first word of the work and echoed again at its conclusion. Socrates goes down into the Piraeus to see the torchlight procession in honor of the Goddess Bendis, and is waylaid on his journey home.[56] Bendis, associated with flame and darkness, was a Thracian goddess who conducted souls down into Hades. The concluding myth of Er is itself a symbolic journey. Er travels with the souls of the dead to the point where, having chosen their future lives, they go through ascending or descending tunnels, and Er is returned to the land of the living that his knowledge may be disseminated.[57] Again, throughout *The Republic*, scattered references are made to sight, light, and journeying. The image of the nearsighted man is the device that marks the shift from the discussion of justice in the individual to that of justice in the *polis*.[58]

Our life is seen, like Er's, to be a journey. Gyges, too, descends into a chasm after an earthquake to take a ring from a body.[59] The ship of state is metaphor centering upon the image of a journey, its inherent dangers, and the knowledge needed for the ship to journey safely—thus the *bios politikos* is seen as a life of journeying for which the navigator is essential. In the broader context of Plato's works, as Crombie has pointed out, images of light and sight are frequently used synaesthetically for sense in general and common sense in the world of *to doxaston*.[60] Equally, in more than one dialogue, an arrested journey sets the dramatic scene for discourse: in the *Euthyphro*, both Socrates and Euthyphro are on their way to the law courts (the same destination to different ends), and Plato's spokesman in the *Laws* is the Athe-

[56] *Republic* 327A–D.

[57] Ibid., 614B–621D.

[58] Ibid., 368D.

[59] Ibid., 359D. Before he finds the ring, Gyges has beheld other (unspecified) wonders on his downward journey.

[60] I. M. Crombie, *An Examination of Plato's Doctrines* (London, 1962), 2: 86.

nian traveler. In short, in their broadest terms, images of light and travel constituted centers of metaphorical expansion for Plato just as perhaps flood imagery did for Shakespeare.[61] In a broader context still, such images of light and journeying have always been pregnant with possibility. In Homer pain is dark, and as C. S. Lewis remarked, it is of more interest to inquire how the age-old associations of light and dark with good and bad, respectively, became separated rather than to consider how they first came together.[62] They are, in Frye's nomenclature, monads, archetypal images pregnant in cross-cultural possibilities[63] (see Chap. 9, p. 270). As a distinctive literary mode, allegory has habitually exploited the suggestive imagery of light, dark, ascent and descent, geared to the device of a difficult and revealing journey. Allegories whose tenors are as distinct as the *Comedia*, *Pilgrim's Progress*, *The Faery Queen*, *Gulliver's Travels*, and *Moby Dick* are all linked through such shared imagery.[64]

Such a clustering of images is, of course, organized into the journey of revelation found in the Cave. It constitutes a concentration of the patterns of imagery and allusion that are woven through *The Republic*,[65] and indeed, it may be seen as a part of an aesthetic strand of discourse which may be unraveled from the more obvious ply of philosophy and ideology. The Cave story itself, compressed as it is, nevertheless has a narrative autonomy

[61] On Shakespeare's centers of expansion, see Caroline Spurgeon, *Shakespeare's Imagery* (Cambridge, 1935), on floods, pp. 93ff. On the notion of metaphorical centers of expansion, see Ullmann, *Semantics*, p. 201, who cites Spurgeon; the vocabulary is H. Sperber's, ibid., pp. 149–150. See n. 74 of this chapter for further reference to Plato's specifically discursive metaphor of sea-travel.

[62] C. S. Lewis, *The Allegory of Love* (New York, 1964 ed.), p. 44; in more depth, R. B. Onians, *The Origins of European Thought* (Cambridge, 1953), is invaluable on the semantic fields of life, death, and pain.

[63] Northrop Frye, *The Anatomy of Criticism*, pp. 71–128.

[64] See at length Edwin Honig, *The Dark Conceit* (London, 1959). Roger Hinks, *Myth and Allegory in Ancient Art* (London, 1939), is full of valuable comment well beyond the realms of pottery and painting.

[65] On the general processes of metaphorical transference at work, see Ullmann, *Semantics*, pp. 226–274; his *Principles of Semantics*, pp. 227ff. L. Bloomfield, *Language*, p. 429. What I have argued here concerning synaesthesic imagery in *The Republic* seems to cohere with the linguistic patterns discussed by Ullmann, Bloomfield, and others.

and momentum which enables it to be placed under the auspices of allegory proper. Leyburn could almost be writing of the Cave when she defines allegory as

> the particular method of saying one thing in terms of another in which the two levels of meaning are sustained and in which the two levels correspond in pattern of relationship among details.[66]

And again, in her comment that "[it] is in the inter-relations of tenor and vehicle that the peculiar interest of allegory consists."[67]

It is exactly here that the difficulties of interpreting the meaning of the *Simile of Light* are compounded. Plato's vehicle is well sustained, detailed, and imaginatively rich, making use of a concentration of archetypally suggestive metaphors which for this very reason need careful signposting if they are to be tied *precisely* to a single tenor. But Plato's signposts are tantalizing and elliptical, and his vehicle as a whole is introduced not to convey tenor or even tenors already clear, but to elucidate them. Thus "what has gone before" may be the elliptical Line, the Line plus Sun, and or the ship of state metaphor. The signpost that the prisoners are "like ourselves" is similarly indeterminant, but as a society of corrupt *doxai* can exist only in the world of *to doxaston*, it is possible that Plato wanted to convey both a philosophical and an ideological tenor, and by its very suggestiveness the imagery is sufficiently emotive, but too discursively indiscriminate, for him to do so.

Such a process of shifting between discursive unities was a habit with Plato: a discussion of the theory of forms immediately precedes the diagnosis of Athenian politics in the ship of state;[68] the discussion of the relationship of mathematics to philosophy is bound up with an exercise in academic timetabling.[69] But whereas elsewhere the shifts are detectable, the marks of a complex mind that do not necessarily result in any ambiguity of statement, the imagery of the Cave prohibits the full and certain

---

[66] Leyburn, *Satiric Allegory*, p. 6.
[67] Ibid.
[68] *Republic* 474B–489B.
[69] Ibid., 521C–541B.

disentanglement of its component strands. This is compounded by the fact that as the story has a degree of autonomy, we cannot be certain which parts in the stages of its unfolding are intended to convey anything, apart from the requirements of a properly extended metaphor.

We may see the Cave as a center for discursive attraction from which various interpretive possibilities emerge, each qualifying and balancing the claims of the others. But this consequence of coalescent ambiguity is precisely what we must expect, if we take the Cave seriously as allegory. We may agree with Henry James that allegory is apt to spoil both story and moral, meaning and form, or conversely with Edwin Honig that it is precisely when allegory to coalesce discursive unities both forewarn us that al- are . . . inseparable from the context of some physical circumstance, or action."[70] These polar appraisals of the propensity of allegory to coalesce discursive unities both forewarn us that allegories in threatening to erode the denotative functions of language are by no means ideal as means of communicating complex and rigorous conceptions.

Accounting for the ambiguity is less easy than it was with Marsilius, whose *legislator* is most plausibly seen as a function of polemical dexterity. In this case, three main possibilities emerge. It may be that in Plato's case, through the simple erosion of time, we no longer have what he could assume of his audience, in Hawthorne's expression, that "faery land" of extrinsic associations which render redundant the detailed signposting and ensure virtually automatic decoding of an allegory.[71] To put the matter more abstractly and to recall the earlier argument (see pp. 181–185), this may be a case where ambiguity in effect describes the hermeneutic circle forewarning of its incipient viciousness.[72]

Certainly, the meaning of individual words is often contentious and, like much of the remaining literature of Greece, flawed

---

[70] Honig, *The Dark Conceit*, quoting James, p. 52, and his own statement, p. 131.

[71] Ibid., p. 101; Hinks, *Myth and Allegory*, chap. 2, esp. p. 63.

[72] Paul Ricoeur, "The Model of the Text: Meaningful Action Considered as a Text," *SR* 38 (1971): 560–562, esp. 562 on the potential viciousness of the circle. See also Appendix.

by random opacity. Added to which, even when an extrinsic meaning appears to us relatively stable and transparent, Plato is apt to give it an undisclosed twist of stipulation without thinking it necessary to warn his readers, since it may not have been when he wrote.[73]

Secondly, it may be simply that the suggestiveness of his imagery escaped the tight control he wanted. Experimenting with language and concerned with style as he still was in his middle period, he overreached what could be clearly conveyed. We must, said Socrates, go wherever the winds of argument blow us.[74] In writing this, Plato was paying testimony to an exploratory rather than a doctrinal emphasis in philosophy, between which alternatives his work was often pulled. In the Cave, the winds of argument may have tossed the ship of discourse momentarily out of the navigator's control.

Thirdly, we must remember that language is never indiscriminately communicative. For various reasons an audience is always exclusive, but the Greeks were much concerned with exclusive communication as well as with the socially and generically delineating power of language. The mysteries of Eleusis involved a progressive process of exclusion, and it may be that the *Simile of Light* confronts us with a discursive analogue to Eleusis;[75] no matter how far we follow there always is something withheld or cloaked in metaphor—a case of *graphos*[76] (see Chap. 8. II). Ra-

---

[73] For example, *eikasia*, on which see the discussions of Nettleship, *Lectures*, p. 241, and the comments of Cornford, *The Republic*, p. 217; and *logos*, on which see J. E. Raven's remarks, in *Plato's Thought in the Making* (Cambridge, 1965), pp. 12–13.

[74] *Republic* 394D. This is only one of the more explicit examples of the use of sea-travel as a metaphor of discourse and knowledge (a modification of a metaphorical pattern already mentioned). See also the metaphor of the three waves (445B–473); the ship of state metaphor.

[75] Cornford, *The Republic*, remarks on the association of caves with initiations into religious mysteries, p. 222.

[76] Stanford, *Ambiguity*, pp. 74–75 and 18. This, then, is to disagree with Oddone Longo, "*Metafore politiche di Platone,*" in D. Goldin, ed., *Simbolo, Metafora, Allegoria* (Padua, 1980), that Plato's metaphors are a means of appealing to an exclusive and ideologically unified class. Compare Whitlock on *Beowulf* as cited in Chap. 1, n. 19.

ven has perceptively remarked that we often feel we are getting to Plato's most deeply held beliefs when he confronts us with a myth or a metaphor—almost, one might say, as a barrier to further intrusion into a world of secret doctrines.[77] With the *Simile of Light* we have this phenomenon in a complex form; a tentative exploration of the relationships between forms, Good, and the visible world is converted into a simile, which is then converted to another, adding another dimension, and this is then explained with reference to the most elaborate and extended figure of the three, an allegory. The permeating and gradually elaborated imagery of light gives an aesthetic coherence to the whole, but at each principal stage in its threefold elaboration, the light passes through a prism, which radiates a spectrum of interpretive option, and it is with this that we must be content.

The three explanatory possibilities for this situation render the genesis of the ambiguity of the Cave itself ambiguous, and in pointing beyond the structure of textual ambiguity, they suggest a consideration of the diverse motivations and circumstances lying behind ambiguous discourse.

---

[77] Raven, *Plato's Thought*, pp. 66 and 144, concerning Plato's becoming more elliptical as he becomes more profound, which puts a considerable barrier in the way of achieving a single correct reading, to which end Raven is prepared to resort to a "psychological hypothesis" rather than accept that the correct reading lies precisely in accepting the limits that Plato seems to be imposing. Cf. also Longo "*Metafore politiche*", who similarly starts from the sound premise that metaphor is an essential means of Plato's mode of argumentation (p. 51), only to orchestrate a violent simplicity (as Derrida might have it) on Plato's figures and his class. The *Simile of Light*, however, is not discussed.

CHAPTER 8

Ambiguity:
Generation and Context

The Arts and Sciences thus have their birth in our vices.
J.-J. Rousseau,
Discours sur les Sciences et les Arts, 1750

. . . complexity complexed. Ponder that, O ye
synthesisers and sophisticators!
Max Lake, *Cabernet*, 1977

———————— I ————————

Most simply, ambiguity may be purposive or circumstantial: the
result of *virtù* or *fortuna*—a tricky distinction in practice, but
my intention here is only to refine a vocabulary of classification
in the process of which I hope to cast some light on the illustrative texts. Purposive ambiguity refers to a family of specific communicative devices: deliberate attempts to control audience reaction through the structure of discourse. More precisely, purposive
ambiguity is that for which reference to a hypothetical intention
has explanatory force. Circumstantial ambiguity amounts to a
residual classification for ruptured communication, for, that is,
an audience's room to maneuver around a recognizably fixed
point despite what we may hypothesize of authorial intention.
There is, however, a further rough distinction relevant to the
realm of *fortuna*, which hitherto implicit in the argument now
requires a word of explication: it is between the ξ we may hypothesize an author would have understood as ambiguous and
that which we now feel obliged to designate so. Echoing what

209

has gone before, we may call the former autochthonous, for it springs from the author and his world; the latter is synthetic, as it is a function of the way in which we impose sense upon it. Autochthonous ambiguity covers the realm of *virtù* and may also encompass ambiguities arising from inadequate control and linguistic seepage (see pp. 212–213). Synthetic ambiguity, however, has its generation in physical or intellectual changes independent of the author and his times. It provides, as it were, an Ozimandian effect (see Chap. 7, pp. 183ff.) and is exemplified immediately below.

————————— II —————————

Discursive Drift

I have argued previously that coalescent ambiguity is that which is located at the junction of our major discursive classifications, being a function of the general categories under the aegis of which we classify the world of discourse. What may be called discursive drift provides a potential explanation for what can appear to us as coalescent ambiguities. Since this ground has been covered before, I shall treat it but briefly here. The gradual refinement, redefinition, abandonment, and realignment of our general categories of discourse may result in the genesis or the clarification of ambiguities. At a given time, an item may be placed under the auspices of a species of discourse and be seen to be in no way ambiguous; but as language and our perceptions of the world change, the same item may later be placed at the intersection of different species of discourse, one or both of which did not exist when the item was originally created. So Hobbes used the terms 'philosophy' and 'science' as synonyms where we have learned to distinguish them. So, more pointedly, the Greeks drew no clear intellectual distinctions between what we classify as science, religion, mathematics, and philosophy. It is, of course, important to realize such differences in the ways in which the intellectual world is organized, and by so doing we can minimize the consequences of discursive drift. We can note that Greek science was infused by religion (and, for the modern mind, the conventional distance between science and religion is great). We can further note that Empedocles' scientific fragments are in hymnodic form; that Pythagoras was a religious leader; that numbers were numinous and that numerical imagery could function politically. But to note these things is itself to presage ambiguity by the application of our own discursive categories at or near the limits of their classificatory power. We may dissolve the ambiguities by sleight of hand, by discarding any incovenient discursive dimension, thus rendering Empedocles simply a scientist, Pythagoras a mathematician,[1] or by forgetting that Newton believed in alchemy—when alchemy was still 'science.' We may also attempt to abandon all reference to, and reliance upon, our own discursive discriminations. But the very fact that we need to hold such discriminations in abeyance means that in a strict sense we can never re-create the thought of the past, and the *theoretical* price paid (not the historiographical price asked) for the thoroughgoing attempt may well be too high. We may be left, in short, with the conclusion that our own discursive classifications are, albeit imperfect, the most appropriate for us, and the recognition of the possibility of ambiguity generated by discursive drift symbolizes the conclusion as it marks our options.

Erosion

Ambiguity may simply be the result of the erosion of substantive evidence, or the incomplete form in which we have a work. The worms of time may bore through a text to such an extent that their trail of random ellipses render the work ambiguous, if not as Soheil Afnan remarks of Avicenna's *Oriental Philosophy*, "full of promise but serving no useful purpose."[2] Much of Aristotle's

---

[1] S. Sambursky, *The Physical World of the Greeks* (London, 1963 ed.), e.g. on Empedocles, p. 16; cf. G. T. R. Lloyd, *Polarity and Analogy* (Cambridge, 1966), pp. 12–13, on the caution with which we can equate the scope of Greek and modern notions of meteorology; or see M. Buettner, "The Reformation and Geography," *History of Science* 17 (1979): 151ff., for the interrelationships between Protestant notions of providence, cartography, and geography.

[2] S. Afnan, *Avicenna, His Life and Works* (London, 1958), p. 290; cf. Shen

canon is so marred. His polished works totally lost, we are compelled to treat as finished his teaching notes in less than perfect manuscripts, added to which (perhaps the single most important methodological difficulty about the study of the whole of Greek society) time has taken much of the surrounding evidence. Reconstructions of fragments are sometimes founded on fragments. In this context also, Munz's analysis of Hooker's *Laws of Ecclesiastical Polity* is pertinent, inasmuch as Munz opened the question of whether the incompleteness of the manuscript was indeed a consequence of contingent destruction (either of the work or of Hooker) or whether, as Munz brilliantly argued, its incompleteness was a tribute to both Hooker's intellectual failure and honesty.[3]

Inadequate Control

It may be that an author fails to build into his argument adequate safeguards against ambiguities that he was at pains to avoid, and that this failure can be explained simply with respect to the immediate linguistic context provided by the text. It is doubtful if the ambiguity of Hitler's slogan *"millionen stehen hinter mir"* was any more than the price paid for compression. The sacrifice of a safeguard for *"millionen"* was capitalized upon by Heartfield in his telling montage in which Hitler's salute appears as an open hand accepting payment from the overshadowing "millions" of big business with Hitler's slogan printed neatly behind him.[4] The possibility of inadequate control is clearly a consideration to be borne in mind whenever we have a putative ambiguity, and it is a possible explanation for the ambiguity of the Cave. But the peculiarity of reference simply to postulated inadequate control is that ambiguity is always dependent directly upon the absence

---

Pu-hai's *Shen-tzu*, which has survived only through its fragmentary quotation in the works of others, which fate has not deterred H. G. Creel from attempting a reconstruction in terms of the work's alleged coherence (by modern standards), anticipation, influence, and originality. H. G. Creel, *Shen Pu-hai: A Chinese Political Philosopher of the Fourth Century B.C.* (Chicago, 1974).

[3] Peter Munz, *The Place of Hooker in the History of Thought* (London, 1952), although the structural problems he sees may be a result of discursive drift.

[4] Margaret Rose, *Parody: Meta-Fiction* (London, 1979), p. 117.

of textual safeguards; to say merely that an author inadequately controlled his argument is to explain very little, since it always invites further lines of inquiry. Thus Warnock points to the equivocation between two senses of the term 'idea' in the writings of Bishop Berkeley: the first stipulating that ideas are sensible perceived things, and the second referring to things as they seem in the mind. This may be left much as it is, but a comment of Coleridge's—all the more interesting for not referring to Berkeley—indicates that Berkeley in his use of the term 'idea' was evidencing and augmenting a wider linguistic phenomenon. English metaphysicians, remarked Coleridge, were apt to use the word 'idea' vaguely, its becoming "the cause of much error and more confusion."[5] Here we can see that the explanation of the generation of ambiguity can carry us well beyond the confines of a given text into what becomes, from the perspective of such a text, its linguistic context.

Linguistic Seepage

All languages change and have at different times and in different ways areas of indeterminacy and excessive flexibilty—the breeding grounds of circumstantial ambiguity. Sapir, remarks Ullmann, spoke of a self-moving drift of language; it is a drift that is apt to have uneven and uncertain flow. Or, again, an author by reflecting upon a specific institution in a state of perplexing transition, a confused area of human activity, or an uncertain physical circumstance may reflect a diversity of possibilities through ambiguity. The complex history of the Latin term for hip (*coxa*), which gave rise to the French for thigh (*cuisse*), was, arguably, conditional upon the proximity and the difficulty of maintaining a clear distinction between the hip and the thigh.[6] Many of our words which retain blurred edges can reflect a world resistant to clear classification. As Wittgenstein asked rhetorically, "Isn't the

---

[5] G. J. Warnock, *Berkeley* (Harmondsworth, 1953), p. 188, who argues that unconsciously Berkeley shifts between these meanings where the context of argument makes his theories most plausible (for a parallel case see Chap. 9. ɪɪ); Samuel Coleridge, *Biographia Literaria* (London, 1930 ed.), p. 52 n.

[6] Stephen Ullmann, *Semantics: An Introduction to the Science of Meaning* (Oxford, 1972), p. 125.

indistinct [picture] often exactly what we need?"[7] Sometimes the ambiguous might reflect physical reality; but this is not to suggest a nonlinguistic determination for ambiguity. If textual ambiguities may be seen to reflect specific social situations, institutions, or physical circumstances, these are of necessity always mediated through language or an associated symbolic mode. For by what may loosely be called an ambiguous situation (one independent of language), we refer to possibilities which are strictly speaking no more than the extralinguistic analogues of ambiguity. The more a phenomenon may be adequately defined *sans* a linguistic component, the less direct bearing it can have upon the generation of any ambiguity. So the more we make reference to such phenomena as a means of explaining ambiguity, the more we string the bow of metaphor further than we need.

Beyond any text, then, the context of ambiguity must be linguistic, but this is as diverse as the possibilities for distinctive ambiguity. For the linguistic context for any given text is itself a static segment cut and shaped by the interpreter from the various ways in which people have used words. All I shall attempt here is to instance some of the ambiguities which may plausibly be accredited to linguistic seepage, beginning with an illustration which more than many has an institutional point of reference.

Gellner has argued that in order to understand states of social transition, without specifying the transition in such a way as to prejudge and dissolve its problematic character, the world must be seen "not through the vision of men or beetles, but through the doubts of men-into-beetles."[8] Such doubts of men-into-beetles about their institutions and traditional practices may not only act as vital stimulants for theorizing but, as Mill's conception of liberty suggests, may also be translated into ambiguous theorizing.

---

[7] Wittgenstein, *Philosophical Investigations* (Oxford, 1968 ed.), par. 71. Ambiguity may legitimately be said to exist in symbolic forms functioning in ways analogous to language—hence Jastrow's drawing of the duck/rabbit (discussed in *Philosophical Investigations*, chap. 2, p. xi); but the point is still a linguistic one, designed to represent an aspect of language and depending for its effectiveness on the coalescence of the categories of duck and rabbit.

[8] E. Gellner, *Thought and Change* (London, 1964), p. 58.

In the nineteenth century, a potent received rhetoric functioning to justify the direction of parliamentary activity centered on
the terms 'liberty' and 'freedom.' This rhetoric of freedom ultimately reflected a widely held conception of the function of Parliament as being ideally an institution for the redress of individual grievance and a protector of individual liberty, an institution
properly concerned with second-order rather than first-order activity. That is, Parliament was seen as concerned with maintaining peace and law as well as providing a stable framework for the
adjudication of the various claims of those engaged in first-order
activities with substantive ends (commerce, industry, farming,
education). Now, as the nineteenth century wore on, this
conception of Parliament's proper function (libertarian, or 'liberal' in a neo-Hobbesian or Humean sense) cohered less and less
with its increasingly first-order activities: its involvement in education, public health, and the direct participation in the economy for economic goals rather than in the name of political
stability. Parliament was arguably and, according to Sir Henry
Maine, lamentably metamorphizing.[9] Significantly, this process
of institutional change was not accompanied by any concomitant
rhetorical bifurcation. Rather, the potential ambiguities in the
terms 'liberty' and 'freedom' could be used to mediate the institutional change. The rhetoric was flexible enough to remain relevant in a period of considerable transition because it could accommodate a change of emphasis and tolerate supplementation
with a rhetoric of efficiency. Liberty and freedom remained *clefs
mots* in the justification of parliamentary activity, but it seems
appeals to efficiency were gaining in persuasive power.[10] If, for
example, the franchise were greatly extended, compulsory elementary education could be justified in terms of giving the people a more effective freedom to participate in society. The im-
perative that we must educate our masters has a dual appeal, in
terms of liberty in a positive mood and efficiency. Conversely,

---

[9] Maine's reflections on the changes in the parliamentary system, and its elec-
torate, are set down in his essays in the *Quarterly Review*, 1883–1885.

[10] On the increasing importance of a notion of efficiency, see Shirley R. Letwin, *The Pursuit of Certainty* (Cambridge, 1965), especially on the thought of
the Webbs.

as Parliament continued to perform its traditional second-order activities or, from time to time, declined to take on first-order responsibilities, it could nevertheless continue to utilize the rhetoric of liberty, the people at least being free from government interference. We do not have two opposing concepts, let alone concepts reflecting two distinct stages in parliamentary history (such a situation would certainly have effected a greater rhetorical discontinuity in English parliamentary history than we have), because, albeit with occasional verbal infelicity, any claim concerning freedom can be couched in negative or positive terms; rather, we have the different sides of a universally available rhetorical token, and therein lies the source of its currency and mediatory power. There was, as it were, a single cloth that covered the body politic's hip and thigh. Similarly, because there is little that cannot be dressed in liberty's garb, a supplementary rhetoric, a corset of efficiency, was worn. In use it reflected the increasingly substantive first-order activities pursued by the institution, but it suggested ultimately a different conception of Parliament from the second-order libertarian ideal of Halifax, Hume, and Maine. We may tentatively locate Mill's *On Liberty* during this rhetorically cloaked period of institutional metamorphosis. Mill's conception of liberty is not unambiguously at one with those who stressed it as the ultimate value that Parliament must preserve by interfering with, and controlling, the substantive activities of social intercourse as little as possible; and neither (to reflect the processes of metamorphosis more completely) is liberty unambiguously an ultimate political value for Mill. To be sure, both these positions sound typical of him, but as Maurice Cowling and Shirley Letwin have persuasively argued, such a reading is too simple; it reflects his position as inadequately as Maine's unambiguous ideal reflects the drift of parliamentary practice.[11] It is not certain that Mill regarded liberty as more

---

[11] See at length, M. Cowling, *Mill and Liberalism* (Cambridge, 1958); Letwin, *The Pursuit*. My brief characterization of the role of Parliament in the nineteenth century is somewhat at odds with the common notion (*à la* Dicey) that there was a distinct period (in theory and practice) of *laisser faire* followed by a more collectivist or paternalistic one. Any notion that the state was tending to wither away until the latter part of the nineteenth century simply ignores the

important than efficiency; neither is it certain that Mill regarded the increasing amount of first-order activity undertaken by Parliament as an abrogation of its proper responsibilities and as an erosion of liberty. Freedom to participate in a society, as much as freedom from governmental interference, may depend upon government control. If the talented are to rise and supervise, and if human resourses are not to be wasted through the poverty and ignorance that only a government can efficiently eradicate, then in the name of efficiency, and perhaps of freedom, government must act.[12] It is in this way that Shirley Letwin is able to locate Mill far closer to the Webbs than to Hume, or even Bentham.

The ambiguity of Mill's *On Liberty*, she suggests, reflects a deep-seated division in Mill traceable to his being educated as a Benthamite with a faith in untrammeled individual liberty, but by a Calvinist father who believed in the superiority of a guiding few. The consequent dilemma was disguised, however, by Mill's appeal for the superior minority to be given greater liberty being dressed in a general libertarian rhetoric acceptable to all manner of individualists. *On Liberty*, she concludes, was thus a classic statement of "late Victorian and twentieth century liberalism."[13] It is possible to suggest, however, that the ambiguity was circumstantial and reflects the institutional changes in English politics with which Mill was explicitly concerned, and in which he was involved, more directly than a residue of personal educational tension. The two possibilities are perhaps ultimately linked. But the ambiguities in the rhetoric of parliamentary liberty were very much public property, and preceded and surrounded *On Liberty*. Mill's failure or reluctance to rid his own argument of ambiguity in fact crystallized the potentialities of a metamorphizing institution; through ambiguity he smote between hip and thigh.

---

direction and increasing scope of parliamentary activity; it is likely to oversimplify Mill and leave Maine somewhat difficult to explain. For some pertinent remarks see Mark Francis, "The Nineteenth Century Theory of Sovereignty and Thomas Hobbes," *The History of Political Thought* 1 (1980): 517–519.

[12] Consider in general chaps. 4 and 5 of *On Liberty* and in particular the closing peroration, chap. 5, lines 900ff. Reference to the A. Castell edition (New York, 1947).

[13] Letwin, *The Pursuit*, pp. 307–308.

A writer sensitive to the ambiguous and fluxing possibilities of language can build protective dikes of definition or stipulation, and stress his dissociation from diurnal connotation and vulgar use. That he attempts to do so may well indicate the state of his language, as it may have consequences when a work becomes itself an item in the flow of discourse. Irrespective of a writer's efforts and their consequences of destabilizing or stabilizing a sector of language, he is unlikely to be more than partially successful in maintaining the rims and walls of his protection. Defenses crack, dikes seep, ambiguities occur to leave *fortuna's* stigmata on the text. Hobbes stressed more than most the importance of formal defense against the illogical and confusing drift of language, the fundamental importance of taking all words back to first reckonings. As Wolin has argued, Hobbes himself was the theoretical, linguistic analogue of his own *Leviathan*, something of an ideologue of definition, waging a philosophical war in a world of linguistic chaos and theoretical absurdity;[14] and if he exaggerated and somewhat overdramatized, he did little more. Hobbes wrote just after a period of unprecedented semantic explosion in England—a period in which the sheer size of the vernacular vocabulary increased as it had never before nor has done since (and how many political theorists have paid attention to this?), a period in which, moreover, word usage, grammar, and punctuation were flexible and encouraged complexity and allusiveness of discourse. Leaving aside the metaphysical poets, this was true of the philosophical, scientific, and political vocabulary of seventeenth-century England, a situation which could easily be seen as integral to philosophical and political chaos. The scientific revolution of the seventeenth century, of which Hobbes was a part, was nothing if not a process of redefining the conceptual vocabulary of inquiry, both in its scope and the interrelationships of its principal terms. Similarly, both the French religious wars, which attracted Hobbes' attention,[15] and the Eng-

[14] Sheldon S. Wolin, *Politics and Vision* (Boston, 1960), chap. 8 (see Chap. 6, this study pp. 152ff.).

[15] J. W. H. Salmon, *The French Wars of Religion in English Political Thought* (Oxford, 1959); Leatherdale, *The Role of Analogy and Metaphor in Science* (New York, 1974), has stressed the relationship between scientific and linguistic change.

lish Civil War involved differing attempts, backed by force, to impose an authoritative uniformity upon uncertain and fluid political vocabularies. Clear guidance concerning *loyalty, right, justice, obedience, conscience, subject, state,* and *individual* were all contingent upon the stable interrelationships of these terms, and stable or uniform in connotation, denotation, and area of operation they were not. To build upon such an ethical structure was to build upon shifting sands; thus Hobbes saw a world of distinctions without meaning, and argument lacking the distinctions and definitions to give it sense. Consequently, he was concerned not just to define individual words, but whole interrelated fields of terms, the currency of distinctive patterns of discourse. His dream, of course, was an impossible one, notwithstanding his heightening of the surrounding chaos, which tumbled old sediment with recent refuse: not every word can be taken back to first reckonings; no one can anticipate all that may later need to be made clear (Guicciardini, *Ricordi*, 143). The arithmetical paradigm provided an optimistic metaphor, and through the most impressive of dikes seeped the ambiguities that are associated with the laws of nature, the grounds of obligation, the character of the state of nature, and his diverse use of the notion of freedom. If there can be deviant possibilities, and interpretive difficulties attendant upon the work of a definitional paranoiac such as Hobbes, how much more might we expect the ambiguity of linguistic seepage in a writer relatively insensible to the fortunes of the language he uses?

In contrast to Hobbes, Machiavelli took little interest in the consequences of loose and equivocal language in politics. His attention was taken by the fortunes of men in action, for whom his own words were but the means to better action. Hobbes, for all his intellectual arrogance, was not sufficiently vaunting to think his arguments would be rendered lucid by the sheer compulsive flow of his prose; he understood the realities of intellectual life too well. Machiavelli, for all his acute perceptions of political affairs, was apt to overlook the importance of language as a dimension of political activity; his effective truth of things was more abstract than he would have us believe, and he reflected the language of his times more clearly than Hobbes. He built no dikes or, perhaps typifying the arrogance of the supreme stylist, thought the beauty of his prose defense enough against the flow of a linguistic contingency which he was to stress in the *Discorso alla nostra lingua.* In either case, the consequences for the understanding of his theories have been considerable; the ambiguities that infect his work make him invaluable evidence for what was happening to the moral vocabulary of Italy and Christendom at the beginning of the sixteenth century.

None of the concepts associated closely with Machiavelli's name does he define or formally isolate from the drift of his own arguments, let alone does he separate them from the variety of common usage. Some we must grasp only by the recurrent contexts of their usage (*ordini*),[16] some by metaphorical excursus (*fortuna*), some by a combination of both. *Virtù* is such a term— one of such significance that no Hobbes could have left it undefined or undiscussed without mentioning a polemical context of previous (inferior) usage. As J. H. Whitfield clearly demonstrated a number of years ago, Machiavelli's extensive use of the term *virtù* and its cognates is at times ambiguous.[17] *Virtù* had an important place in the moral and political vocabulary of Christendom, and its importance and the complexity of its functioning are reflected in Machiavelli's theoretical works. The point here, then, is not to labor what Whitfield and others have amply shown about Machiavelli's deployment of the term, but to suggest that the problem of *virtù* in Machiavelli may properly be

---

[16] J. H. Whitfield, *Discourses on Machiavelli* (Cambridge, 1969), chap. 8.

[17] J. H. Whitfield, *Machiavelli* (Oxford, 1947), chap. 6; see also Russell Price, "The Senses of Virtù in Machiavelli," *European Studies Review* 3 (1973): 315ff.; and "Virtù in Machiavelli's *Il Principe* and *Discorsi*," *Political Science* 22 (1970): 43ff., which lists the occurrences of the term in both works; and Neal Wood, "Machiavelli's Concept of Virtù Reconsidered," *Pol. Stud.* 15 (1967): 159ff. These specific studies I have found invaluable. See Fredi Chiapelli, *Nuovi Studi sul linguaggio del Machiavelli* (Florence, 1969) for an important general account of Machiavelli's style and vocabulary as the outcome of linguistic traditions in crisis. See also B. Lauretano, *Ambiguità e Metafora* (Naples, 1964), esp. chap. 2, for a tangential discussion focusing on the realtionships between metaphor and ambiguity, in the context of a Vicoesque or Bachofian understanding of metaphor and ambiguity's debasing dangers for science and logic.

seen in terms of linguistic seepage, reflecting and evidencing the drift in the language of his times.

In largely moral and political terms, the use of the word *virtù* in and beyond Machiavelli's works was controlled by certain qualifying, or opposing, conceptions such as *vizio, fortuna, sapienza*; it subsumed specific qualities, such as *giustizia* and *liberalità*. It could have different areas of reference, such as warfare, artistic or technical and intellectual enterprise. The term, moreover, existed on a familiar vector of use enabling it to be deployed for overtly rhetorical purposes at one extreme, or to be used as an organizing category of experience at the other.

Now when Machiavelli wrote, it appears that *virtù* was becoming dissipated in extension. Hence the need for explicit definition was all the greater if ambiguity was to be avoided. Machiavelli's writings, however, reveal not only an absence of all definition, but concomitantly a failure to capture or recapture a sufficient intension to avoid both ambiguity and the occasional inconsistency. This may initially be illustrated with respect to *fortuna* as a consistent lexical qualifier. Traditionally, the role of *fortuna* was varied. It received theological sanction as a sort of divine intermediary or, as Commynes had it, *"une fiction poétique"* for God's grace;[18] it could even function as a sort of emotional buffer which enabled the unfortunate to avoid holding God responsible for disaster;[19] and, uneasily, it could take on capricious existence, independent of any divine order, having an inexorable momentum of its own. Whatever its force, it was usually presented metaphorically.[20] Much of this, to the confounding of *virtù*, is found in Machiavelli. Of the seventy times

[18] Cited in A. Gilbert, *Machiavelli's Prince and Its Forerunners* (Durham, 1939), pp. 205–206.

[19] Chaucer's *The Book of the Duchess* provides a clear example of this, for a discussion of which I am indebted to Geoffrey Cooper's paper, "Grief Work in *The Book of the Duchess*."

[20] The inexorable wheel was a common image; compare its use in Mortimer's last speech in Marlowe's *Edward II* and in *Il Principe*, chap. 26. Louis Green, *Chronicle into History* (Cambridge, 1972), pp. 24–25 and 57–59, discusses perceptively the relationships of God and fortune with respect to the work of the Villani brothers; see Chiapelli, *Nuovi Studi*, sec. 10, for *fortuna* in the context of Machiavelli's metaphors.

221

virtù is used in *Il Principe,* on twelve occasions it is explicitly and immediately paired with *fortuna*—more than with any other term in the same lexical field. Yet *fortuna* is defined no more than is *virtù.* Where it enjoys some excursus it is metaphorical, and the metaphors are not always consistent. *Fortuna* is like the earth to be shaped, it is like a river; it is like a goddess, and a woman. Although both pairs of metaphors are aesthetically coherent, they are used to opposing effects. The earth metaphor (echoed in the dikes that can be built against the raging river) emphasizes the control of *fortuna* by *virtù*; the emphasis of the river metaphor has an opposing force. The goddess is imperious, the woman responsive. Each of these images, however, carries the impression of *fortuna* as independent of God's divine order, yet in the final chapter of *Il Principe, fortuna* is found as a mediating concept and God himself is portrayed as taking a direct interest in human affairs. At least, we might still be left with the impression that *fortuna* is a category which can be used for all human actions and circumstances, on which basis it might seem possible to say that *fortuna* is a matter of other men's *virtù*—a matter of perspective, but even this is not so of Cesare Borgia's ill fortune. We have, in short, a term in Machiavelli which reflects different uses and fails to stabilize *virtù* even though it is frequently found in formal opposition to it.

Sapientia, as Rice has shown, was also an unstable item of Renaissance discourse; it could be contracted to complement *virtù* and thus help to define its limits, or it could be expanded so that true wisdom could include some senses of *virtù.*[21] *Sapientia,* or its vernacular forms, could involve intelligence, or be opposed to it, and when Machiavelli uses *virtù* to refer to superior intelligence (*Discorsi* 1. 56), the relationship with wisdom is obscure. Yet for Machiavelli prudence is sometimes wisdom, and prudence is a virtue or, in its Roman sense, *virtù.* There is at least no doubt that if *Il Principe* and *i Discorsi* could be subtitled "on political virtue," they could equally be subtitled "on political wisdom, . . . or prudence or fortune." In terms of the subsumed

[21] Eugene F. Rice, *The Renaissance Idea of Wisdom* (Cambridge, Mass., 1958), passim.

qualities of *virtù* (its mundane specification), there are still problems; Machiavelli is not always specific and we cannot with safety presuppose the exclusion, or only provisional inclusion, of traditional Christian moral values, even where such a reading provides a distinct possibility of interpretation. When Machiavelli writes of *virtù* at *Il Principe* 15, we cannot invoke any wider range of virtues than those listed and then discussed. Less still, on the basis of this, can we take him to be skeptical on all occasions of Christian virtue per se; and less than this can we take Machiavelli's use of *virtù* to be referring to a free-floating universal morality which is or is not separate from politics. It has been on the assumption that one can so read his comments in chapter 15 (with its associated lack of attention to his failure to specify particular virtues elsewhere) that the whole *question mal posée* concerning the autonomy of politics has been based.[22] Whitfield, I believe, was right; sometimes Machiavelli's usage of *virtù* is predicated upon an acceptance of Christian virtues *qua* virtues, or his tone presupposes specifically Christian virtues (here *vizio* often acts as an effective lexical qualifier). Thus we get the ironic comment on Vitellozzo, *"maestro delle virtù e scelleratezze sua"* (*Il Principe* 8). The overall result is an occasional ambivalence of attitude to a given figure—hence at *Discorsi* 1. 20, Phillip of Macedon is among *"i principi virtuosi,"* and six chapters later, un-Christian and inhuman.

But even here the matter is too simply expressed; there is a further range of possibilities. Because the term was used with reference to much more than moral and political activities, the specific qualities it could subsume could be of yet different orders. Thus Leonardo uses the term to refer to the principle through which a thing (a mechanism or a muscular system) works;[23] Machiavelli, to refer to the skills which mark an activity—the principles by which it works. In a related sense it is talent at *Discorsi* 1. 57, and in the introduction to Book 1 it refers to that

---

[22] John H. Geerken, "Machiavelli Studies Since 1969," *JHI* 37 (1976): 366–367, refers to the Crocean question in these terms, in an essay marked by shrewd judgment.

[23] F. Gilbert, "On Machiavelli's Idea of Virtù," *Renaissance News* 4 (1951): 53–55.

which excites interest and curiosity—initiating the discussion of the principles by which Rome achieved her greatness. Yet success by one's own endeavor is not necessarily *virtù*, as Machiavelli's explicit judgment on Agathocles shows (*Il Principe* 8). These remarks scratch the surface, but to round them off it is possible to see *virtù* as existing at the center of a number of different human activities, each requiring a different specification of the term, and some requiring different lexical qualifiers. Understandably, as Machiavelli is talking about politics, warfare, and largely through reference to antique societies, the field is circumscribed, and Wood is correct in arguing that Machiavelli tended to run Roman military and stoic virtues under the mantle of *virtù*. However, he did so without attempting definition, without entirely resisting countervailing forces, by occasionally calling upon Christian connotations and specifications, and even others associated with medicine, art, and oratory. The overall result is that ambiguity may seep into Machiavelli's usage with respect to three sorts of linguistic relationship: with respect to *virtù*'s formal lexical qualifiers, its subsumed qualities, and its areas of reference.

What is perhaps surprising is that, under the circumstances in which he wrote, Machiavelli's apparent semantic insouciance should result in no more than occasional ambiguity. The possibilities are always limited, and limited by his concern for the effective truth of things, largely to a single area of human experience. He is often perfectly clear, though not always consistent. The seepage, however, is at times evident, and it has consequences not just for our interpretation of him, but for his understanding of the world around him. At *Discorsi* 2, *Proemio*, Machiavelli laments in familiar terms what he sees as the manifest collapse of morality and *virtù* around him. Men, he tells us, are forever extolling the past and condemning the present, usually wrongly and on insufficient evidence, as Burke was also to suggest in *The Causes of the Present Discontents*. Even after the fall of Rome, its concentrated virtues were scattered widely among different *nazioni* so that we still see the *virtù* that is much lamented and much praised (*che si desidera e che con vera laude si lauda*). But not so Italy (and Greece) where there is nothing to compensate for the misery, infamy, and degradation of the whole period, where there is no religion, obedience to law or discipline, where the present is stained (*maculati*) by every form of brutality, and all these vices (*questi vizi*) are made worse by existing in the highest in the lands, who judge, command, and expect adoration. Such sweeping claims cannot be taken at face value, but more than this, it is difficult to index clearly any process of degeneration as that of which Machiavelli, not untypically, writes. It is at least possible here that Machiavelli is mistaking a partial collapse in the ethical structure of his society (that is, a received appraisive vocabulary of morality) for a total collapse of morality. It must indeed often seem that when we cannot use such terms as *goodness, virtue,* or *vice* with confidence and trouble-free reference, there is something amiss with the way people are in fact behaving. Certainly, when *virtù* can be used with the variety and ambiguity of a Machiavelli, we may expect men to bemoan the vices of their age. Fittingly, since his own works were tossed into the flow of discourse, he has often suffered the fortune of being castigated for his immorality. Vice has been mistaken for use of *virtù*.

In some respects, Hobbes and Machiavelli provide us with complementary variations on a theme: both are victims of linguistic seepage, one despite his efforts, the other because he was apt to write *"sanza argini è sanza alcuno riparo"*; the one doing something to stabilize and purge a sector of political vocabulary, the other reflecting and even exacerbating the difficulties of a political vocabulary. But in none of these respects are they alone, nor do they belong to categories which themselves cannot give rise to ambiguity.

Dante's closing insistence in *De Monarchia* (3. 16. 134–136) that the Emperor should hold the Pope in reverence as a first-born son must respect his father (*Illa igitur reverentia Caesar utatur ad Petrum, qua primogenitus filius debet uti ad patrem*) conjours the specter of Roman Law and the father's right of *potestas puniendi*—clearly, a possible case of linguistic seepage which would vitiate much of Dante's case against the Church.[24] But an

---

[24] Michael Wilks, *The Problem of Sovereignty in the Late Middle Ages* (Cam-

earlier use of *reverentia* (an uncommon word in *De Monarchia*) couched in strikingly similar analogical terms precedes and provides the apologetic ground for the attack upon the temporal claims of the Church: "*[cum] quibus illa reverentia fretus, quam pius filius debet patri, quam pius filius matri . . . pro salute veritatis in hoc libro certamen incipio*" (3. 3. 128–134). Could this be a more disingenuous or ironic maneuver? If it is, Dante's final stress upon Ceasar's proper reverence for Peter is cast in a rather different light. That is, the vocabulary of Roman Law which may be seen as undermining the force of his argument may also be seen as a subject of his ironic manipulation. Such a display of reverence as Dante shows kept *De Monarchia* on the Papal Index until the twentieth century, while his apparently unselfconscious use of *reverentia* from the stable context of Roman Law usage still enabled a reassertion of the very papal claims Dante had argued so strongly against. There is, then, not only an uncertainty about *reverentia* but whether Dante is the victim or manipulator of his language. In this we nudge the world of purposive ambiguity. To make the transition we can turn again to *The Republic*.

Plato, like Hobbes, was acutely conscious of the instability of language, of the need for and the difficulty of achieving proper definitions. In other respects, like Machiavelli, a supreme stylist, he relied on metaphor or the context of argument to make the meanings of crucial terms clear. Sometimes there is covert stipulation, sometimes the potentially ambiguous diversity of common and fluid usage is imported into the text. But in Book 1 of *The Republic* (335b–336a) there is the possibility, as it were, of a controlled seepage.

The term *blaptein*, and related terms (*blaberos, blabe*), referred in Greek to hurting, damaging, or making worse; thus *blabes dike* was an action for damage done and causing a worsening in one's circumstances. As hurting and making worse are not necessarily the same things (there is a parallel with *malum*

---

bridge, 1963), p. 145, forcibly makes this point, stressing Dante's familiarity with Roman Law and his equation in the *Convivio* 4. 9 of *reverenza* and *suggetti*. Wilks also notes the earlier use of *reverentia* (which I shall discuss), but not its place in Dante's argument.

here, see Chap. 7. v), the *blaberos* family of words could be used in different contexts to ambiguous effect—much more obviously, as Cross and Woozley remark, than in English.[25] As they also remark, a refutation of Polemarchus hinges precisely on the ambiguity of *blaptein*—a word commonly discussed in Plato's works.

There are three distinct possibilities here: first that Plato has lost control of the argument, and that there is a simple case of linguistic seepage, and second that it is an attempted dissimulation—an improper philosophical procedure. Thus Cross and Woozley remark: "Socrates has exploited an ambiguity. . . . as an argument designed to produce rational conviction it leaves much to be desired."[26] But then, as they have already told us, "Socrates's counter-arguments contain a number of mistakes or even dishonesties, which a better philosopher than Polemarchus would have challenged":[27] tabloid headlines in *Mind*. It is perhaps a tribute to Plato's dramatic genius that philosophers should write of Socrates and Polemarchus in this context as if they could have argued this or that, should have taken this line, or surprisingly have failed to take some other. It smacks somewhat of biographical Macbethery.

We might, instead, be advised to look for the point of what Plato was doing in making his characters blunder and dissemble, harm each other's arguments with ease, and get caught in the simplest ramifications of their own positions; specifically we may ask, *if* it was deliberate, what was the point of making Socrates exploit such an obvious ambiguity in *blaptein*? And what was the point of having Polemarchus collapse and retire in confusion? Certainly, it adds plausibility to the expostulations with which Thrasymachus erupts into the argument—he is not fooled by Socrates' sophistry any more I suspect than the reader is supposed to be; his irritation underlines Socrates' trickery—just in case we have missed the point.[28] Moreover, I suggest the exploi-

---

[25] Cross and Woozley, *Plato's Republic*, p. 21.

[26] Ibid., p. 20.

[27] Ibid., p. 4.

[28] *Republic* 336B. That is, there may well have been an extension from a very common dramatic technique of using ambiguity to unify an audience and author against a character (discussed in sec. III). See W. B. Stanford, *Ambiguity in*

tation of the ambiguity is intended to show the ease with which people in moral discourse can be fooled. It is intended to point to the state of the ethical vocabulary of Athens, and to prepare the ground for, and emphasize, the importance of definition in the search for a *paradeigma* of justice.

Given the dramatic context, it is precisely the success of a bad argument—a whole series of them in fact—which can make this point best. The third interpretive possibility, in short, is that Plato is drawing attention to the consequences of ambiguity in political language, by allowing an obvious ambiguity from diurnal usage to seep into the fabric of his argument, and to harm and make worse the argument of his characters.[29] Indeed, if this was the point, he could hardly have chosen a more appropriate word to act as a synecdochic clue to the argument. This, in turn, indicates the significance of the sequence of characters and their arguments in Book 1: they constitute personifications of a wider problem, a dramatic intimation writ small of the ethical linguistic background to the remainder of the work.

The father, sure of his beliefs, though ungrounded in philosophy, passes on to the son (who literally inherits the argument before it has started) a morality which is uncertain and easily confused. Such a son, such a generation, becomes the game of the sophists who dominate the moral discourse of the *polis*, who can exploit the ambiguities of language and make the worse argument appear the stronger, and who, in Thrasymachus, extol as virtue unjust behavior. A hapless continuity, of fathers, sons, and sophists, seems mediated, then, through a purposive ambiguity. But if this is so, it is a use drawn of a rich poetic inheritance and is designed neither to trick nor convince the reader.

Greek Literature (New York, 1972 ed.), p. 76, and the discussions of numerous instances drawn from Aeschylus, Euripides, and Sophocles. That such precedent is ignored is arguably a function of discursive drift. Some modern philosophical perspectives preclude such a context as immediately relevant or proper when unraveling a sequence of propositions.

[29] It is curious that a related expression, *blaphtheisen ozo*, meant to be trapped in branches, or (mentally) to mislead. Hobbes, making a similar point about the confusion of language *sans* adequate definition, refers, of course, to birds caught in lime twigs, and may be alluding to the Greek.

Instead, it seems designed to encapsulate the consequences of an ambiguous political and moral vocabulary as part of the Heraclitean flux of language with which this chapter has been much concerned.

———————— III ————————

Purposive Ambiguity

I shall begin by circumscribing the most likely areas of discourse in which purposive ambiguity is found. As a specialized stylistic device in poetry, ambiguity has been much explored in writers as far apart as Sappho and Shakespeare. Cocteau's notion that any genuine piece of poetry required as much creative effort from audience as from creator, in order for it to be fully finished, derives most of its plausibilty from awareness of ambiguity, which often belies apparent simplicity and directness.[30] Under a clear surface poetry is obscure. If purposive ambiguity is common in poetry, its transference to, or reinforcement in, other realms of discourse is also a possibility—especially in societies in which the poet carries a potent social authority. Although, then, we are not directly concerned with poetic ambiguity, it is to be noted that ambiguity in one area of discourse may help generate it in another.

Similarly, I am not directly concerned with the piecemeal forms of purposive ambiguity which are so useful on an *ad hoc* basis in diurnal discourse—of the sort that abound in advertising copy (and which have related functions to those found in poetry); nor with the sort that become the legendary *bons mots* of later generations. At a dinner one night, the Prince of Wales described graphically how he was with Wellington at the charge down the hill at the battle of Vittoria. He turned to Wellington for corrob-

[30] A similar point to Cocteau's was made by Lord Kames, *The Elements of Criticism* (Edinburgh, 1792), chap. 3, p. 112, cited in Leyburn, *Satiric Allegory, Mirror of Man* (Westport, 1969). The position is strongly associated with the symbolist poetry of Mallarmé, and is intimated in the *Essais* of Montaigne.

oration, who replied "Steep sir, very steep."[31] This operating area for ambiguity also provides a relevant background to political theory. Frequently, people, like Wellington, find themselves in situations where response is expected and perhaps where they would prefer to remain silent. Ambiguity can become a substitute for silence, as to an extent it is always structured on a partial silence. The Wellingtonian retort has its unforced extension in the studied literary ambiguities of Cosimo de' Medici's reply to a papal request for money to finance a crusade against the Turks. As a banker he would agree, as a private citizen in a free republic his hands are more tied; he remains uplifted and flattered by the Pope's vision.[32] So, room for interpretive maneuver is preserved; an option for action is kept open and also a justification for inaction. In short, an eye is being kept on the realm of contingency, which compromises silence less easily than sound. The extension from Wellington to Cosimo is the extension into a sort of political theory (at least the letter is a politically significant one), exploiting the possibilities of political commitment and reality, indicating how in the world of high politics and diplomacy, no less than in that of poetry, ambiguity is a most important tool of trade. A work like Mattingly's *Renaissance Diplomacy* could not have been written without an acute awareness of just this point. And Huxley, for example, in his essays, *Method and Results*, suggested (though in typically disparaging terms) that it was the very vagueness of Rousseau's literary evocations of equality which commended themselves to practical politicians like Robespierre and Baboef, who wanted to use Rousseau's name.

The two worlds of politics and poetry come together most clearly in the utterances of the oracles. Their ambiguity was widely recognized, even mocked, but Isocrates, perhaps, and certainly Plutarch were prepared to defend their ambiguity precisely in terms of diplomatic necessity.[33] The oracles, more clearly and formally

---

[31] This anecdote is to be found in vol. 1 of Elizabeth Longford's biography, *Wellington: The Years of the Sword* (London, 1971).

[32] Cited in G. Hibbert, *The Rise and Fall of the House of Medici* (London, 1974), p. 86.

[33] See Stanford, *Ambiguity*, chap. 8, esp. p. 123 on Plutarch, p. 12 for his

than the bardic poets, functioned and maintained their position as guides for this life and mediators of a divine sanctioning order by being able to combine the ambiguity of poetry with prognostication. This was possible partly because of the permeating authority of poetry in Greek intellectual life. The *sophistes*, whose own notorious ambiguity originated not with him but with the *poietes*, was, as Guthrie has suggested, poetry's self-appointed heir. Aesthetic canons of judgment as well as poetic devices were transferred to the realms of political discourse.[34] Solon reviewed his political career through poetry, and *Gorgias* codified Greek aesthetic experience as a rule of rhetorical *praxis*. But if poetry had a permeating importance in Greek moral and political life, it could maintain it only by encompassing the future, and the political future, if significant, was uncertain—hence Sir Harold Wilson's prose comment on the weekly eon. So, too, the ambiguity of the oracles was sanctioned by poetic practice and political sense. For the act of unraveling, and effectively selecting, the appropriate from sometimes several differently intelligible possibilities, or of being able to exploit the ambiguities to one's

comments on Isocrates. More generally on the role of the oracles see H. W. Parke, *The Greek Oracles* (London, 1967); on their diplomatic importance see Sir F. Adcock and D. J. Mosley, *Diplomacy in Ancient Greece* (London, 1975), chap. 17.

[34] Stanford, *Ambiguity*, p. 1, for an invaluable discussion of the transference of ambiguity from poetic to rhetorical practice, and chaps. 1 and 2 for the indiscriminate theoretical hostility to the ambiguous; W. K. Guthrie, *A History of Greek Philosophy: The Sophists* (Cambridge, 1971 ed.), chap. 3, for the sophistic inheritance of the poetic mantle. On aesthetic canons of judgment see esp. Nancy Struever, *The Language of History in the Renaissance* (Princeton, 1970), chap. 1, which also passim intimates the importance of poetry as an idiom of political theory. More specific, though very different, treatments are to be found in David Nichols, "Aeschylus' *Oresteia* and the Origins of Political Life," *Interpretation* 9 (1980): 83ff.; the scattered remarks of W. Forrest, *The Emergence of Greek Democracy* (London, 1966), and the very suggestive study by Jacqueline de Romilly, *Magic and Rhetoric in Ancient Greece* (Cambridge, Mass., 1975); and G. Thomson, *Aeschylus and Athens* (London, 1941). All these underline the importance of poetry and the tragedians as political thinkers. Historically speaking, Aeschylus would seem a better starting place for the tradition of political theory than either Plato or Socrates. The fact that he does not normally provide such a point is yet another indication of how far the tradition is an arbitrary projection of a contemporary discursive balance.

own ends, involved a combination of poetic and political skills which gave a derivative authority to the interpreter. The recipient of oracular utterance, like the reader of poetry, had to do as much as the oracle. In this way, the oracles' reputations were protected and controlled, and the men of *arche* in the *bios politikos* could galvanize and justify the action they required . A sort of division of labor necessitated by oracular ambiguity helped insure a sort of distribution of authority. Athens was indeed saved by her wooden walls, but only because Themistocles, to his everlasting fame (and immediate advantage), had the flair for effectively exploiting the oracle. Such gods have dwindled into newspaper astrologers.

In general, we may anticipate that if the world of politics can pivot upon reading, constructing, exploiting, and combating ambiguities, then the theories devoted to that world—often constructed by people of literary, if not even poetic, sensibility—will exhibit purposive ambiguities of their own. Perhaps we may even expect that the more intimately involved is theory with practice (and much political theory is intrinsic to political practice), the more we may expect to be confronted with pivotal and purposive ambiguity. I shall now list and illustrate what I take to be its main forms.

Protective Ambiguity

In Hobbist terms, the desire to strike a balance between fear and pride may well lie behind some purposive ambiguities. It was no doubt from such an awareness, and from a knowledge that people sometimes believe themselves to be persecuted and seek to communicate with each other discriminately, that Leo Strauss developed his ramified theory of esoterica, which trades grandly in the currency of ages of persecution, exoteric and esoteric doctrines, disguise and the art of decoding.[35] The hypothesis on which his theory is built is surely not unreasonable—books and people have been burned; and Strauss has certainly enriched the vocabulary of interpretation. But the theory in its more ambi-

---

[35] I am drawing generally on Leo Strauss' *Persecution and the Art of Writing* (Chicago, 1952) and *Thoughts on Machiavelli* (Chicago, 1958).

tious forms has proved somewhat difficult to apply, and the attempts to do so have proved susceptible to devastating criticism.[36] This is perhaps one of the ironies of intellectual life, indicating some of the difficulties of transferring commonsense awareness into the study of texts long since written. The hypothesis of persecution may seem plausible to us, as it must especially have done to Strauss and many of his generation, but to build much upon it is to build almost systematically upon the edge of Ockham's razor; there are usually simpler and more plausible explanations than those requiring the detailed decoding of a hypothetical esoteric doctrine—we return to a mode of reification. In the last analysis, if the theorist was unskilled, there is little that is going to be secret about his work; whereas insofar as he was skilled we are unlikely to be able to uncover the doctrine cloaked in a bland exterior.

Attempts to do so are likely to look arbitrary and perverse. Conversely, any interpretation can claim to be a revelation of an esoteric doctrine. Decoding can be a euphemism for the willful disregard of evidence. One does not, however, have to go to the extreme of searching for (and finding) whole esoteric and morally subversive theories cloaked in a publicly acceptable doctrine in order to recognize that writers may rely on a degree of protective ambiguity. They may, indeed, hold some fears for their safety (though to hypothesize this we must identify a specific audience to be excluded from some interpretive possibilities and one which we can show has understood the different meanings). William Hone's *Political Litany* (1817) is a case in point. The work was a blend of religious and political comment at a time when there was a lower tolerance of blasphemy than political satire. He was brought to trial but argued successfully that the Bible, which he reverenced, was being used only to make a political point—in

[36] See e.g. Skinner's comments in "Meaning and Understanding and the History of Ideas," *Hist. & Th.* 8 (1969): 21; Felix Gilbert, "Politics and Morality," *Yale Review* (1959): esp. 468; G. L. Moses, "Review of Thoughts on Machiavelli," *AHR* (1959), at length; see also Peter Laslett's symptomatic complaint, Introduction to Locke's *Two Treatises of Government* (Cambridge, 1963 ed.), p. 105n.; for a more sympathetic reading of Strauss and his significance, see Allan Bloom, "Leo Strauss," *Pol. Th.* 2 (1974): 372ff.

effect, a mere and traditional vehicle for a political tenor. Similarly, the potential ambiguities of allegory may have had a protective purpose for both Heine and Karl Kraus writing, respectively, in the troubled 1840s and in the censorious enthusiasm of Hitler's Germany. Heine used animal fable in *Atta Troll* to avoid censorship; Kraus an explicitly Aesopian form in *Dritte Walpurgisnacht*—which was not quite protection enough to risk publication.[37] Alternatively, writers may fear for their reputations lest events confound their theories, as well as their physical well-being.

In either case, ambiguity may lay up treasures in heaven against contingency, treasures for which writers pay in the coinage of clarity and an extensive, admiring audience. Thomas More may well have been one such, not once, but with respect to three of his major works.[38] The *Utopia*, as has long been recognized, was a well-designed construct for oblique criticism of society, but as the form was to become a genre, with a literary momentum of its own, the need to reinforce indirection with an element of protective ambiguity has diminished. In *Utopia*, however, it is not always clear what in fact represents a criticism of Tudor England, how far Hythloday is More's political mouthpiece, and, conversely, what in fact constitutes the free play of literary fancy, especially as Hythloday is a rounded character with a voice distinct from More's. The form provides ample opportunity to develop both a practical strand of political theorizing and an aesthetically autonomous one; where they coalesce the work, like *The Republic*, shimmers in equivocation. More knew his Plato well enough, and there is a striking surface parallel between *Utopia* and one of the consequences of the discursive structure of

[37] Rose, *Parody*, pp. 32, 111, 115ff., on whom I am drawing with respect to Heine, Kraus, and Hone. There is, of course, an added irony that Orwell (*Animal Farm*) drawing on the tradition of Heine and Kraus did not need the protection animal fable was developed to afford when he attacked the sort of society in which it would be necessary.

[38] My discussion of More here draws freely on Damian Grace, "The Political Thought of Sir Thomas More, 1509–1520" (Ph.D. thesis, University of N. S. W., 1980); and "On Interpreting Sir Thomas More's *History of King Richard III*," in N. Wright and F. McGregor, eds., *European History and its Historians* (Adelaide, 1977), pp. 11ff.

the Cave—but we need not postulate any tendentious process of influence. If the structure of *Utopia* is informed by a tactical indirection, this can be found also both in the *Richard* and the *Epigrammata*. There is, then, it seems, a family resemblance between the three works radiating from a persistent sense of the protectively ambiguous—a sense befitting a court politician in the orbit of an uncertain prince. In writing explicitly about a past king, More, in his portrayal of the tyrant, could turn the armory of humanist rhetoric tentatively toward immediate objects. An account of the past having an intelligibility and point of its own could have a politically supporting role in the present, or an admonitory and hortative one. By his exaggerations and use of rhetorical figures, More shows he was not writing about Richard the historical being, for only Richard as sustained image can be portrayed to stare so fittingly janus-like in the present. Again it has been shown that the political content of the *Epigrammata* is far greater than has hitherto been supposed. More, through free translation from the Greek, intensifies political content and gives noticeable political import where in the Greek there is little. Thus, where possible, the epigrams display in general terms and in continuity of imagery the evils of the times. The epigrams are arguably his, and not his, as are the words of Hythloday and his interlocutors, as well as the words and actions of Richard.[39]

Sectarian Ambiguity

The need to exclude a potential audience from a range of possibilities within a work—or in the last resort to claim some textually justified disassociation from that audience's realization of them—hardly exhausts the range of purposive ambiguity. A range of higher or inner meanings may be available only to an audience of initiates. Circumspect and sectarian impulses may in fact be closely connected, as they may well coincide in the writings of More or Heine. Nevertheless, a notion of sectarian ambiguity

[39] Grace, *The Political Thought of Sir Thomas More*; for Hythloday as the butt of More's satire see also W. W. Wooden, "Satiric Strategy in More's *Utopia*: The Case of Raphael Hythloday," in *Renaissance Papers* (Durham, 1977), pp. 1ff.

can be treated separately. Here we are concerned, then, not with ambiguity as a consequence of a felt need for protective exclusion, but as a consequence of an author's sensitivity to a publicly graded audience, for which he attempts to provide a work that is variously intelligible according to the reader's degree of initiation into a body of knowledge or some mode of writing, and which, potentially, the entire audience may be presumed to seek.

This, of course, excludes from consideration here a related, though with respect to ambiguity, a quite contrary phenomenon, namely, the process of writing for an entirely exclusive and specialized audience. The physicist does this when writing for other physicists. To the uninitiated he is opaque, and he is indifferent to his opacity. To the initiated he is ideally transparent, and much of his language is designed to render him so.

The poet's opacity is different, and more closely related to the problems of ambiguity. The Eliot or Pound who builds on biblical econometric allusion, and who slides with facility from English to Greek or Italian, is *ipso facto* excluding a less or differently educated audience from much of his meaning, adopting "the methods of the cuttle-fish retreating under cover of an opaque cento of purple patches."[40] In doing so, though he may remain unmoved, he is likely to suffer accusations of deliberate exclusiveness from those who recognize the house for what it is and see the door closed in their faces. A little Latin would get us through a portal, a good Christian education, perhaps, into an inner sanctum.[41] What appear to be similar processes at work in Marlowe would not have been so regarded by his contemporaries, who, if they could *read* his English, would be likely to have understood the allusive Latin hurled into the flow of his prose "O lente, lente currite, noctis equi!" The opaque and the transparent are largely functions of an audience's education, but it is precisely this that can be turned into a device deliberately to limit, and gradually filter, a potentially indiscriminate audience. The possibilities revealed in a work depend very much

[40] Stanford, *Ambiguity*, p. 81.

[41] Compare "Vacant Shuttles weave The Wind" (Eliot: *Gerontion*) with "My days are swifter than a weaver's shuttle and are spent without hope. O, remember that my life is wind," Job 7: 6–7, cited in Stanford, *Ambiguity*.

upon the stage of initiation reached by a reader, but insofar as they are various and interrelated we may well look for specific ambiguities; for the ambiguous will function ideally as a means of grading the audience and controlling entry into the sect. Much medieval erotic poetry, it is said, held inner meanings of divine religious significance, the full possibilities of which, radiating from a single set of images, only the cognoscenti could appreciate. Or there is the still puzzling case of Mozart's *Magic Flute*, intelligible though apparently trite on the surface, carrying inner meanings of considerable political import that were fully available only to those initiated into freemasonry.

A more pertinent instance to political theory, as it is traditionally understood, is to be found in what I have taken to be a likely explanation for the culminating ambiguities of the *Simile of Light*.

The Greeks were much preoccupied with the paradoxes and the potent opacity of language. Their language per se was an exclusive mark of genuine civilization and a necessary condition for the *bios politikos*.[42] But within it the unraveling of obscure utterance was, as has already been suggested, of great significance. Hellenic society, in which cults and exclusive sects and associations flourished, in which the line could be very thin between what we see initially as scientist, philosopher, and religious leader (see also pp. 210–212), was thus subdivided in part by exclusive and excluding idioms of discourse. Participation was a matter of initiation; education, in part, a matter of the art of progressive decoding.

Plato's works, available and intelligible to a fairly wide public, were possibly intelligible in different or supplementary ways to his followers. We must bear in mind here less the evidence of the *Seventh Letter*, if it is genuine, or its insight, if it is not, than Socrates' comments immediately before the *Simile of Light*, which do something to explain his resorting to allegory for his listeners. Socrates states that he is uncertain if he really knows much about the relationships of the Good to ideas, between this

---

[42] The term *barbarian* has, of course, a distinct linguistic core to its etymology, and for Aristotle man is above all *homo loquens*; while for Gorgias it is through language that the world itself takes what shape it has.

world and the intelligible, and even if he could, such arcane and mighty matters could hardly be explained to those lacking the requisite education.[43]

The best he can do is provide what he thinks may be a likeness. These comments must be taken seriously; they come close to announcing that only those initiated into Plato's ways of thinking will be able to unravel the following images properly. To be able to do so speaks of complex preparatory education, without which there are meanings, possibilities, and approximations, but nothing more certain or central. If Plato's attitude seems unreasonable, or unduly secretive, we must not only consider the sectarian background to his thought, but also the logic of his position as it is presented in *The Republic*. If Socrates is the possessor of such a stupendous understanding, and if to achieve a full understanding of all things real and significant there must be so much education for so long for so few, then we can hardly expect to be given more than crumbs from the table. We, the uninitiated readers, are the recipients of a myth which makes more or less intelligible the riddles of the universe, and as such we are the theoretical *doppelgangers* of those denizens of the *Kallipolis* who are given the noble lies. A clear statement of the full meaning of the *Simile of Light* would, if this is so, be in contradiction to its stipulated significance—to say nothing of its being, like the final definition of *dikaiosyne*, an anticlimax.

Having stressed to his own and his interlocutors' satisfaction, and having abundantly illustrated the sheer awesomeness of understanding, Socrates is then asked, in effect, for a digest of the truth. Plato makes Socrates react with commendable patience, which is the excuse for providing the *Simile of Light*.

When Clarendon, according to Aubrey, asked Hobbes why he had written *Leviathan*, Hobbes was less tolerant of such a crass request made of such a monumental statement of political and philosophical principle. He condescended to answer at a level of mere mundane motivation, saying he has a mind to be home. The question itself prohibited any answer on the level of philosophical explanation; for by his request Clarendon, if the story is

---

[43] *Republic* 507A.

true, revealed his lack of philosophical initiation; a man (like Ibsen) more dismissive than Hobbes might well have replied, "Because I had to." If Plato was indeed writing in such a way as to interest the excluded, stimulate the sympathetic, and communicate with the initiates into his understanding, then for us to continue to ask for the simile's ultimate or inner or correct meaning is close to being an act of theoretical crassness, of Clarendonian or kingly proportions.

Dramatic Esoterica and Pseudoterica

Sectarian and protective ambiguity has its dramatic counterpart in the use of ambiguity not only within plays, but with respect to the author's identification with an audience against a character—a situation in which a character is limited to the perception of one possibility of an *équivoque* where the audience may contemplate its various possibilities. So Macbeth is stilled into a false sense of security; thus "again and again in Sophocles' play King Oedipus innocently reminds the omniscient audience of his impending doom. Poet and audience are drawn together like conspirators by this technique."[44] As Stanford remarks, such ambiguities may be called esoteric, the surface meaning being restricted to the character, and deceptive inasmuch as the character is almost invariably deceived. The point, however, is not to deceive or exclude the audience. To pick up Stanford's apposite image, through such ambiguity the poet reveals himself as puppet master, overthrowing the illusion of the play as "a real happening."[45] But the effectiveness of such dramatic conspiracies against the puppet-characters depends upon the knowledge of the audience—its awareness of strings. When, however, the dramatic esoterica is extended far in a satiric direction, even this becomes a moot point and we have what becomes, in effect, the bastard counterpoint of sectarian and protective ambiguity proper: some-

---

[44] Stanford, *Ambiguity*, p. 75. John Gardner, *Grendel* (London, 1973), provides some brilliant variations on this device.

[45] Ibid., p. 76. Extensive examples of dramatic esoterica are analysed in chaps. 10 and 11. Cf. Roland Barthes' remarks on J.-P. Vernant and P. Vidal-Naquet, *Mythe et Tragédie en Grèce ancienne* (Paris, 1972), in *Image, Music Text*, trans. S. Heath (London, 1977 ed.), p. 148.

thing akin to the cylindrical side of Arbuthnot's "plano-cylindrical speculum," in *The Art of Political Lying,* which for want of a less Arbuthnotian term we may call *pseudoterica,* noting which takes us toward the marginalia of political theory. However, its thematic connection with sectarian and protective ambiguity suggests an important link with a centrally significant form of political ambiguity.

The context of pseudoterica is satire and parody, and its mode of ambiguity may be seen as a device in that species of narrative through which an author lampoons or pillories the people of his times. Such narratives are most obviously associated with the works of Dryden, Pope, Swift, Aristophanes, and with those of numerous and often anonymous medieval satirists.[46] Typically the narrative is concerned with conveying a story, and with displaying a range of characters unconnected with the author's own political milieu, or with the telling of a 'history' or fantasy even unconnected with his own world. On such levels the narrative will be largely intelligible. To those, however, sufficiently familiar with the political and social world of the author, the narrative takes on additional significance and a greater range of meaning.

Insofar as the work pivots on a range of ambiguities, then different tenors are carried economically and simultaneously in the same vehicle. As is the case with *Absolem and Achitophel,* a pointed satire can be elegantly conveyed through the disingenuous retelling of a familiar story, begun with the innocence of a fairy tale.[47] Thus far it may seem that only wit divides pseudoteric from sectarian ambiguity, or even from dramatic esoterica, but this is not so. The motivation behind pseudoterica is to be understood in terms neither of fear nor of elitist intellectual sectarianism, but in terms of a desire to amuse and flatter. The

[46] I have in mind here such works as *The Gospel According to the Silver Mark* (probably twelfth-century French); *The Story of Saints Gold and Silver* (anon. under the name Garcia of Toledo, circa 1100), and the *Propter Sion non Tacebo* of Walter of Chatillon, which is to be found in F. J. E. Raby, *The Oxford Book of Medieval Latin Verse* (Oxford, 1959). These and other similar items I have used through annotated translations and copies produced by The Sydney Medieval and Renaissance Group.

[47] Leyburn, *Satiric Allegory,* chap. 2

audience participates, as with dramatic esoterica à la Cocteau in the full creation of the work by its ability to unravel arcane possibilities, and is flattered by its ability to do so. By following the range of possibilities generated from a specific *équivoque*, such as a pun or an allusion contained in the name of a character (a device typical of the *Gospel According to the Silver Mark*), the audience is given the means of turning the translucent into the transparent. The process itself is exemplified and parodied brilliantly in Swift's *Tale of a Tub*, a work which makes clear that we are not just dealing with a species of sectarian ambiguity. For the purpose is not to narrow an audience, or to appeal only to one which possesses certain serious intellectual credentials; it is to flatter any reader with a modicum of wit (hence the clues are well signposted) that he is part of an inner group.[48] Whereas for sectarian ambiguity there is an inner meaning to be grasped by the few, and whereas for protective ambiguity the possibilities of the ambiguity may not agree with each other, and whereas in dramatic esoterica there is a knowledgeable conspiracy against a character, in pseudoteric ambiguity the center may well be hollow and without exclusive direction. This mode of purposive ambiguity, which helps render especially satiric allegory effective, is worth mentioning here less for the sake of completeness than because the line between catering for a variously aware audience by a series of ambiguously portrayed characters and situations and providing a series of variously exploitable symbols (a display of caps that can fit where we please) is a narrow one. It is the difference between Sporus and Napoleon Pig. The crucial point is that, in crossing it, we shift from the consideration of ambiguity as a means of narrowing and discriminating within an

---

[48] "Satire is a sort of glass wherein beholders generally discover everybody's face but their own; which is the chief reason for that kind reception it meets with in the world, and that so very few are offended with it" (*The Battle of the Books*, Author's Preface). Consider also Swift's use of notes in *The Tale of a Tub* with their pseudo-elucidations and mock confusions, and the whole persona of the Bookseller, ignorant of Latin (*Bookseller's Dedication*) and not knowing quite what to do with the book or how to understand much of it (*Bookseller to the Reader*). Leyburn's comments, *Satiric Allegory*, pp. 24–25, are pertinent.

241

audience to the consideration of it as a device adaptable to the process of widening and unifying an audience.

Amphiboly

The political writer who is involved in identifying with what he takes to be a discrete and homogeneous audience, who, perhaps, is writing to reinforce its sense of security, to encourage, or to warn, who is involved, that is, in preaching to the converted, most properly trades in clichés and most appropriately writes in an idiom free from significant ambiguity. Conversely, the writer whose appeal is to a heterogeneous audience, or whose purpose is to enlarge his audience, or to redefine an agenda of dispute, is greatly aided by a sensitivity toward the ambiguous. He must cast words like nets, to augment, and to gather in.

The processes of augmenting a potentially small, and often politically insignificant, audience are markedly problematic, not least because the received language as a whole (its syntax, grammar, its potent myths and symbols, its abstract structures of ethical conceptions) always constitute a series of challenging and partially restricting variables. They require careful use if an audience is not to be alienated and fragmented, and equally discriminate use if the audience is not to be inadequately or disadvantageously defined. As James T. Boulton has shown, the stylistic differences between Burke and Paine are, in part, functions of the different sorts of audience to which each appealed; or, rather, that each was able to appeal to supplementary segments of an English-speaking political audience can be explained stylistically as well as doctrinally.[49] Their success in reaching extensive, and otherwise often divided, audiences and setting down the terms of debate over the French Revolution rested in large part upon their ability to select and manipulate an adaptable, but by no means entirely malleable, inheritance of political vocabulary comprising such symbols as the Norman Yoke and the Glorious Revolution as well as such abstract *clefs mots* as *reason, custom,* and *nature.*

---

[49] See at length James T. Boulton, *The Language of Politics in the Age of Wilks and Burke* (London, 1963).

Such clusters of terms and expressions come to a writer radiating connotations, the residue of past political conflicts, and
the markers of present political division. Some words, by being
closely, even exclusively, associated with a specific sect or political party, may well inhibit a potentially broad appeal (see pp.
256–259). Others, having enjoyed such an obvious and widespread prestige that most political groups will have tried to manipulate and appropriate them, may afford an insufficient control. Whether he is writing for related though differing sects within
a narrow range of the political spectrum, or seeking to appeal to
a widely divergent audience, the augmentive writer has an unen-
viable task that is easily overlooked by those who disparage ideology and its rhetoric as per se dubious modes of thought; and it
is a task that is lost altogether on those who think that all political
theory must be seen as a matter of logical proposition. The amphibolous theorist has to tread the line between the totally uncontrolled dissipation of his argument and its undue restriction
to a single grouping.

By virtue of the ambiguous he can bypass, or mask, politically
divisive issues among the audience to which he would appeal.
By virtue of the ambiguous he thus gives the different sections
of his audience the creative opportunity of deciding for themselves ways in which they may identify with him. The ambiguous, then, can provide an important mechanism by which otherwise different groups can find salvation under one banner and
share a common vocabulary for the variety of future actions and
expressions of belief. In sum, the resort to amphiboly constitutes
both a recognition of the limitations of political language and of
the discrepancies between the potential size of a political audience and its homogeneity in an attempt to overcome such limitations. Rooted in the logistics of persuasion and perhaps in the
notion of author as *makar,* amphiboly offers the text as a flexible
tool rather than as a monument to its creator.

To illustrate such ambiguity we need look no further than to
Marsilius of Padua's elliptical amphiboly the *legislator humanus*
(see Chap. 7. vi). There are, however, other possibilities which
may be suggested briefly. Locke's argument in *The Second Treatise on Government* is, despite its abstract language, largely di-

rected against the Stuart monarchy. The immediate force of the *Treatise* is to say that unless the king (executive) behaves in keeping with his trusts, namely, to protect property and to maintain a state of peace, then he can and must be corrected or removed. What is important to note here is the significance of the English Civil War, not as a past event, but as a potent symbol of stasis and destruction. Its existence in the memories and vocabulary of Locke's contemporaries made arguments of resistance difficult and, to many, potentially unpersuasive. It is understandable that Locke should therefore not argue on the level of historical symbol which put the cause of resistance at a polemical disadvantage and activated old sores rendering it mere rebellion. His argument operated on a level of what might be called euphemistic abstraction. Like Marsilius he used an idiom of abstract philosophical argument to pursue a theory for the sake of action.

In this context, then, there is a clear sense in which Locke's abstract conceptions of "government," "society," the states of "nature" and "war" should not be seen as more or less successful alternatives to Hobbes' stark biads of peace or war, government or anarchy (pace Mabbott).[50] His conceptions constitute a second mode of circumnavigation.

Locke appears to have been intent of squeezing through the Scylla of broadly Hobbist philosophy and the Charybdis of civil war memory to assert with a bland and lucid reasonableness (which is even more remarkable for proving ultimately correct) that an objectionable king could be removed, despite all his claims and pretentions, and be replaced without the anarchy and destruction of civil war.[51] Thus (despite the lessons of history) because the government of the king is little more than a potentially securing superstructure for a preexisting (English customary) society, it may be removed. What is more, the people have a per-

[50] See e.g. W. D. Mabbott, *The State and the Citizen* (London, 1948), pp. 20–25. James Tully, *A Discourse on Property: John Locke and His Adversaries* (Cambridge, 1980), adduces important additional reasons of a much more metaphysical nature for Locke's circumnavigation of history. It may be, then, that philosophy and ideological advisability coincided conveniently for Locke.

[51] Hence Dunn's challenging remark that Locke was haunted by Hobbes, *The Political Theory of John Locke* (Cambridge, 1969), pp. 86–87.

fect right, even a theological duty, to do so if necessary. In the context of religious ideological discourse, in which I believe *The Second Treatise* most properly belongs, Locke was presenting an extraordinarily ambitious thesis under difficult circumstances, and much of its success, and its appeal, depended upon the room for interpretive movement allowed. How precisely and uncompromisingly the reader was prepared to relate it to concrete contemporary political issues was a matter which the level of abstraction left open to choice.[52] How far Locke's argument could seem acceptable to how many depended in particular upon his well-recognized extensive and potentially ambiguous usage of property.[53] In one sense Locke tells us property is to be understood as life.[54] In this sense the trusts of the executive to maintain

[52] Locke's possible use of George Lawson's *Politica Sacra et Civilis* (1660) is relevant and instructive, for his position is strikingly similar (saving the explicit references to English secular and ecclesiastical affairs), and it was precisely such specific reference that Locke seems to have been at pains to avoid. On the similarities between Locke and Lawson see A. H. Maclean, "George Lawson and John Locke," *Cambridge Historical Journal* (1947): 68ff.; see also the claims of J. Franklin, *John Locke and the Theory of Sovereignty* (Cambridge, 1975).

That there was potentially a diverse and actively interested audience for Locke's *Treatises* has been shown by Mark Goldie's invaluable survey of the pamphlet literature immediately preceding the publication of Locke's ,work, "The Revolution of 1689 and the Structure of Political Argument," *Bulletin of Research in the Humanities* (1980): 473–564.

[53] The discussions of Locke's use of the term *property* are, as befits such a slippery notion, extensive and various. A representative number are cited in Laslett's Introduction, p. 103n.; and on p. 102 he refers to Locke's "extraordinary vagueness." Locke's usage was not unique, and thus if the vagueness to which Laslett refers was not part of a deliberate strategy of argument, it represents a fortuitous case of seepage (see pp. 213ff.).

The use made by his contemporaries is discussed by J. Richards, L. Mulligan, and J. Graham, "Property and People: Seventeenth Century Usage," *JHI* 42 (1981), and by Tully, *A Discourse*, who has done most to circumscribe the limits of Locke's usage in such a way as to make much metaphysical sense of him. My few comments here are restricted to a more rhetorical rationale for Locke's writing.

[54] ". . . yet every Man has a *Property* in his own *Person*." His rights to this property are, Locke says, absolute, and "The *Labour* of his Body, and the *Work* of his Hands, we may say, are properly his" (*Second Treatise*, chap. 5.27). It is from this famous proposition that property is extended to include whatever a man can mix his labor with. Cf. Richard Baxter, *A Holy Commonwealth* (Lon-

245

peace and property run into each other, and not even a Hobbist required obedience to an authority which directly threatened life. The notion of a property in one's life provided, then, a bedrock justification for resistance (a right of self-defense) which could appeal to virtually all within the political community. On the basis of this, Locke could build property as a right into an edifice fit even for a Whig magnate or a tax-controlling Parliament. For Locke also uses property in the sense with which we are all familiar, referring to the accumulated interests, holdings, and artifacts that society, and its acceptance of money, makes possible on a large scale.[55] In this sense, property had a particular relevance to the Whig aristocracy which felt so threatened by James and was most likely to attempt his removal. However, by degrees (measured partly upon a tax scale) it was of less relevance to those beyond the ambit of the court and its religious political policies, and to those with less property to be taxed.

Now Locke, like a number of his contemporaries, was well aware of the significance of the shift from Latin to the vernacular, and of the instability and uneven expansion of this vernacular. *The Essay on Human Understanding*, Book 3, should be read with such a background of linguistic change as well as self-conscious reform in mind; in particular he was acutely aware of ambiguity in discourse and the use of words with uncertain areas of meaning (*Human Understanding*, 3, 9–10). He also showed a marked hostility to inherited scholastic conceptual fields and a predilection for operating within the realms of established Eng-

---

don, 1659), thesis 52, p. 69: ". . . and each man hath that propriety in his life and faculties, and children, and estate and honour, that no rulers may justly take these for him; which Right as it is secured partly by the Law of Nature, partly by other Laws or institutions of God, and partly by the specyfying Fundamental Contracts of the Commonwealth, are commonly called the liberties of the People." Richards et al., "Property and People," do not mention this passage, though they cite a more tangential one, pp. 40–41.

[55] Ibid., pp. 36–37. For Locke, unlike Harrington in *Oceana*, the acquisition of property is not limited in the name of civic virtue although it may be limited and potentially redistributed (a point noted by Laslett years ago but often ignored since). Locke's theory is in some respects closer to theology than economics and as a distant cousin to the fourteenth-century Franciscan poverty controversy shares some of the moral ambivalence associated with property owning.

lish vocabulary. By using the vernacular *property* largely in place of the more elaborate and discriminatory scholastic conceptual field comprising *ius, dominium, possessio, proprietas,* and *usus,* he ran together matters of degree, type, object, and right; and he enabled others to effect a similar conceptual collapse. Whether for broadly metaphysical reasons (as *Human Understanding* could furnish), for those associated with political eristics, or from a fortuitous coincidence of both, Locke was thus able to appeal to those who feared for their property in differing senses of the word; he provided a means by which a defense of property in one sense could seem reasonable when couched in another, namely, that of right and religious duty. After the overthrow of James II, I suspect that the uneasy rationalization of his removal was helped by the exploitation of Locke's ambiguity; *property* separated rebellion from the rhetorically distinct notions of self-defense and obedience to God, and could do so in a way that encompassed the interests of the few as well as those of the whole society of the living.

This is to say that Locke's conception of property is not a defense of capitalism. However, the amphibolous character of the concept does extend to encompass a good deal of what we now call capitalism or associate with it, and once we have made the conceptual simplifications, Locke can be tailored to fit. By the early nineteenth century, it seems that the requisite conceptual simplifications had been effected. Lord Macauley, for example, in his critical review of Mill's *Essay on Government* in the *Edinburgh Review,* 1829, reflects a bifurcation of the notions of property and persons in his accusation that Mill has forgotten that government has obligations to persons as well as property. By property, Macauley clearly means objects possessed, apparently exclusively by people, and intimates that property possession is a mark of class. Because on its own the *Second Treatise* lacks sufficient safeguards, it has proved easy to read such notions as Macauley voices back into Locke and thus create a potent lineal stereotype.[56] Despite the Laslett edition of the *Two Trea-*

[56] See e.g. the readings of R. H. Tawney, C. B. MacPherson, and belatedly in the latter's idiom, Ross Poole, "Locke and the Bourgeois State," *Pol. Stud.*

tises and, for example, the work of Dunn and Tully, we can expect such simplified projections to continue to circulate. The conventional structure of political theory can even be seen as underwriting them. Political theorists have an academic interest in discussing Locke and such neoterically important concepts as capitalism, and one can easily be a means of talking about the other. Similarly, they have an interest, legitimately, in the concept of democracy and have combined this repeatedly with discussions of Marsilius. Nevertheless, Locke's conception of property is better understood, like Marsilius' *legislator*, as an elliptical amphiboly, in its structure, its contextual suggestiveness, its rhetorical functioning, and its interpretive fate.

Consider also the *Communist Manifesto:* Marx and Engels begin the work dramatically by exaggerating the role of their movement in the context of contemporary history. Communism is a specter, haunting and elusive, and doubly dangerous to the establishment for that reason. Yet if there is a specter in the text, it is the bourgeois. He and his class are not simply portrayed through and defined with the objective criterion of economic class distinction—that is, as those who have under their control the means of production and *ipso facto* the power in the political superstructure. The bourgeois is rather the principal external threat to the socialist movement of which Marx and Engels' own party was an aspiring part, a threat indeterminately related to the means of production. The distribution of the term *bourgeoisie* can either have a fairly concrete economic point of reference or indicate synoptically and generally socialism's principal and pervasive danger, the more evocative for having no persistently clear focus and the more usable for being a relatively free-float-

---

28 (1980); A. Rapaczynski, "Locke's Conception of Property and the Principle of Sufficient Reason," *JHI* 42 (1982); Robert Nozick, *Anarchy, State and Utopia* (New York, 1974), on whom see S. B. Drury, "Locke and Nozick on Property," *Pol. Stud.* 30 (1982). The fate of Locke, in this context, is by no means isolated. Mandeville has suffered a similar simplification. Because he provided a defense of various activities under some of which we subsume capitalism, he has been seen as specifically justifying it. See M. M. Goldsmith, "Mandeville and the Spirit of Capitalism," *Jnl. of British Studies* 17 (1977).

ing term of traditional vituperation.[57] Groups internal to the movement, or competing with the Communists (if such clear-cut distinctions be allowed), were identified succinctly and doctrinally.[58] The bourgeois, however, who acted with such subtlety and single-mindedness to maintain his position, and to destroy the emergent threat, was sufficiently ambiguous to provide in a fragmenting and fragile movement a continual point of hostile reference, and some negative means of affirming an identity. The reference to obscure threats and conspiracies has for centuries been a rhetorician's stock-in-trade—not least because on occasion there are such threats and conspiracies. In large measure their success depends not on total fabrication, less still on an abundance of unambiguous and concrete references (which are apt to render the polemicist redundant). Rather, the success of such tactically conjured hauntings depends, as Arbuthnot so brilliantly elaborated, upon the exploitation of plausible ambiguities in evidence and points of reference. It is not so much surprising, then, as a further ironic manifestation of a venerable rhetorical device, that Senator McCarthy understood communism in much the same way and to similar effect as Marx and Engels portrayed the bourgeoisie—as a specter. We have (to cut a thin *ad hoc* segment from the many faceted history of socialism) a series of reverse mirrors, though not quite in Arbuthnot's wicked sense, variations upon a haunting theme. The opening statement of The *Manifesto* is a reverse figure for the conception of the bourgeoisie, while for McCarthy the similarly amphibolous Communists, who could almost haunt and threaten the soft un-

---

[57] See P. Corcoran, "The Bourgeois and Other Villains," *JHI* 38 (1977): 447ff. The vituperative inheritance is clear in the *Communist Manifesto*, trans. S. Moore (Moscow, n.d.), chap. 1, in which are canvassed a number of general identifications of the bourgeois: in terms of economic structures (p. 41 and p. 53, where it is equated with the abstraction Capital); historical significance (e.g. chap. 1, p. 44); moral character (pp. 43, 46, and 54–56); and definitional power (pp. 43 and 59), where the notion of the bourgeois is itself the means of defining the proletariat, and from which is generated the notion of bourgeois objections to communism (identified with the proletariat), in chap. 2, p. 79.

[58] Contrast with the aforementioned, the precise discriminations made in chap. 3 and the names of authors as well as representatives specified. The bourgeois remains, however, as he appears in the prefaces and in chap. 1.

derbeds of each household, became, in turn, a means of purging and unifying that most evocative abstraction, the American Way of Life. This, in turn, is something of an inverse figure of the Communist movement which Marx and Engels would have us believe already haunted Europe when they wrote, and which they sought to purge and unify in partial reference to the bourgeoisie.

Reliance, however, on a specific concept or related set of abstractions by no means exhausts the possibilities of augmentive ambiguity. At the level of grammar, anaphora can be used to amphibolous ends. Gill Seidel has explored the generation of ambiguity through the selective use of pronouns to be found in the French political tracts produced during the crisis of May 1968, some of which themselves are connected with the notion of the bourgeoisie.[59]

In one tract, produced by the *Comités de Défense de la République*, Seidel notes how the potential ambiguity in the pronoun *on* (as in *"on part,"* inclusive, or *"Est-ce qu'on va mieux aujourd'hui?,"* exclusive of the speaker) is actualized through its unspecific use to suggest "an elusive and menacing presence."[60] Or, again, she notes how in student tracts the use of *nous* and *vous* can have ambiguous reference, and can be used to find a common platform against a clear enemy for those who (it may be added) in the received idioms of Marxism would appear, *prima facie*, to be themselves class enemies.[61] The students, largely bourgeois in one sense, were sensible of their vulnerability to accusations of being bourgeois in another sense. The fear of bourgeois irrelevance required an emphasis on action, not on abstract class categories, and to this end classless paired pronouns could be employed. The selection and use of pronominals Seidel says is rarely innocent,[62] being used as part of *"strategy and masking."*[63] In the cases Seidel discusses, as well as in the in-

---

[59] Gill Seidel, "Ambiguity in Political Discourse" in M. Bloch, ed., *Political Language and Oratory* (London, 1975), pp. 205ff.

[60] Ibid., p. 222.

[61] Ibid., pp. 210–213.

[62] Ibid., p. 222.

[63] Ibid., p. 211.

stance of Locke, Marsilius, and Marx, however, the success of the appeal to an extensive and heterogeneous audience depends not upon the author's ability to exercise power over his reader (on this point Seidel seems confused),[64] but upon giving its segments room for interpretive maneuver and facilitating changes in political priorities under the auspices of a single evocative vocabulary, upon, in short, the most effective distribution of the means of persuasion. Such maneuvers are more familiar to rhetorical theorists and literary critics than they have been to political theorists traditionally in search of the sorts of correct reading that their use of established appraisive categories together with their doctrinal fixations have lead them to expect. The symbolically blank pages in *Tristram Shandy* ("The motley emblem of my work"); the alternative endings to *The French Lieutenant's Woman*; and Milligan's parody of the author's struggle to control his text in *Puckoon*—we accept all as literary license. Yet Kermode, in a passage which could well have been about Marsilius, or perhaps Locke, Marx, or the pamphlets examined by Seidel, writes of Hawthorne that "his texts with all their . . . controlled lapses into possible inauthenticity, are meant as invitations to co-production on the part of the reader."[65] His conclusion, however, is that we have no right to expect, or any possibility of finding, a correct reading.[66] But I would suggest, rather, that close attention to the appraisive category of ambiguity redefines the terms through which we must look for 'correct' readings. As Kermode recognizes, in Barthes' expression, in the last analysis (though only in the last analysis) "*L'oeuvre propose, l'homme dispose,*"[67] which is to say, great books are not written, they are read (see p. 3), and it is a notion of ambiguity which helps draw the line between the recognition of this fact and the advocacy of

[64] Ibid., p. 206.

[65] Kermode, *The Classic* (London, 1975) p. 113; but see also E. Garver, "Machiavelli's *The Prince*: A Neglected Rhetorical Classic," *P. & R.* 13 (1980): 115–116.

[66] Ibid., explicitly *contra* E. D. Hirsch, *Validity in Interpretation* (New Haven, 1967).

[67] Roland Barthes, *Critique et Vérité*, cited in Kermode, *The Classic*, pp. 137 and 141; see also Barthes, *Image, Music, Text*, pp. 147–148 and 155–164.

a millennialist anarchy of interpretation.[68] There is a sense, close to Cocteau's or Malarmé's symbolist, Barthes' semiotic, Empson's or Lewis's critical, in which a given author's work is 'completed' in the exploitation of the ambiguities and equivocations he has created or made possible given the conventional networks in which its readers operate. With this last comment, the essay flows directly into a consideration of ambiguities, purposive or circumstantial, elliptical or coalescent, and their exploitation once a text is bequeathed to the world. Hence we come to the final stage of the argument, namely, to the framework for the historical explication of the classic nature of some of political theory's rich and ramshackle inheritance.

[68] Although this is a very thin line at times, it is to recognize that the reader can always do what the reader wants with a text; the restraint lies in the reader wishing to be read in turn, which requires some compliance with extant conventions of what constitutes a 'reading.' "*La parole est moitié à celuy qui parle, moitié à celuy qui l'escoute,*" wrote Montaigne with typical balance, but the listener, he continues, should be prepared to receive according to the spirit of the offering (*De l'Expérience, Essais* 3.13).

CHAPTER 9

Towards an Explanation
of Classic Status

Oh yet we trust that somehow good
Will be the final goal of ill.
Tennyson, *In Memoriam*, 1854

And with that I awaked, vowing I would never
write any more such idle toys, if this were well
taken: praying the readers to regard it but as the
first lyne of Isops Fables.

Gallus gallinaceus dum vertit stercorarium
invenit gemmam.
Sir John Harington,
A *New Discourse of a Stale Subject,*
called the Metamorphosis of Ajax (1596)

———————— I ————————

It is at this point, preliminaries concluded, that I might happily
embark upon yet another history of political thought from Plato
to Nato. Such an enterprise is beyond my competence, though
the continuing attempts to push such tomes up a slope of historical credibility indicates that Camus was right, *"il faut imaginer
Sisyphe hereux."* I shall instead hazard something less Sisy-
phean by returning to the question posed much earlier: what is
it that bestows classic status upon a political theory text?

The question arises naturally and starkly from a consideration
of the appraisive field of textual analysis shared by political the-

ory and related lineal activities, though it has been shrouded in a certain obscurity by the established though important themes of methodological dispute among political theorists and historians of ideas: thus Schochet saw as a shortcoming of Skinner's methodological principles the fact that they provided no clear means of distinguishing great from small.[1] Nevertheless, when Hacker offered his "straightforward" grounds for discussing only the elite of the former, he invoked the central items from the established appraisive field of textual analysis (see Chap. 3, pp. 77–78). When Sanderson directly confronted the question of classic status, he provided an annotated catalog of the field (see Chap. 4, p. 100 and Chap. 5, p. 140). When Levin puzzled over the classic status of Locke (see p. 78), it was in part his belief that great writers should be original and coherent and influential which led to his conclusion that Locke had been lucky.

Here I shall attempt a path between Hacker's assumption of *virtù* and Levin's acceptance of *fortuna*. *Virtù* must be shunned because the virtues of the appraisive field are largely unsatisfactory; *fortuna*, though less irrevocably, because it explains nothing. A reformed appraisive field suggests a further hypothesis and it is this—a sort of synthesis *manqué* of necessary vice—which I wish to sketch in, thereby drawing earlier threads together.

Why is it, then, that a cluster of apotheosized figures has endured to be constantly analysed, to become the rhetorical tokens we reckon by? Why are some books always read even if, as C. S. Lewis remarked of Bacon's *Essays*, we are not often found reading them? In the simplest form these constitute the central questions of classic status. This is also to say that endurance, usage, or suitably refined a sort of relevance (see Chap. 5, pp. 128–129, sec. VI) is not, *pace* Sanderson, a status-bestowing quality, an answer to such questions; it is a minimal testimony to the fact of classicism. The quintessential question, then, is what aids endurance?

[1] Gordon Schochet, "Quentin Skinner's Method," *Pol. Th.* 2 (1974): 270.

To begin with, the works with which we are mainly concerned have been typically used in, or generated largely by, political and religious controversy. This piece of conventional wisdom is worth mentioning precisely because in such contexts of dispute the received academic field of textual appraisal as such has rarely been noticeably dominant or even important. Insofar as before the formal academic study of political theory the context of text use was combative, and frequently unqualifiedly polemical, then it is important to understand such usage in terms of the relevant intellectual conventions rather than the (habitual) failure of past figures to achieve our standards of honesty, interpretive accuracy, and logical coherence—that is, to achieve originality and to acknowledge properly debts and influences like the good professors of political theory they should have tried to be.

What I suggest, in short, is that we use general categories of explanation appropriate to the diversity of political and religious dispute which has provided the immediate contexts for the employment of what are now the classic texts. Here the safest generalization appears to be that the status of x was a function of the rhetorical and ideological resonance that stemmed from his being effectively exploited as an authority. Such authority, when considerable, could be compressed in the flow of argument because a writer could assume a familiarity with the name and its associations, and in making that assumption, he reinforced his identity with a discrete audience. The greatest names in political theory have all been elevated to the status of adjectives.

These schematic remarks have provided us with two explanatory categories—those of authority and exploitation—with which we can now begin to approach the question in more detail. I use the term *exploitation* in the sense of the use (see Chap. 5. VI) of available resources—and I do not wish to connote any aura of misuse. It is unhelpful to inculcate the impression that the interpretations of the eristic nonacademics of the past are the works of intellectual spivs and second-hand concept salesmen. Authority initially refers to those resources in the context of eristic debate which a given author feels obliged to use, or is virtually required to use, if he is to be taken seriously by a given audience. The exploitation of authorities exists then on a sliding scale. At one extreme (and the role of medieval political thought and possibly some schools of Marxism is paradigmatic here), authorities are inescapable, the mere use of their words constituting *prima facie* proofs of argument. Only the uses, not the authorities, are challenged. In this way, we can see that, in the overlapping areas of literature and officially sanctioned language use, Eliot's classics such as Virgil and Dante are authorities in which Eliot in fact believed. At the other extreme (a phenomenon with which we are certainly more familiar), the authority may provide little more than a range of evocative expressions to be dropped into an argument which is strengthened by the association with a name. That is, although an authority may remain a guide and a seminal figure to whom respect is due, it will be recognized that his words and thought are not (even if properly unraveled) the last. The spirit, not the letter, becomes the point of emphasis; the authority's words become credentials more than proofs; he anticipates rather than answers our problems; and so status rests on the weak analogy of the religious prophet. We are negligent in our devotions, albeit still fulsome in praise. Now it is not my purpose to attempt to locate precisely the exploitation of past thinkers along this continuum which stretches from inescapable authority to sage anticipation. It is enough here to suggest that the 'classics' of political theory have spent most of their histories being shifted along it. It has provided us, at it were, with one axis of a crude graph. To say as much, however, has not taken us far; for if the durability of the thinkers of the past was a political one, the results of an effective authoritative embalming, we may still seek that in the body which facilitates the embalmers' art.

Here, within the general ambit of exploitation, there is a consequential and functional distinction to be drawn between the emblem and the authority, and this provides us with a second axis for the graph in Figure 5. A figure exploited as an emblem is a badge of a cohesive group, an abridgment of its values and a mechanism for maintaining identity. One used as an authority, however, carries weight across dispute and is part of a shared but

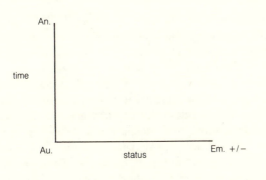

FIGURE 5

contentious vocabulary. Such a figure may even amount to a personification of the significant items in an ethical structure of discourse and become a name to be co-opted or distributed as a surrogate for abstraction among groups (see also Chap. 3. I; Introduction, Part Two, sec. II). An authority, then, is fought for, an emblem has been captured; an authority is an index of ideological dispute, an emblem (an ideological scar perhaps) one of unity. An authority carries uniformly laudatory or pejorative connotations, while those of the emblem are a function of attitude to the possessing group.

To which point a figure gravitates depends both upon the size of the relevant group to which the exploiters belong and upon the period of time over which we trace analysis. The authority may be an erstwhile emblem of a once-cohesive group; an emblem an exploded authority—a white dwarf in Young's firmament of genius. The distinction thus concerns the consequences of the exploiter's art and is a function of time and scale of analysis. It may be illustrated by the difference in status between a Lord Cecil and an Edmund Burke. The first is an emblem of identification shared by members of the British Conservative party, but Cecil's name carries no automatic authority for groups beyond the party. With Burke, however, the situation is different, insofar as his name carried weight across party distinctions during the late nineteenth and early twentieth centuries. If he was an emblem, it was at the level of Parliament as social group, not party. With respect to party he was an authoritative and legiti-

257

mizing figure whose name was to be co-opted. To Morley, Burke was, albeit a faltering one, a prefiguration of Gladstone; to Hugh Cecil, who did so much to restructure the beliefs and sense of identity of the Conservative party, Burke was spiritually at one with Disraeli.[2] It is something of this ambivalence of authority status which Mazlish expresses in referring to the "dualism" of Burke which has made it difficult to place him irrevocably in either a conservative or a radical camp. In the context of his status, it was certainly appropriate that when Nigel Nicholson wrote his defense and justification for rebelling against his party over the Suez Crisis in 1956, he appealed to and employed the authority of Burke, one who, because he had been effectively and permanently co-opted by no party, could be seen as a figure transcending party allegiance, and in the shadow of whom Nicholson could place himself.[3]

What has been said so far with respect to the status of a figure as an authority is intended to indicate the uncertainty of the status, the difficulty of achieving it, and the ease with which it is eroded into anticipation or emblematic existence. The willingness to exploit an authority in the name of a cause is not enough; the exploiter's art is difficult, and the reluctance of the exploiter to create his own authorities can similarly be attributed to political *nous* rather than an inherent 'conservatism'. To try and elevate a new figure to the status of authority is to admit the failure

[2] A. Cobban, *Edmund Burke and the Revolt Against the Eighteenth Century* (London, 1929), pp. 38 and 9, or consider the remarks of Seymour Drescher, *Tocqueville and Beaumont on Social Reform* (New York, 1968), Introduction, concerning de Tocqueville's status in the nineteenth century. "He left behind no sect . . . to maintain his authority and its own coherence by means of constant reformulation or ritual invocation" (p. x). His fate in the twentieth century is to have become something of an anti-Marxist emblem. Drescher cites, among others, George Probst, *The Happy Republic* (New York, 1962), p. xiii: "To those who ask, 'What is the importance of Tocqueville in modern world politics?' it is enough to reply that he is the answer to Marx." In the light of such comments, Andrew Lang's *Method in the Study of Totemism* (Glasgow, 1911) is additionally suggestive.

[3] Bruce Mazlish, "The Conservative Revolution of Edmund Burke," *RP* 20 (1958): 22–33. It is, however, Mazlish's intention to resolve the dualism and reveal Burke's coherence and originality. See Nigel Nicholson, *People and Parliament* (London, 1958), at length for a number of relevant remarks on Burke.

to co-opt the old, and before the new can function like the old it has to acquire a patina of use and somehow achieve a requisite resonance when touched upon. This appears to have been one of the problems confronting the Levellers; having failed to co-opt the widespread authority of the Ancient Constitution, they attempted to elevate a counter-authoritative image of the Golden Age, which, as the resonant Ancient Constitution remained usable by other groups in seventeenth-century England, established itself only as an isolating emblem. They thus abandoned the Golden Age for direct appeal to the abstract *clefs mots* of English political debate and made direct appeal to disembodied *rights*, *justice*, and *freedom* which they had been unable to house in any authoritative image relevant to English society. The shift into a more modern idiom of discourse was, as it were, a result of ideological defeat, at best, a consequence of strategic withdrawal.[4]

There is a simple but complicating conjunction which above all else makes the successful use of authorities a creative and uncommon skill.[5] On the one hand, over time and across societies, the substantive living issues of politics change. On the other hand, the ideas of those we call the 'classics' of political thought are fixed in the mordant of ink. They are dead and dyed. It is overcoming their fixity in the face of new problems and possibilities that is difficult even for the most willing of authority exploiters. If problems of adaptation cannot be overcome, then authority must dwindle to anticipation, and as fewer groups can

---

[4] I am drawing here freely on Pocock, *The Ancient Constitution and the Feudal Law* (Cambridge, 1957), and "The Origins of the Study of the Past" in *CSSH* 5 (1962–1963). See also M. I. Finley, *The Ancestral Constitution* (Cambridge, 1971). For a more detailed analysis of the logic and strategies of authority citation, see Condren, "Authorities, Emblems, and Sources: Reflections on a Rhetorical Strategy in the History of History" in *P & R* 15 (1982). Alan Bradford's "Stuart Absolutism and the Utility of Tacitus," *Huntingdon Library Quarterly* 40 (1983), offers valuable independent illustration.

[5] For a suggestive awareness of this see e.g. E. Kohak, "T.G. Masaryk's Revision of Marxism," *JHI* 25 (1964): esp. 520–523, and Julius Kovesi, "Marxist Ecclesiology and Biblical Criticism," *JHI* 37 (1976): 93ff., for a subtle exploration of some of the protective strategies shared by Christian and Marxist apologetics.

see its relevance, an authority is contracted to an emblem; the name of the work once tossed upon the seas of political dispute will finally sink into the sediment of the archives:

> We must cope with the paradox that the classic changes, yet retains its identity. It would not be read, and so would not be a classic, if we could not in some way believe it to be capable of saying more than its author meant; even if necessary, that to say more than he meant was what he meant to do. (*The Classic*, p. 80)

Notwithstanding both the loose use of paradox (for change and identity are relative) and the dramatic exaggeration of "would not be read" (for historians live on a diet less ambrosial than a glut of unending classics), Kermode's peroration does point to the problem of transcending fixity in the face of flux which threatens authors with *almost* total oblivion. It is the well-telegraphed hypothesis here that the means of transcendence is to be found not in any edifying catalog of academic and literary virtues, but in the sleazy ambit of the most venerable of academic vices, ambiguity. This is not only, or even mainly, because what may be deemed ambiguous, vague, uncertain, or unclear provides a flux for the mordant of ink, mechanisms for the diverse relationships into which texts can be seen to enter when proffered to posterity; it is also partly because ambiguity in particular and by definition suggests a balance between interpretive options. This, in turn, affords some protection against the totally effective co-option of an authority by a single group, with the consequent diminution of his status to that of an emblem: a change which is both a less sure and less public purchase on immortality.[6] Authorities, like ambiguities, are essentially contestable.[7]

[6] See e.g. Bruce Mansfield, *Phoenix of His Age: Interpretations of Erasmus, 1550–1750* (Toronto, 1979), which would seem to support this hypothesis. Mansfield suggests that it was Erasmus' very ambivalence, his ideological "shiftiness" (p. 300), which is crucial to explaining first the erosion of his name to the status of an emblem of a few isolated figures (to revert to my terminology) and then his rehabilitation among a diversity of those of irenic disposition to something approaching authoritative status.

[7] W. B. Gallie's well-known expression, *Philosophy and the Historical Understanding*, chap. 8. A similar point was made in a context of rhetorical theory by Quintilian, *Institutio Oratia* 7. 9. 14.

Here a qualification is crucial: I am not saying that the classics of political theory are so simply because they are, as it were, pathologically ambiguous, and because a specific locus of ambiguity or a kindred characteristic has proved for any one of them a necessary and sufficient reason for successful and continued exploitation. My understanding of the structure of ambiguity alone would prohibit anything so simple. Rather, I am suggesting that there is a triadic relationship between the willingness to search for, elicit, or even impose ambiguity and the effective exploitation of an authority. The relationships between the notions of authority, exploitation, and ambiguity, in short, may provide us with the means of organizing the single most significant thematic continuity in the historiography of political and social theory. Put another way, the permutations and interrelationships between these terms can provide us with explanatory vocabulary for confronting Blakey's "promiscuous heap" and its transformation into a tradition which has been the subject of so much concern in the twentieth century, and for Kermode's "paradox" of classicism.

The general point here is applicable well beyond the realms of political theory. One can, for example, note the obvious possibility of a strong correlation between the high number of *cruxes* in Shakespeare's plays and his being the most widely discussed and diversely performable of playwrights—a very Janus, Dryden called him. Similarly, one can suggest that a vital clue to the widespread fashionableness of Kuhn's earlier theories lies in the ambiguity of his notion of a paradigm while the attention given to Wittgenstein's private language theory seems generated by a tantalizing aura of obscurity. Or (to draw on two discussions by Stephen Toulmin) Kant's use of *vorstellungen* to refer ambivalently to sense perception and (safely) to the dependence of all knowledge on forms of judgement has given rise to different interpretative schools and has facilitated his assimilation to differing metaphysical traditions. Chomsky's much-discussed nativist thesis of the generation of language, Toulmin similarly suggests, has two forms. In a strong sense (that language is "specific and unitary") the thesis has been vulnerable to attack on biological grounds; but defenders of the thesis can retreat to an altogether more innocuous and widely acceptable version (that language involves a complexity of infinite capability).[8] The structural parallel here between Toulmin's analysis of this potentiality for equivocation and Warnock's discussion of Berkeley's ambiguous notion of 'idea' and his shifts between its two main senses is striking (see Chap. 8. III and n. 5). In these cases, we do seem to have, in short, theories whose controversial public buoyancy is maintained by ambiguities. Naturally, these suggestions cannot substitute for a detailed study of the relevant texts and their histories, but in turning again to political theory, the following may serve as synoptic illustrations of the hypothesis and the general reflections preceding it.

III

To begin with a simple case: in the fourteenth century, St. Augustine was a sufficiently potent authority for political argument to be carried on through his words and in reference to his name. Marsilius, who had an acute awareness of the importance of exploiting ambiguities in the strategy of authority use, found him inescapable, and more than effectively exploited Augustine in his work. Yet turning the saint upon his halo and directly against the established Church was not always easy. At one point where St. Augustine is perfectly clear, and as clearly unacceptable to Marsilius, he is glossed to render him ambiguous, and then Marsilius takes the least likely but preferred possibility as Augustine's essential meaning.[9] Thus Augustine, who had been writing against the heresy of the Manichees in the name of the Church and its

---

[8] Stephen Toulmin, *Human Understanding* (Oxford, 1972), vol. 1, pp. 193ff. for the discussion of Kant; and Rorty, *Philosophy and the Mirror of Nature* (Princeton, 1979), pp. 148ff. and 161, for comments of Kant's differently read authority; and Toulmin, ibid., pp. 448–477, on Chomsky.

[9] *Defensor Pacis* II. xix. 8. See also Condren, "Rhetoric, Historiography and Political Theory: Aspects of the Poverty Controversy Reconsidered," *Journal of Religious History*, forthcoming, for the ambiguities of Bonaventura's *Apologia Pauperam* and their conflicting exploitation by Pope John XXII and Marsilius, in the context of authority use during the poverty controversy.

authority over Christians, is made to deny that Church's authority over his own belief. Where authorities are inescapable or at least desirable, an inherent ambiguity is itself desirable, but can be provided by skillful hands. The establishment and the exploitation of an authority, however, are much easier where less ingenuity is involved.

I have discussed Marsilius' elliptical amphiboly of the *legislator humanus* in terms of its structure and putative generation, but it is instructive also to look at its fate. The work itself became notorious, and the two hundred and fifty heresies which Clement VI detected in it, as well as the replies that were hurriedly and officially penned against it, did not stop its dissemination or its translation into both French and Italian by the end of the fourteenth century. The precise use to which Marsilius was put is obscure, but in the conciliar crisis of the fifteenth century this is no longer the case. As Paul Sigmund has argued, Marsilius' arguments are much in evidence in the writings of Nicholas of Cusa and Dietrich of Niems.[10] Indeed, Marsilius must have been appealing to men who wished to make the Pope accountable to a larger body within the Church. Nicholas in particular thus exploited the aristocratic possibilities of the *legislator humanus (fidelis)*, reading for the community the Church as a whole, and for the weightier part of the *legislator*, the College of Cardinals. Thus far he provides us with a relatively straightforward example of the exploitation of an ambiguity, except that Marsilius was no authority within the Church—rather, he was an emblem *renversée* whose name could be used as a token of opprobrium by any group within the Church.[11]

Nicholas, therefore, I suggest, capitalized on Marsilius' own extensive use of Aristotle as an inescapable authority and upon the explicit suggestion that the *legislator* could be determined according to the counsel of Aristotle, simply by citing Marsilius and calling him Aristotle. Sigmund believes that Cusa misinterpreted the *legislator* (which is really a democratic concept) and

[10] Paul Sigmund, "The Influence of Marsilius of Padua in Fifteenth Century Conciliarism," *JHI* 23 (1962): 392ff.

[11] Thus, as Gewirth points out, Luther was accused of being a Marsilian. Gewirth, *Marsilius of Padua* (New York, 1964 ed.), p. 303n.

believes that Cusa, in mistaking the Stagirite for the Paduan, was not quite as careful a scholar as his reputation suggests.[12] In other contexts this last point might be so, but in the use of Marsilius something more subtle and more attuned to the logic of authority usage is, I suspect, going on, which will be apt to escape us if we trade in canons of appraisal appropriate to modern scholarship. Nicholas, in short, was not 'influenced' by Marsilius, nor did he fail to understand a democratic concept, or mistake Marsilius for Aristotle; he exploited an ambiguity in the name of reform and did so under the authority of another name. In doing so he treated the Paduan in the spirit of his own writing.

It was, then, in part, ambiguity that facilitated exploitation just as it was a lack of plausible ambiguity in the right places that necessitated William Marshall's omissions when he translated the *Defensor* in 1535. Marshall was one of the scholarly humanists who were gathered around Thomas Cromwell and used to defend the Henrician reformation.[13] Cromwell commissioned the translation from the Latin, and twenty-four copies of *The Defence of Peace* were suitably distributed.[14] Marshall, unable to gloss significant portions of *Dictio* 1 in a way which would not have been offensive to the king, left them out.[15] The definition of the *legislator*, however, is left intact, and it receives a marginal gloss which ties it effectively to English circumstances. Marshall comments: "In all this longe tale he writes not of the rascall multitude, but of the Parliament." As it stands it is, of course, a reading which fits as well as any other: a group of men, repre-

---

[12] On Cusa's alleged misunderstanding of the democratic concept see also Sigmund's *Nicholas of Cusa and Medieval Political Thought* (Cambridge, Mass., 1963), pp. 153–154 and 191; on which see Condren, "Democracy and the *Defensor*: On the English Language Tradition of Interpretation," *IPP* 13 (1980): 313.

[13] See J. K. McConica, *English Humanists and Reformation Politics* (Oxford, 1968 ed.), pp. 136ff.; H. S. Stout, "Marsilius of Padua and the Henrician Reformation," *Church History* 43 (1974): 308ff.

[14] McConica, ibid.; A. P. d'Entrèves, "La Fortuna de Marsilio da Padova in Inghilterra," *Giornale degli economisti è annali de economia* 2 (1940): 141–142. G. Piaia, *Marsilio da Padova nella Riforma e nella controriforma* (Padua, 1977), pp. 143–164, for the most detailed discussion.

[15] Piaia, ibid., Gewirth, *Marsilius*, 1:195n., both following Previté-Orton's edition of the *Defensor* (Cambridge, 1927).

senting the community over which the laws are made effectively, stands for the rest of the people and, in such a position, is legitimized through the appeal to custom.[16]

Again we see that the appeal of Marsilius is in the practical range of argument he can organize against the Papacy; again the flexibility of the concept of the *legislator* facilitates its wholesale use. In a society, however, which is in process of breaking with Rome, there is no need to be coy about the anathema of his name: Marsilius can come into his own. But he was not to become a mere emblem. Marshall's resorting to extensive censorship (in a work which was fully available in Latin) indicates the exploitation of a figure operating at the limits of plausibility. Thus for anyone who objected to the aspiring absolutism of Henry (to which the omitted sections of the *Defensor* were an affront), Marsilius was also co-optable. Starkey made judicious use of him, taking the *legislator* to refer potentially to England, but taking seriously the *legislator's* controls over the *pars principans* as guidelines for the proper relationship between Parliament and the king.[17]

John Ponet also may have drawn on Marsilius when confronted with the unpalatable combination of a monarch who was also a Catholic, and Hudson has argued that it is likely that in fact Ponet's *A Shorte Treatise of Politicke Power* drew on Marsilius with respect to the locus of authority. The severe limitations on the authority of the monarch are clear, but there is no con-

---

[16] *The Defence of Peace*, p. 28a.; the clause referring to the quality and quantity of citizens was not in the *Editio Princeps* used by Marshall, but his case is arguable without it. Indeed, still working on the basis of corrupt texts, Maxwell, writing well after Marshall, correctly translated *valentior* as "greater and better," as modern scholars failed to do until after the Previté-Orton edition (Cambridge, 1928). See *Sacro-Sancta Regnum Majestas* (Oxford, 1644), pp. 14–15.

[17] It is perhaps an exaggeration to say that we can see the lines of English seventeenth-century political dispute being drawn up through the attempts to use Marsilius, though Van Baumer has gone further, arguing in effect that the reason why Starkey received so little attention in his own century was because he was ahead of his times and this because he used the fourteenth-century Paduan (extraordinary chronology). "Thomas Starkey and Marsilius of Padua," *Politica* 2 (1936): 186ff. On Starkey's use of Marsilius see also Piaia, *Marsilio da Padova nella Riforma*, pp. 167ff.

clusive evidence.[18] Be this as it may, the Marsilian flavor of portions of Ponet,[19] plus the Paduan's diverse employment by Marshall and Starkey and others, indicates his adaptability even within sixteenth-century England. Certainly, he never reached the authoritative heights of an Aristotle or a Plato; he was never as much reprinted or translated as Machiavelli, perhaps in part because, as Starkey aptly said, Marsilius was of "grete iugement," "in style rude."[20] Even so, he was used by Burghley, and possibly Hooker.[21] Skinner refers to his "long-term influence";[22] d'Entrèves and Gewirth both suspect that such an 'influence' was upon Hobbes;[23] and there is no doubt that he was used by George Lawson, whom, it seems, John Locke had the wit to co-opt.[24] An emblem *renversée* for patriarchalists such as Owen and Maxwell, Lawson appropriately thought highly of Marsilius.[25] More

[18] W. S. Hudson, *John Ponet: Advocate of Limited Monarchy* (Chicago, 1942), pp. 167–168.

[19] *A Shorte Treatise* (facsimile of 1556 ed., pp. 105–110 in Hudson). This is the only possibility of which I know not discussed by Piaia.

[20] Thomas Starkey, *Life and Letters*, cited in R. Eccleshall, *Order and Reason in Politics* (Oxford, 1978), p. 43. Marshall's translation is prefaced by a similar remark.

[21] On Burghley, B. W. Beckinsale, *Burghley: Tudor Statesman* (London, 1967), p. 211; on Hooker, P. Munz, *The Place of Hooker in the History of Thought* (London, 1952); Piaia, *Marsilio da Padova nella Riforma*, for some sound skepticism, pp. 207ff.; Hudson, *John Ponet*, and Piaia, ibid., p. 168, cite Cranmer also as a promoter of the *Defensor*.

[22] Q. Skinner, *The Foundations of Modern Political Thought* (Cambridge, 1979), 1: 65 and 2:37 and 101.

[23] D'Entrèves, "La Fortuna," p. 152; Gewirth, *Marsilius*, 1:310.

[24] *Politica Sacra et Civilis* (London, 1660 and 1689). I have discussed the use of Marsilius in "Lawson and Resistance," *HJ* 24 (1981), and more extensively in "George Lawson and the *Defensor Pacis*: Reflections on the Use of Marsilius in Seventeenth Century England," *Medioevo* 6 (1980): 595-618. But see also Lawson's unpublished *Amica dissertatio* (manuscript in an unknown hand), *Baxter Treatises*, 1ff. 99–150b, item 9. I believe Lawson owned a Frankfort, 1592 edition of the *Defensor*. For illuminating comments on Baxter and Lawson, see William Lamont, *Richard Baxter and the Millennium* (London, 1979); for Lawson and Locke, A. H. Maclean, "George Lawson and John Locke," *Cambridge Historical Journal* (1947).

[25] David Owen, *Herod and Pilate Reconciled* (London, 1610); John Maxwell, *Sacro-Sancta*. The pattern of emblematic usage is discussed in more detail in Condren, "George Lawson and the *Defensor*."

than this, Lawson, who cites him twice,[26] appears to have structured his argument concerning the locus of authority and the distribution of power in churches and in states around Marsilius' distinction between *legislator humanus* and *pars principans*. In effect, Marsilian categories are cashed into terms (with certain modifications of emphasis) directly relevant to English post-Interregnum circumstances, the *legislator* becoming the (English) people, a residual authority beyond the claims of kings, Parliaments, or established Churches, to whom (or its *sanior parte* or *weightier part*)[27] such established powers were all in some way answerable. Thus: "Marsilius in his *Defensor Pacis* determines the power of Legislation to be *in Populo, aut valentiorem partem*, or their Trustees."[28]

These scraps of usage or putative employment do not constitute a great deal, but there is certainly enough to indicate a general pattern which fleshes out the bones of this chapter's initial hypothesis. The context of argument in which Marsilius was used was one of politico-religious dispute, and it is the ambiguity of the *legislator* which facilitates his effective employment and enables a sense of association between the words of a dead Paduan and the problems of those who came after him: it allows both *"l'oeuvre propose"* and *"l'homme dispose"* within the conventional bounds of persuasive possibility.

When interest in Marsilius intensified in the late nineteenth century and continued into the twentieth, a continuity with this earlier period of interpretation remains apparent. What I have elsewhere called the authoritative-anticipatory tradition of Marsilian study remains the dominant one.[29] Marsilius is no longer seen as an authority who speaks directly and clearly to us of our

---

[26] *Politica* (1689 ed.), pp. 219 and 340.

[27] Ibid., p. 383; cf. *Defensor* I. 12.

[28] Lawson, *Politica*, p. 340.

[29] "Marsilius of Padua's Argument from Authority: A Survey of Its Significance in the *Defensor Pacis*," *Pol. Th.* 5 (1977): 206–207. The democratic simplification of Marsilius seems to begin with the French Revolution. In a paper as revealing of modern commitments and expectations as it is of eighteenth-century ones, Gregorio Piaia points to Melchiorre Cesarotti, *Lettera d'un Padovano* (Padua, 1796), as providing "the beginning of the rehabilitation of Marsilius" and what

problems, as he was for Marshall, Starkey, and Lawson, but in a weaker sense he can still be held to 'anticipate,' 'herald,' or 'prophesy' our problems and institutional arrangements: he has become part of a pedigree. As Gewirth and Luciano Russi have amply shown, the range of his alleged anticipations is now striking,[30] and many of them hinge upon the interpreter's ability to see in the *legislator* a family resemblance to his own society, interests, commitments, and political vocabulary. The distinction between the *legislator* and the *pars principans* among other functional classes of society suggests an 'anticipation' of Montesquieu and (as well it might) of Locke. An 'anticipation' of 'the division of powers' doctrine suggests, in turn, a prefiguration of the American Constitution. Similarly, it was an understanding of the *legislator* as an organized and conceptually unified part of the people, acting independently yet being the same thing as a numerically larger community, that facilitated Marsilius' becoming perhaps the first political thinker to be called a totalitarian, in the initial laudatory sense of the term.[31] It remains possible to call Marsilius a totalitarian in another sense, though it is fair to say that the overwhelming consensus is that Marsilius was, or was at heart, a democrat—once more good marks or good marks for trying.[32] Cusa—I gather authorities while I may—Marshall, Starkey, and Lawson knew better—possibly because they were closer in spirit to the conventions of argument that ruled Marsilius' own writing and which explicitly invited the diverse exploitation of his most ingenious polemical device. And because he was so exploited, he remained to be rediscovered and reinter-

---

he concludes by calling "the liberal–democratic doctrine of the *Defensor.*" See *"Il Padre Zaccaria, L'Abate Cesarotti e 'actualità' di Marsilio nel Secolo dei Lumi," Medioevo* 6 (1980): 632 and 637.

[30] Gewirth, *Marsilius* 1:3ff.; L. Russi, "Letture e valutazioni di Marsilio da Padova," *Trimestri* 13–14 (1980–1981): 3ff.

[31] F. Bataglia, "Marsilio de Padova è Il Defensor Pacis," *Revista internazionale di filosofia del diritto* 4 (1924): 411.

[32] For details, see Condren, "Marsilius of Padua's Argument from Authority," pp. 215–216; and Gregorio Piaia, "Democrazia o totalitarismo in Marsilio da Padova" *Medioevo* 2 (1975): 363ff., for a discussion of recent Italian and Spanish literature all drawn up in terms of what he calls this crucial theme of Marsilian criticism and its (two) opposing solutions.

preted as an intellectually and historically significant figure in the more academic context of a 'democratic' age. Exploitation placed him in the heap; continued flexibility rooted in ambiguity has transformed him into a member of a lineage. Through exploitation comes immortality.

—————————— IV ——————————

In considering Plato briefly, over approximately the same period of time it is possible to detect a pattern of usage and reference which can be encompassed within the same conceptual framework, though there are manifest differences between the reputation and treatment of Plato and Marsilius. Throughout the whole Middle Ages, Plato's name was one to be conjured with, even if his works were largely unavailable and clustered with accretions of forgery. Klibansky detects three main traditions of use and reference, the Arabic, Byzantine, and the Latin, in which Plato could be most things to most men.[33] His name was associated with magic, astrology, and prophecy, but, above all, in Western Christian society, if there was a dominating attitude, it was that suggested by St. Augustine—namely, that of all the pagan philosophers, Plato was the most congenial, even that he was a *figura* of Christian wisdom.[34]

Now because a handful of fragments and interpretive rumors float more accommodatingly on the seas of time than the whole weight of a documented mind, we might expect there to be something of a shock and a discontinuity when Plato's works became available in their complete forms during the Renaissance. One might expect Plato's image to suffer badly, when men both predisposed to employ Plato and familiar with a received body of Platonic meanings needs must confront the Athenian's own words. Klibansky detects no such sense of shock

[33] R. Klibansky, *The Continuity of the Platonic Tradition During the Middle Ages: Outlines of a Corpus Platonicum Medii Aevi* (London, 1939), pp. 15ff.
[34] Ibid., p. 32.

or discontinuity—indeed, if anything, the authority and kudos attached to Plato's mind increased; despite the baggage of his reputation he was adaptable to sixteenth- and seventeenth-century concerns.[35] One can at least get a clue as to why this was so by referring to the *Simile of Light* in *The Republic*; one of the first of Plato's works to become available, and remaining one of the most authoritative, it has since the fifteenth century enjoyed unbroken interpretive attention. The imagery that is both characteristic of the simile, and an intrinsic part of its ambiguity, was also particularly amenable to Christian translation. As has been suggested (see Chap. 7, p. 204) the imagery was monadic; that is, it functioned both cross-culturally and habitually in a religious context of belief.[36] Via neo-Platonism, Plato's Good became associated with a concept of God, the forms were then translated as spiritual beings and then angels.[37] These conceptual translations are reinforced precisely by the images which Plato shared with the Hebrews and the Christians: Malachi (4:2) speaks of Sun of righteousness; John (1:5) speaks of God as Light. Christ ascended into Heaven, Hell is placed below in the dark and associated with fire, and echoing Platonic imagery, Augustine could write "God is the intellectual light who climbs like a sun in the soul."[38]

It was easy, then, for writers such as Ficino, Valla, Colet, More, and Erasmus to use Plato, each in his different way, to draw on and reinforce the Athenian's authority in the name of political and religious reform, thereby modifying the age-old religious distinction between the ages of light and dark. As Charles Trinkhaus remarks, because of their criticism of Greek society, Ficino placed Socrates and Plato "almost on the same level as

---

[35] See e.g. L. Miles, *John Colet and the Platonic Tradition* (London, 1962); F. J. Powicke, *The Cambridge Platonists* (London, 1926).

[36] Northrop Frye, *The Anatomy of Criticism* (Princeton, 1973 ed.), pp. 71ff.; the expression "monadic" is Frye's. C. S. Lewis, *The Allegory of Love* (New York, 1964 ed.), chap. 2.

[37] H. A. Wolfson, "Extradeical and Intradeical Interpretations of Platonic Ideas," 22 (1961), at length.

[38] Cited in Miles, *John Colet*, pp. 97–98.

St. Paul."[39] In his *Prohemium* to the *Theologica Platonica*, Ficino claimed generally that there was nothing considered by Plato that did not lead directly and piously to the contemplation of God[40] and, in particular, that it was through the theory of forms that Plato knew divine truth and made it available to the Greeks before Christ[41]—hence the flame that Ficino kept burning before an image of Plato.[42]

Lorenzo Valla, more famous for the literalist philological acumen he directed against the use of an authoritative past in the present, nevertheless resorted to a Christian allegorical interpretation of Plato's *Simile of Light*. Ironically, it was used to stress the vain labor of trying to clarify the enigmas and allegories of Christian truth, which shine like the rays of the Sun into which we are unable to look, not because it is obscure as in other things but because it is too bright.[43] This, states Trinkhaus, "is the same transformation of Plato's metaphor . . . which Calvin later used to express the weakness of the human mind in perceiving celestial things."[44]

For Colet, Christ was the Sun, and the Light, in the simile, became Grace from God. Plato himself became an authority used to attack paganism.[45] For Erasmus, Socrates was a saint;[46] for Sidney, Plato, the most poetic of philosophers, was the patron of true poets who mediated Christian truth.[47] Later still, the

[39] Charles Trinkhaus, *In Our Image and Likeness* (London, 1970), 2:745.

[40] Ibid., citing *Theol. Proh.*, 1:35–36, quoted n. 6, p. 778.

[41] Ibid., p. 746. The parallel with the authority of the Old Testament prophets is made explicit. Referring to *Republic VII*, Finico writes: "God manifested Himself through a common knowledge of divine things, just as he revealed Himself to the Jews through the Prophets so he made Himself manifest to the Gentiles through the Philosophers" (Trinkhaus, ibid., the Latin at n. 75, p. 882).

[42] Miles, *John Colet*, pp. 8–9.

[43] Cited in Trinkhaus, *In Our Image*, 1:144 and n. 97, p. 378: *Quod cernitur in radiis solis, in quos intueri nequimus, non quia obscurus ut in ceteris rebus sit, sed quod nimium clarus est.*

[44] Ibid., p. 143.

[45] Miles, *John Colet*, pp. 101 and 27.

[46] Erasmus, *Convivium Religiosum*, *Opera* 1. 683, cited in H. Spiegelburg and Q. B. Morgan, *The Socratic Enigma* (Indianapolis, 1964).

[47] Sidney, *Apologie for Poesie*, on which see R. Howell, *Sir Phillip Sidney*,

turgidly learned Theophilus Gale almost dissolved the distinction between the ages of light and dark through reference to Plato. As one who believed that Old and New Testaments were literally true, and for whom Plato was also a potent authority, Gale set out to show that there was no discrepancy between Plato and Christian truth because Plato had read and understood the Bible.[48] Here there is an echo of Cusa's masking strategy which cited Marsilius under the authority of Aristotle. In such close ranking of received authorities, the allegory of the Cave must have been an uncommon blessing, but its general amenability to Christian reading and allegorical unraveling now needs little stressing. Leaving aside the epistemological reading of Valla and Calvin, the allegory was amenable to a message of an almost Bunyanesque simplicity: the prisoner is a sinner freed by grace who journeys to see the Light and is initiated into momentous knowledge. He returns to his fellows, to save, and perhaps to die a martyr's death. Some modern scholars have themselves been taken by the structural similarity between Plato's Cave image and his more literal treatments of the mission and execution of Socrates, particularly in the *Apology* and the *Phaedo*, and, deeming the form an aretalogy, have suggested that it may have been Mark and Luke who modeled their accounts of the crucifixion upon a knowledge of Plato.[49] Gale upon his head.

Again we may say, generally, that the context of usage was one of practical polemical argument, where the effective use of an authoritative name was itself a tactical victory, and required a sort of counteroffensive to regain possession; and thus Hobbes had seen Plato as among the least objectionable of ancient philosophers, and was in his turn attacked by Cudworth through the Athenian.[50]

The Shepherd Knight (London, 1968), pt. 2, esp. p. 176; and Lily B. Campbell, *Shakespeare's Histories: Mirrors of Elizabethan Policy* (London, 1964 ed.), pp. 94ff.

[48] *The Court of the Gentiles*, on which see Powicke, *The Cambridge Platonists*, pp. 28–29; Clement of Alexandria and Pico della Mirandola also believed in a Platonic connection with the Old Testament. See Craven, *Pico Della Mirandola: Symbol of His Age* (Geneva, 1981), p. 107.

[49] H. C. Kee, *Jesus in History* (New York, 1970), p. 121.

[50] Powicke, *The Cambridge Platonists*, p. 125.

In the twentieth century, it would be a gross distortion to suggest that an authoritative-anticipatory tradition of interpretation dominates Platonic scholarship as it has Marsilian scholarship. Even so, the most popular and most printed books on Plato are in this ideological mode—Popper's *Open Society,* Crossman's *Plato To-day.* Moreover, as Plato has always been so philosophically suggestive, he has been seen as anticipating various twentieth-century interests and developments in philosophy, and reference to him, in the name of interpretation, has proved a way of exploring them further.[51] Finally, we may say that just as the *legislator* and its character is arguably *the* central problem in Marsilian scholarship, so, too, there remains probably no more vexed and controversial topic in Platonic studies than the *Simile of Light.*[52]

We may hazard, then, that when Blakey found his promiscuous heap of great political writers, he had found an oft-exploited cluster of political authorities and emblems of significant causes, and that their promiscuity lay in his looking for the wrong sort of connection (Chap. 3. II). Certainly, when the tradition

---

[51] R. C. Cross, "Logos and Forms in Plato," in R. E. Allen, ed., *Essays in Plato's Metaphysics* (London, 1965), and D. Wiggins, "Sentence, Meaning, Negation and Plato's Problem of Non-Being," in G. Vlastos, ed., *Plato: A Collection of Critical Essays* (London, 1972), 2:268ff., provide good and convenient examples. Plato, however, is not exceptionable.

[52] I am deliberately echoing a commonplace which prefaces many of the essays on the problem. It provides, moreover, the only issue in Cross and Woozley's study which gives rise to dissent between the two authors; Plato's *Republic,* A *Philosophical Commentary* (London, 1964), chap. 9. In an enthusiastic piece of paradigm grabbing, Sheldon Wolin, "Paradigms and Political Theories," in P. King and B. Parekh, eds., *Politics and Experience* (Cambridge, 1968), has argued that the "great" political theorists provided a series of paradigms in terms of which their lesser followers worked, a pattern which he holds to be directly analogous to the "paradigms" he believes to be at work in science. This view may seem to have a family resemblance with my own position. Its plausibility, however, resides only in the misconstrued fact that thinkers we call 'great' for some reasons have habitually provided centers of co-optive expansion. But as should be clear from the nature of my argument as a whole, that any historiography of political theory which holds that there is a tradition of thinkers, great by virtue of their displaying intellectual qualities at one with our appraisive criteria, must be closer to the fanciful historiographies of Blakey, Sabine, and Hacker than to my own position, even if a linear incremental 'progress' is replaced by a Kuhnian framework.

was made of the heap of writers, links were formed between those figures who have been most used and effectively exploited, have been most capable of having ambiguities foisted upon them or elicited from them, and *ipso facto* of being manipulated into a plausible show of a tradition. It is these figures which form the backbone of the ancestral dimension of an academic *oikos*—whose classicism lies perhaps less in any undisputed authority than in the diversity of claims scholars can now make about them, or in the context of their still having some authority. They are, in short, part lineage, part academic residue of past dispute from which political theorists extract new life and through which they can project their own identity with the aid of rhetorical devices (see Chap. 3, p. 73) analogous to the strategies of exploitation that authority status required. And it seems more than likely that there is a high correlation between centers of academic expansion and centers of ambiguity, whether or not the centers of ambiguity are coextensive with the specific ambiguities that have enabled the uncertain balance of authoritative status to be maintained.

I have suggested that the criteria of judgment that operate and have operated in the context of political and religious dispute have been by no means coextensive with those operating in academic life, but that the political theory community exhibits in a modified form the standards of ideological discourse found before and beyond it. It is precisely this that is manifested in the authoritative-anticipatory tradition of Marsilian scholarship, in *The Open Society*, and *Plato To-Day*.

It is important to note, however, that the ideological disposition is often marked by the search for 'contributions' modified by what I have broadly labeled historical and philosophical reasoning. 'History,' or more properly, the widely disseminated legacy of orthodox historicism, has placed a barrier against thinking that a Marsilius can speak directly to us of our problems, and it is thus that authorities are diluted (respectably) to the status of anticipators of recognizably different things which we either like or abominate. The 'contributions' of the masters of political thought are safest seen in terms of questions rather than answers.[53] The emergence of an attitude to the past as a whole which deprecates its use simply in and for the benefit of a political, religious, or moral present and which stresses complexity and discontinuity between past and present, which has as its ideal the understanding of a discrete past, has been disruptive. It is associated largely with the nineteenth century, with the great increase in available archival materials, as well as the increasing professionalism and academic orientation of the study of the past.[54] But such professionalism and such a cornucopia of materials do not explain any change of attitude on their own, any more than myths of exiled Greek professors carrying antique scrolls to Italy explain the Renaissance in their day.

V

By way of an epilogue, which puts the present chapter in some sort of context and which also takes us back to the discursive character of political theory, I shall suggest that a clue to the 'emergence of history,' that is, the historicist orthodoxy, lies, somewhat like the key to understanding the tradition of political theory, in the problems of exploiting authority. A self-conscious alternative to the ideological use of the past, and also to its positivistic reaction, lies in the fate of ideological theses about the past. Such a suggestion must draw much of its force from John Pocock's analyses of the breakdown of "past-relationships,"[55] al-

[53] Schochet, "Quentin Skinner's Method"; even Segall, *Der Defensor Pacis des Marsilius von Padua* (Wiesbaden, 1959), who has no time for the vocabulary of anticipation. Kermode, *The Classic*, p. 114, makes a similar point in distinguishing old from new conceptions of classicism; and Soheil Afnan, *Avicenna: His Life and Works* (London, 1958), p. 290.

[54] George Nadel, "The Philosophy of History Before Historicism," in G. Nadel, ed., *Studies in the Philosophy of History* (New York, 1965), p. 73, and G. Gomme, *Folklore as an Historical Science* (London, 1908), for the extra-archival dimension of this phenomenon.

[55] See esp. Pocock, "The Origins of the Study of the Past." If I were attempting a fuller treatment of historicism, however, much greater stress would have to be placed upon its relationship to positivism, on the one hand, and the more aes-

though historians have been obliged to see the genesis of their own activity as a matter of advance—a commitment which raises a peculiar form of logical problem.[56] This itself, however, is not to side with those who would wish to see the past uniformly pressed into the service of the present, and who thus have an interest in denying that the study of the past can be any different from what it normally has been—who would, that is, eliminate the conventional distance between historical writing and ideology. For there is a great difference between the difficulty of shedding an ideological perspective and the methodological ideal of doing so.

In the principal claims of what may be called historicism (expanded into the dominating conventions of twentieth-century Western professional historians), we do have something different from the practical exploitation of the past in the name of a present cause. Although obviously we do not have anything hostile to the study of the past, or any of its texts, we do have something quite inimical to even diluted authority exploitation and to accepting at face value the amaranthine aura of classicism. We have also a difference between such historicist claims and those

---

thetic historiography of writers such as Burckhardt, on the other. On the antagonisms between positivism and historicism, see e.g. L. Rubinoff, Introduction to F. H. Bradley, *The Presuppositions of Critical History* (Chicago, 1968). But in some fields, by a process of analogical flow, science and historicism could at least seem to be assimilated. See D. R. Oldroyd, "The Rise of Historical Geology," *History of Science* 17 (1979): 191–213 and 227–257. By and large, historicism has been more successful in theory than in practice in delineating itself from positivism (because in practice positivism is apt to collapse into historicism). At the same time, historicism has yet to disentangle itself from the Nietzschean and Burckhardtian tradition of aesthetic history, and into the literary use of the past. On this area, see Hayden White, *Metahistory* (Baltimore, 1973); and also the pertinent remarks of Stephen Bann, "Towards a Critical Historiography," *Philosophy* 56 (1981). These entangled relationships help explain the difficulty of sorting out literary from historicist expectations in reading a text and help explain some of the differences, in particular, between e.g. Gadamer and Hirsch, Pocock, and Gunnell (see Appendix).

[56] Thus e.g. Pocock, who sees the end of normative backward-glancing history as an advance; review article in *Hist. & Th.* 13 (1974): 89–97. On the logic of this oddity, see Condren, "An Historiographical Paradox," in F. McGregor and N. Wright, eds., *European History and Its Historians* (Adelaide, 1977), pp. 89ff.

of the positivist who seeks, in the past, universal laws and strictly causative connections, by the discovery of which (perhaps) he hopes, like Comte, to provide a foundation for the moral guidance of society. In terms of what they believe should characterize and legitimize their studies, there is, in short, a world of difference between, for example, a Stubbs and a Holt, a Freeman and a Brooke, or between a Buckle and a Droyson, or even a Bloch.[57]

Conversely the 'rise' of historicism is dubiously portrayed in terms that both the traditional ideologue and the positivist understand all too well—the loaded vocabulary of progress with its attendant rhetoric of freeing genuine history from the shackles of the past, with the achievement of methodological autonomy, even with marches along the highway of history,[58] all of which (signposted with erstwhile authorities) provide direct analogues of the hallowed sagas of political progress which the historicist shuns. One only has to compare *The Whig Interpretation of History* with *Man on His Past* to get the full flavor of the oddity of a historicist history of history.

Now, if what I have said is true, that is, that the dominant way of looking at the past as a whole and its authoritative figures in particular has been largely a matter of exploitation guided by the political, moral, and religious needs of the present, then so far we have been dealing with a microcosm of something altogether more significant than the lineage of ex-authorities which political theory will not let rest in peace. If exploitation is a fact of life, overexploitation, as Marshall's censorship intimates, is

---

[57] J. C. Holt's comments on Stubbs in *Magna Carta* (Cambridge, 1976 ed.), pp. 175–177, and at greater length his attitude to the Whig legacy of interpretation, chap. 1. C. Brooke on Freeman, in *The Saxon and Norman Kings* (London, 1960), pp. 22–23, J. G. Droyson, *Art and Method*, contrasted with H. T. Buckle, *History of Civilisation* (1856–1861), on both of whom see F. Stern, *The Varieties of History* (New York, 1956), pp. 120–144. Marc Bloch is mentioned here because, among twentieth-century historians, he was not unsympathetic to positivism. In *Le métier d'historien* (Paris, 1948) he argues that the historian's purpose is to maintain for history *"au nom scientifique"* minus the extremes of *"positivisme mal compris."*

[58] The imagery is common; see "An Historiographical Paradox," pp. 88 and 93n., and Ch. Perelman, *The New Rhetoric and the Humanities* (Dordrecht, 1979), pp. 57–58.

always a danger. Once an authority does not mean always an authority, and it is precisely when the past in large segments (like the single authority) is overexploited in the name of a cause that both its relevance and the cause's viability are threatened. Pocock's structure of overexploitation bears repeating: people search the past for the guidance they need, and the more they reveal of it, the more likely it is to exacerbate their problems in the present. As the authorities of the past are tied more clearly to their own times, and those times become more fully documented in the name of the present, so those times can well become more alien. The Bartolan ideal of recapturing Roman Law for application in the present gives way to the Valla's methodological rejection of its authority.[59] Here, apart from a continued faith in the threatened past, à la Machiavelli, two main defensive possibilities arise. One is to abandon a historical idiom of contemporary social reflection, and to bypass its manifest inconveniences as Locke, the Levellers, and the American Colonists on the eve of the Revolution did, all by resorting to more abstract terms. If one cannot talk about the traditional rights of Englishmen because the notion of an Ancient Constitution in which those rights were sacredly housed has been exploded, or effectively co-opted by antagonistic groups, then one can still talk about the rights of man per se. This possibility leads directly and immediately to the sort of abstract mode of ideological discourse with which we have become particularly familiar at least since the American and French revolutions. Moreover, because there is a considerable overlap in terminology it may lead to varying degrees of independent philosophical speculation. The second possibility is to accept the difficulties of using the past as any substantial source of practical guidance and to study it regardless. Past or present, one of them is apt to give.

Both possibilities have led to, or rather been rationalized through, different strategic methodological reflexes which have hardened into complex intellectual positions. The first possibility which has had a long, if intermittent, history can be associated

[59] Quentin Skinner, *Foundations*, 1:104–105, who quite properly characterized this matter in terms of methodology.

with a similarly long-standing methodological reflex to the effect that the past is irrelevant to what is really right and wrong, and reference to it provides at best illustration or an inferior means of practical guidance. It is to be found, naturally enough, when an authoritative past is proving difficult to manipulate. In particular, it is to be found in Coluccio Salutati's dismissal of John of Salisbury's authority-dependent arguments on tyrannicide. John proved only that tyrannicide had frequently happened, argued Salutati, not that it was justifiable.[60] It is to be found, albeit fleetingly, in Marsilius when for once even he finds an authoritative voice from the past difficult to manipulate, and he reminds the reader that there is a difference between the fact that a thing has been done or said, to which an authority can attest, and the question of whether something is right, wrong, or useful.[61] It is to be found in Sidney's *Apologie For Poesie* where he seeks to undermine the claims of the "historians" to some intellectual authority in and for the present.[62] Similarly, it is to be found in Hobbes, among many others, as Skinner has brilliantly shown, who attacked the use of authorities per se, and who distrusted in particular the lessons drawn from ancient republican history.[63] In Hume something strikingly similar to these methodological reflexes is transformed into a genuinely philosophical challenge to the religious ideologies which he abhorred, by the insistence on the difficulty of establishing logical principles of connection between facts and matters of moral sentiment.[64] Thus he sug-

[60] *De Tyranno* 2.

[61] *Defensor* 11. xix. 8.

[62] Sidney, *Apologie*, p. 12, referring to authorities based upon authorities based ultimately upon hearsay.

[63] Quentin Skinner, "History and Ideology in the English Revolution," *H.J.* 8 (1965):151ff.

[64] A *Treatise on Human Nature*, 3. 1. 1. On his attitude to his own native Church see Letwin. See also D. Forbes, *Hume's Philosophical Politics*, pp. 61ff., for the function of religion in his politics. The recent history of Althussarian Marxism may provide a further variation on this methodological reflex: see the concluding comments of M. Sawer, *Marxism and the Question of the Asiatic Mode of Production* (The Hague, 1977); and Kovesi, "Marxist Ecclesiology," pp. 104–105.

gested a passage through the methodological nexus into realms of persistent philosophical interest.

When George Nadel surveyed the philosophy of history before nineteenth-century historicism, he could find no opposition to the affirmations of the practical ideological value of the study of the past, and concluded that the almost statutory justifications of the value of studying the past were largely empty rhetoric. I suspect that he was looking in the wrong direction for attacks on ideological exemplum 'history,' namely, to other delvers into past events; in so doing he was looking for anticipatory evidence of the very phenomenon he associated only with the nineteenth century.[65] Rather, it may be that the constant and repetitive justifications for the practical use of the past before the nineteenth century should be read as a response to those who would deny the past any authority, rather than in the context of those who would write about it according to post-Göttingen conventions of historical discourse.

The second methodological reflex is to be found more fleetingly, though it is clear enough, in Guicciardini. Recognizing the difficulty of using the past as an authoritative guide for the present, it stops well short of turning away from the past and investing an authoritative status on some other mode of thought or field of human endeavor; the difficulties become challenges, the irrelevances become the goals of study. It is, writes Guicciardini, perceiving the often minute differences between and within the past that takes "the keen and perspicacious eye."[66] The slightest change in, or discrepancy between, situations may give rise to great differences.[67] The difficulties in using the past, in simply applying it to the present, and in citing the Romans at every turn[68] are on the verge of being rationalized as the neces-

---

[65] Nadel, "The Philosophy of History," p. 73.

[66] *Ricordi*, 117, Cecil Grayson's translation in *Selected Writings* (Oxford, 1965); see also *Ricordi*, 6: a critical allusion to Aristotle?

[67] *Ricordi*, 177.

[68] Ibid., 110 and 69: "*Se voi osservate bene, vedrete che di età in età non solo si mutano e modi del parlare degli uomini . . . ma, quello che è più, e gusti ancora.*" Emilio Pasquini ed. (Milan, 1975). This remains, however, no more than the expression of one propensity among others in Guicciardini.

sary conditions for a genuinely intricate and demanding activity. And this, as Droyson was later to remark admiringly of Nierbuhr, must seem unspeakably tedious for those with an inherited taste for slick answers. Defeat is becoming a skeptic's virtue; the inapplicable past is to be enjoyed, and to have its differences and alien character properly revealed by those who have not enthusiasm, but *"la disrezione."*[69] The attitude is at one with that which more generally is to be found in Montaigne and La Rochefoucault.[70]

An unstable compound of both of these species of methodological reflex is to be found in Cornelius Agrippa's *De vanitate.*[71] Skinner has suggested that the work shows an intensification of Guicciardini's skepticism toward the past,[72] to which is added the strong belief that it is in principle wrong to seek wisdom and guidance in the authorities of the past. But such an apparent coalescence is both indiscriminate and fortuitous. Agrippa's attack on the alleged authority of the past is not so much an instance of the precise location of a problem (as it is with Hobbes); even less is it a manifestation of a Guicciardinian skepticism which encourages the study of the past. Rather, it is part of an attack *toute courte* on all things which may be said to emanate from the human mind, on all branches of learning, on politics, and social structure.[73] It was stimulated and haunted by an erstwhile faith in the authorities of magic and the occult, and was pulled by an intense faith in the authority of the Bible. Thus a variety of arguments against the authority of the past are rehearsed only as a prelude to an assertion of mystical faith in The

[69] *Ricordi*, 6. See W. J. Bouwsma, *Venice and the Defense of Republican Liberty* (Los Angeles, 1968), pp. 597-598, for a similar propensity in Sarpi.

[70] Ibid., where Pasquini quotes La Rochefoucault, *Maximes*, 550; Nadel, "The Philosophy of History," cites Bayle and Bolingbroke as skeptical about ancient examples.

[71] *De incertitudine et vanitate scientiarum declamatio invectiva* (1556) on which see C. Nauert, *Agrippa and the Crisis of Renaissance Thought* (Urbana, 1965). The work was much and variously printed; that available to me has been *De incertitudine et vanitate omnium scientiarum et artum*, in *Opera*, 2, Lugvini (n.d.), *Landmarks of Science*, Readex Microprints, New York.

[72] Skinner, *Foundations*, 1: 220–221.

[73] Nauert, *Agrippa*, pp. 210–211 and 309–310.

Authority.[74] The authority of the past is, in fact, contradictory, confusing, and unreliable, in principle superfluous, because all ye can and need to know is in the beauty of the Gospel.

These two species of methodological reflex, which appear on the glittering surface of *De vanitate*, take on a more discriminate and stable form largely through the theoretical writings of Herder and Schleiermacher, and Dilthey. Through the elaborate conventions of professional historians and historical theorists (e.g. Bradley, Croce, Collingwood) of the twentieth century, they have hardened into two of the most important, though flexible, conventions of that activity for which I have broadly used the term 'history.'

First, there is an objectivity convention, which insists on the categorical distinction between the facts of history and the historians' values, between the truths of history and the moral verities There is also, perhaps more important though at times difficult to disentangle from the first, a diachronic convention, which by definition outlaws that which is deemed anachronistic—a designation which covers the mislocation and characterization in time of events, values, attitudes, and ideas. These conventions of historical discourse are now found in a whole panoply of methodological refinement and justification and have been widely disseminated.[75]

Although the historians of history tell us that the story of this activity is one of progress and development (a liberation from mere ideology and mythology-moralizing in the past tense), such accounts seem as implausible as they are in a special sense self-contradictory. One wonders why people would want to free themselves from an ideological use of the past while it was of

---

[74] Agrippa, *De vanitate*, pp. 225–247. Such attacks on particular authorities masquerading as denigrations of arguments from authority *per se* are not uncommon. See Ch. Perelman and L. Olbrechts-Tyteca, *The New Rhetoric, A Treatise on Argumentation*, trans. S. Wilkinson and P. Weaver (Notre Dame, 1968), pp. 305–310, with reference to both Pascal and Calvin; Condren, "Authorities, Emblems and Sources," with reference to Hobbes and Lawson.

[75] See e.g. Michael Oakeshott, "The Activity of Being an Historian," in *Rationalism in Politics* (London, 1962), which takes care to delineate the historical understanding of the past from both practical and scientific ones.

service. Rather, historicism, a testimony to Foucault's sense of discontinuity, is, I suspect, rooted in an inability to use the past to consistent effect; it is a full-scale rationalization for the results of ideological failure; its genesis makes it cousin to the flight into ideological abstraction, which may terminate in philosophy. But in neither case is character to be judged by genesis. Both parents and children can be reciprocal embarrassments, and certainly the generation of historical discourse, *qua* historicism, through the sporadic failure to use an authoritative past, is in the end a good reason neither for nor against the continuing dominance among professional historians of historicist conventions of discourse. The failure of the Levellers to deploy the authority of the Ancient Constitution is no reason to rewrite the United Nations Charter.

The exploitation of authorities is then part of a broader phenomenon, as is the problem of Blakey's promiscuous heap, and the explanatory bankruptcy of the terms we most naturally employ in asserting, modifying, or accounting for 'classic' status. The broader phenomenon, the practical application of an authoritative past to the present, is germane to political theory not only because its 'tradition' is born of it, but also because its bastard offspring is a legitimate (*de facto*) part of the discursive structure of the community, surviving with its parents in the same *polis* of *academia*, surviving to question their faith in the contemporaneity of vast stretches of the past. For it is an apparent paradox of historicism that because it is so past-centered, it requires us to live in the present rather than to reinforce or rail against our own world with the largely stereotyping props from the past.[76] In this way, political theory exemplifies the larger

---

[76] It is appropriate if a final footnote moves from citing theory to concrete practice. In Skinner's analyses of Hobbes, Craven's of Pico, Segall's of Marsilius, Hexter's of More, Dunn's of Locke, Pocock's of Harrington, Forbes' of Hume, Adkins' of Plato and Aristotle, and many more, one can see a perspective upon the past and consequent lines of enquiry and emphasis which, with more or less deliberation, sever the nexus of an academic present with a truncated and conveniently co-optable past. As Lamont remarks of Baxter, his very "accessibility . . . to later generations may represent a failure of the historical imagination,"

problems of relating past to present which, at one hypothetical extreme, imprison a world in antiquity and, at the other, produce an almost total dislocation in time which renders any reverence for the classic a grotesquely irrelevant absurdity. One's attitude to the notion of classic status is thus virtually a barometer of one's sense of place in time, and *ipso facto* of one's identity.

―――――――――― VI ――――――――――

What then gives texts classic status? At its simplest, the intellectual communities that need them: they are fashioned as man's gods and ancestors have been in his image and likeness. Plausibly, this may be written off as a typically deconstructionist anti-climax, at best, as an echo of the Introduction, and the reader may be forgiven for thinking that I sit closer to Lewis Carroll's protagorean egg than I should; chickens may come and chickens may go, but Humpty Dumpty will inherit the earth. An intellectual community may need a roster of works it calls classics and proves them to be so simply by force of use, as a political society needs its own heroes, villains, demigods, sacred tablets, and scrolls. And reasons can always be provided to justify the status of sanctity, but these, like the myth of metals or Numa's conversation with nymphs, sell rather than explain. Explanations are less inspiring, something we have long accepted with chic skepticism when we are speaking of political communities, but are reluctant to extend to the *poleis* of *academia*. The political religious metaphors which have permeated much of this argument, however, require that we do otherwise. Our classic texts do not testify to any transcendental pattern of intellectual verities after which a community single-mindedly searches, but they do

---

Baxter and the Millennium, p. 21. What have recently been referred to as the "deprivations of historicism" (in a review of Forbes, *Hume's Philosophical Politics* in *Interpretation* 9 [1980]) are aptly named; and in our attitudes to such "deprivations" lies the future of political theory as a discipline and the historian's role within it.

constitute something of an insurance policy against historical dislocation, *anomie*, and intellectual and even literal underemploy-
ment: they, the most used and exploited in the past, continue to
be the most studied because they can be within the bounds of
conventional decorum. It is perhaps only this study, together
with the superstructure of traditional rationalizations which comes
from the values created and fostered by the academic world, which
holds the political theory community together. It is a community
somewhat like a fragile marriage which has only its children and
their praise in common or, more grandly, like Livy's republican
Rome, cohered by the virtues of its *religio* and its Sybilline books.

But sacrosanctity is not everything for one who hovers on the
walls of a community; one may read Numa's tablets, love them,
and still see them as common laws on common clay. Hence
much of this essay has been taken up with outlining a vocabulary
of appraisal, exegesis, and explanation appropriate to what
Machiavelli called (a rough translation) sophisticated times in
which the most plausible converse with nymphs is a touch difficult to swallow. Old virtues like originality and influence have
scant explanatory purchase and their evocation aids the organization of textual analysis but little. Yet to argue this is not to
introduce new gods, even if it is to respect old vices as deifying
agents. It is to distinguish a rhetoric of rationalization from reasons. Even the impious egg, an embryonic omelette perhaps,
sitting safely on the wall, while curing the city of its ills, may
offer some sort of cock to Asclepius.

Intention, Text,
Audience, and Objectivity

"Voicy qui va bien!" s'escria Socrates, "nous estions
en cherche d'une vertu, en voicy un exaim." Nous
communiquons une question on nous en redonne une
ruchée.

Montaigne,
De l'Experience, Essais

The reference in Chapter 1 to the normative force of all statements in terms of a framing vocabulary of intention to affect an
audience; related passing comments on the rhetorical plane of
all public discourse; the discussion of ideas in texts in Chapter
4, and that of purposive ambiguity in Chapter 8—all raise a
number of problems with which it was not appropriate to clutter
the text, but which deserve brief comment here.

Skinner has argued, amending Collingwood, and following a
Strawsonian intention-statement-audience model of discourse, that
the historian should focus firmly upon authorial intention. The
plausibilty of the Strawsonian utterance model of historical interpretation depends upon the specification of ξ as a statement: if
reading a historical document is like listening to a diurnal locution of the sort Strawson, and before him Austin, had in mind,
then the importance of insisting upon the recovery of authorial
intention, a *mens auctoris* in the statement, remains a paramount obligation for the historian. For I believe Strawson has
argued convincingly that the predication of ξ as a statement entails the notion of a stater performing something in stating. The

ξ, in short, becomes meaningful above all else as the act of an author.[1]

There are, however, differences between ξ as an utterance and as a pattern of inherited written words. These are disguised by the fact that the word 'statement' operates in both the verbal and written domains of language and by the (sometimes) harmless convention of writing about dead authors in the present tense ("*x* states"). The crucial point in this context is that whereas ξ as direct human utterance is difficult to separate from *x*'s intention in performing ξ, as written statement by a dead author ξ is only a residue of evidence for some past purposive action. Thus whereas ξ as statement fuses authorial intention, meaning, and utterance, ξ as text indicates a fundamental dislocation between author and receiving audience.[2] Therefore, although we may still say that ξ is the consequence of some pattern of human intention, the business of reading back from ξ to its author's intentions is largely a matter of hypothesizing beyond the only evidence we have.

Thus it may be urged against the utterance model of historical understanding that the mind of a dead author cannot be a subject for investigation; the text has been irrevocably cut off from its author's mind. This notion of textual autonomy comes close to placing intentions in the same class as reified Lovejoyan ideas as constituting a world per se unavailable to the historian; and it has the consequence of writing off as chimerical the historian's search for a true, objective reading of the evidence as something that can be monitored by reference to the authority of the author's intention.[3]

---

[1] See e.g. Quentin Skinner, "Meaning and Understanding in the History of Ideas," *Hist. & Th.* (1969); and his remarks in "Some Problems in the Analysis of Political Thought," *Pol. Th.* 2 (1974): 277ff.; also E. D. Hirsch, *Validity in Interpretation* (New Haven, 1967) and *The Aims of Interpretation* (Chicago, 1976).

[2] Charles Tarlton, "Historicity and Revisionism in the Study of Political Thought," *Hist. & Th.* 12 (1973); John Gunnell, *Political Theory: Tradition and Interpretation* (New York, 1979), chap. 4; Paul Ricoeur, "The Model of a Text," *SR* 38(1971):535.

[3] The general position I am referring to here is to be found in H. G. Gadamer,

Here, too, however, some cautionary comment is in order: first, the impossibility of achieving an ideal does not necessarily invalidate the organization of an activity with that ideal in mind as a criterion for excluding certain sorts of argument. Secondly, the specification of ξ as text may be no more innocent than its specification as a statement. Because the term 'text' is uninformative, as a material topic it cannot determine the way in which it is going to be interpreted. So it cannot be used *a priori* as a magic wand to banish all reference to an author from its consideration.[4] Further, because the term is so general, understanding it requires that we refine it, and in doing so we reintroduce the vocabulary of human agency. A text may refer to little more than a raw datum to be read but, once specified as an argument, it implies an arguer, as a poem a poet, and as a statement a stater.[5]

Thirdly, not everything appearing under the auspices of 'intention' can be written off as redundant in the name of textual autonomy. Indeed, if one looks at the way historians use intention, it is clearly less an extraevidential object of inquiry, like Lovejoyan ideas, or Dilthey's *geist* beyond *objective geist*, than a means of textual explication. Intention is, briefly, a means of specifying a range of problems to which ξ makes sense as a response—of controlling the ideational completion of a text; and in this way it is typically referred to precisely at those points where the text as a gathering of ideas becomes problematic and cannot be regarded as speaking adequately for itself. Thus references to authorial intention within a text, like Fielding's prolegomenous chats to the reader in *Tom Jones*, are anticipatory markers for the problematic; the historian's recourse to reference

---

Philosophical Hermeneutics (Berkeley, 1976); also Ricoeur, "The Model"; and in some of Roland Barthes' essays, e.g., *Image, Music and Text*, trans. S. Heath (London, 1977 ed.). See Gunnell, *Political Theory*, for a good discussion of Gadamer with respect to political theory, and the discussion between Gunnell and Pocock in *Annals of Scholarship* 1 (1980).

[4] Barthes, *Image, Music and Text*, pp. 155f., although his position seems later to be amended.

[5] We can in fact specify the text in other terms (paragraph, sentence, morpheme, or discuss it as artifact through its binding) but in either case this is to take us away from the history of ideas, or perhaps even from history altogether. In any case, it is to move in the ambit of priorities irrelevant to the problems discussed here.

to intention is, in a sense, a means of substituting for the inadequacy of such markers and is a barometer of interpretive difficulty. In this way, the intentional idiom of textual explication is rather like Gallie's notion of the idiom of causation; it is a "voice change" used to isolate the problematic within the text.[6]

Seen thus, it is clear just how difficult it is to avoid the vocabulary of intention and audience even if the text is to be seen as only an isolated residuum of human activity now lost to us. As Ricoeur states:

> What the text says now matters more than what the author meant to say, and the very exegesis unfolds its procedures within the circumference of a meaning that has broken its moorings to the psychology of the author.[7]

Here (and elsewhere) author, statement, and audience are conflated rather than avoided in the name of textual autonomy. We become the audience (rather than the inheritors), and the text becomes the stater by virtue of *its* saying. However misleading in some respects, then, the utterance model properly stresses the importance of what I have called the framing vocabulary of intention and audience in the processes of textual explication. The importance of the notion of textual autonomy, however, lies in its stress upon the passivity of the text in the hands of its readers. What *ultimately* restricts them, to repeat (see Chap. 8), is less the author than the conventions of discourse in terms of which they operate.

The utterance model and the theory of textual autonomy are in contention because both appear as differing structuring metaphors under the ample and flexible aegis of historical convention. They both spring, more specifically, from Dilthey's realization that the central problem of history as a distinctive mode of discourse lies in making the past intelligible in the present without mistaking it for the present—it is a problem of how to predicate time (see Part One, Introduction, sec. III). To put it another way, Dilthey's problem was to describe the hermeneutic

---

[6] W. B. Gallie, *Philosophy and the Historical Understanding* (London, 1964), pp. 105ff.

[7] Ricoeur, "The Model," p. 534.

circle both as a condition for and a central problem in historical understanding. The point can bear some minimal explication.

Dilthey's late historicist theories clearly seek a passage between the claims of ideological, positivistic, metaphysical, and literary discourse upon the past.[8] As I understand it, his position is roughly that the search for mind by mind (*geist*) makes historical understanding (*Das Verstehen*) different from scientific explanation which is restricted to the study of the totally alien. Further, following Schopenhauer, whereas scientific classifications have predictive and explanatory power, historical ones (nominalistically) are shorthands, mere abridgements for classificatory convenience. It is in fact something individual which is always the ultimate object of historical understanding. Thus to treat abstractions such as *class*, *state*, *nation* as historically real and active is (correctly I think) a blunder of reification. So much, in a sense, for positivism. The individual (*ein Eizelnes*) is understood historically only by being located and defined through a matrix of relationships with others in a provisionally understood set, a *Gemeinsamkeit* constituting a manifestation of *gestige welt*. In this way, understanding is an appreciation of contextual connection (*Zusammenhang*).[9] The whole, then, is always a provisional abstraction, and lacking a context, it cannot have meaning. So much (elegantly) for Hegel, Spengler, et al.[10] On the other hand, the individual has meaning also through its contextual relationship with the universal in human nature—the historian's psychological understanding of which is used to judge interpretations of the problematic. At this point it appears that the problems of reification and contextual understanding throw a question mark over Dilthey's own work. The process which seems necessitated

---

[8] I am drawing largely on the following: *Ideas Concerning a Descriptive and Analytic Psychology* (1894) and *The Understanding of Other Persons and Their Expressions of Life* (circa 1910), trans. K. L. Heiges and R. M. Zaner, respectively (The Hague, 1977).

[9] Compare Saussurian or later Wittgensteinian notions of word meaning as a function of the relationships within a given field of language, rather than as a matter of representation, with Dilthey on understanding sentences, *Das Verstehen*, pp. 209–210.

[10] Thus Quentin Skinner's pertinent remarks on the distinction between text and context being a manifestation, not a way out, of the hermeneutic circle, "Hermeneutics and the Role of History," *NLH* 7 (1975): 227.

by the alien and incomplete nature of the past threatens to bring the past back into the present as a reconstruction of the historian's contingent values and personal psychology. It is this constant possibility which threatens, for example, to bring about what I have called categorical anachronism—of which Dilthey's contextualist understanding makes him acutely aware; for a change of context is a change of meaning. History, one may interpolate then, is always being rewritten insofar as it is problematic in a present, because each generation of historians needs to test its own understandings of humanity against the understandings of the problematic past, and at some points it is always likely to mistake its own contingent values for the universal, becoming a victim of ideology and reification alike.[11] Hence for Dilthey, and in Dilthey, making the past intelligible in a contingent present without mistaking it for the present is a knife-edge along which all historical understanding of necessity moves. Historical writing is identified by the affirmation of and the quest to achieve the ideal, not by any permanent success.

Now much of this has passed into historical commonplace, often in a vulgarized form—as when, for example, H. A. L. Fisher suggests that history is only concerned with the individual, science with the general;[12] and it lies directly behind the relationship between what I have called here the structuring metaphors of textual autonomy and the utterance model of interpretation. The intentional idiom of textual explication, however hypothetical (and the more problematic the text, the more it must become so), is a means of reaffirming and attempting to insure the past-oriented drive to inquiry. On the other hand, the emphasis upon textual autonomy is a salutary reminder that all we have of the past is that which remains in the present, to be read by those operating in the present; that history is the creation of historians, good history, that which other historians applaud ac-

---

[11] The universal in human nature, which Dilthey seems to reify into a mysterious absolute, can be taken as directly analogous to his notion of a whole (context) being provisional and hypothetical; both logically and historiographically we are better off doing so.

[12] *History of Europe*, Preface. Conversely, refutations rediscovering the obvious that historians use classifications and make general statements are the appropriate progeny of such commonplaces.

cording to whatever standards they communally accept. The problem was acutely posed by Droysen.[13] Together, then, the two metaphors may, as it were, be seen as the two sides of the blade along the edge of which the somewhat sepulchral dance of history proceeds.

What then of objectivity? It is evident enough how a cry of textual autonomy can lead to a purely subjective set of ruminations upon past evidence;[14] it is equally clear how the apparently firm and objective readings of the past that are sometimes claimed in the name of authorial intention can be written off as illusory. Historiography is a graveyard of definitive interpretations of dead minds. But in neither case should we judge the use and the hypothetical explication of historical evidence by the standards of positivistic objectivity. These are both chimerical and misleading. As was suggested in Chapter 1, objectivity is an appropriate normative mode. The force of the ξ, whether it be hypothesized to be the original author's or the text's own, functions by degrees to tie the reading to a network of conventions adhered to in principle by interpreter and the audience to whom the interpretation is proffered. To predicate a reading objective is to indicate that the reading seems to adhere to a certain pattern of conventions. Objectivity is an economy of values—only those entailed by an activity are manifest in its performance (although such conventional economy is not exhausted by reference to objectivity).[15] That the predication 'objective' is often contentious is apt concomitantly to be an indication that some redress of conventional standards is being required. Slogans to the effect that objectivity is impossible, or subjectivity rampant, are them-

---

[13] See his famous critique of Buckle, *Art and Method*, in F. Stern, ed. *The Varieties of History* (New York, 1956), chap. 8; at length, Michael MacLean, "Johann Gustav Droysen and the Development of Historical Hermeneutics," *Hist. & Th.* 21 (1982): esp. 347, for a valuable account of Droysen's attempt to steer between present-centered ideology and Ranke's critical method.

[14] See i.e. Jacques Picard's pointed critique of Barthes' *Racine* (*Nouvelle critique ou nouvelle imposture* [Paris, 1965]); Barthes' response, *Critique et Vérité* (Paris, 1966).

[15] Richard Rorty, *Philosophy and the Mirror of Nature* (Princeton, 1979), pp. 335ff., and David C. Hoy, "Hermeneutics," *SR* 47 (1080): 649ff., esp. 670, elaborate in much the same direction.

selves not so much simple statements of objective fact as appeals for some discursive reform on the basis of which predicates like 'objective' (and there are a number of other terms in its ambit, such as 'fair,' 'balanced,' 'reasonable') can be distributed in a way that most members of an activity might consider proper; and so it is hardly surprising that objectivity has provided a central *topos* for methodological dispute (Chap. 1. ɪɪ).

All this is *not* to argue—it is merely a piece of clarifying terminal Lutherism (here I finish) indicating: (*a*) that standing at the intersection of different conventional matrices, a 'text' potentially houses contradictory demands for the interpreter; (*b*) that *if* textual inquiry is to be centered on the past *and* upon human activity, some idiom of intention cannot be avoided; (*c*) that the utterance model and textual autonomism have, in the context of (*b*), more common ground than their extreme formulations would lead us to believe. Examined properly, we might end up with a picture something like Figure 6. But justifying this would require a good deal more methodological discourse, and I think I have learned my lesson.

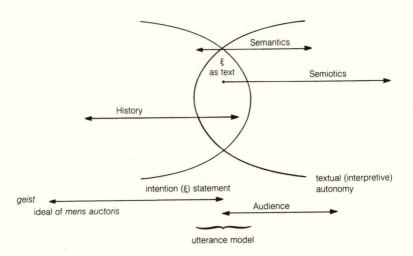

FIGURE 6

INDEX

Adkins, A.W.H., 82, 283n
Aeschylus, 16, 231n
Afnan, S., 211, 212n, 275n
Agrippa, C., 281–282
alchemy, 30, 211
allegory, 178, 179, 202–208, 234, 237, 241, 271, 272
Althusser, L., 132
ambiguity, 3, 85–89, 164, 171–208, 260–264, 267, 269, 270, 274; circumstantial, 209–229, 245n; coalescent, 25, 186–189, 197–208, 210–211, 252; elliptical, 185–197; and equivocation, 177–180, 185, 187–188, 195, 239, 241, 252, 262; protective, 232–235, 239–241; pseudoterica, 239–242; purposive, 171–209, 229, 252, 286; sectarian, 235–241
amphiboly, 242–250, 263
anachronism, 36, 101, 147, 183, 198, 282; categorical, 124, 126, 291
anaphora, 250–251
Ancient Constitution, 259, 278, 283
Anselm, St., 188
anthropology, 26
anticipation, 96, 101, 256–259, 268, 274, 280. *See also* originality
appraisive field, 3–10, 14, 20, 26, 30, 43–44, 83, 85, 91, 95, 99, 107, 117, 140, 167, 174, 198–199, 253–254
Aquinas, St. Thomas, 58, 70, 113, 126
Arbuthnot, Dr. J., 9, 240, 249
Aristophanes, 240
Aristotle, 30, 49, 52, 58, 70, 71, 88, 114, 119, 124–125, 128, 131n, 158, 189, 191–192, 194, 196,

211–212, 237n, 266, 272, 283n, 263–264; *Politics*, 161; *Rhetoric*, 174
Arnold, M., 4
Ashcraft, R., 35n, 38n
Athens, 197, 202, 205, 228, 232
audience, 209, 233–239, 241–243, 255–256
audience-intention model. *See* intention-audience model
Augustine, St., 58, 70, 136, 141, 158, 262, 269, 270
Austin, J. L., 155, 286
authority, 102, 112, 153–155, 231–232; exploitation of, 255–285; text as, 191–194
Avicenna, 211, 275n

Bacon, F., 18n, 43, 94n, 254
Bakunin, M., 58, 70
Barry, B., 37n, 38n, 40, 41n
Barthes, R., 109n, 110, 239n, 251–252, 288n, 292n
Bartolos of Sassoferrato, 278
basic issues. *See* issue-orthodoxy
Baxter, R. (*A Holy Commonwealth*), 133n, 141, 245n, 246n, 266n, 283n, 284n
Bay, C., 38n, 41n, 74
Bentham, J., 58, 69, 70, 130, 217
Bentley, R., 148, 152
Beowulf, 24n, 75, 187n, 207n
Berkeley (Bishop), 54, 212–213, 262
Berlin, I., 21n, 40
Bernstein, R., 8n, 13n, 17n, 37n
Bevan, R., 37n
Bible. *See* religion
bios politikos. See *polis*
Black, M., 172n, 178n
Blackstone, W., 42, 43n, 69

Library of Congress Cataloging in Publication Data

Condren, Conal.
   The status and appraisal of classic texts.

   Includes index.
   1. Political science—Addresses, essays, lectures.   2. Political science
literature—Addresses, essays, lectures.   3. Influence (Literary, artistic,
etc.)—Addresses, essays, lectures.   I. Title.
JA71.C568 1984   320.5   83-43065
ISBN 0-691-07670-7

Conal Condren is a Senior Lecturer in Political Science at the
University of New South Wales.

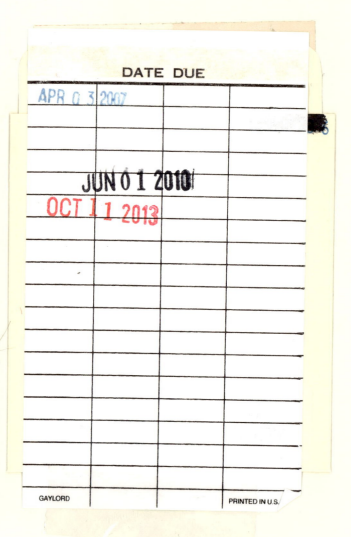

DATE DUE

APR 0 3 2007			
JUN 0 1 2010			
OCT 1 1 2013			
GAYLORD			PRINTED IN U.S.